ANTHROPOLOGICAL PAPERS

MUSEUM OF ANTHROPOLOGY, UNIVERSITY OF MICHIGAN
NO. 31

A PREHISTORIC SEQUENCE IN THE MIDDLE PECOS VALLEY, NEW MEXICO

BY
ARTHUR J. JELINEK

WITH A CONTRIBUTION ON PALYNOLOGY
BY PAUL S. MARTIN

ANN ARBOR
THE UNIVERSITY OF MICHIGAN, 1967

ISBN (print): 978-0-932206-29-9
ISBN (ebook): 978-1-949098-63-1

Browse all of our books at
sites.lsa.umich.edu/archaeology-books.

Order our books from the University of Michigan
Press at www.press.umich.edu.

For permissions, questions, or manuscript queries,
contact Museum publications by email at umma-
pubs@umich.edu or visit the Museum website at
lsa.umich.edu/ummaa.

CONTENTS

INTRODUCTION

The following study of prehistoric materials in east central New Mexico is the result of survey work and excavation carried out during short periods in 1956, 1957 and 1965, and during a full summer field season in 1960. My initial interest in the Middle Pecos area grew from work on the Llano Estacado during the summer of 1956; in a survey of surface sites in Blackwater Draw at that time we collected sherds from a number of localities that appeared to indicate several periods of utilization of the area by peoples with strong contacts in the central New Mexico area. In a discussion of these materials with the late Stanley Stubbs at the Laboratory of Anthropology in Santa Fe, I learned that virtually nothing was known of the eastern border of the Southwest in the area in which we had been working, and of this area of the Pecos Valley in particular. As a result of this conversation I decided to undertake a brief survey of the valley between Fort Sumner and Roswell, to collect materials for comparison with our material from the Llano Estacado, and to determine whether any settlements more complex than the campsites of the Llano were present in the valley.

This survey located four sites in the valley and also visited Site LA2707, located earlier by the Permian-San Juan pipeline survey, but at that time not reported. The time period represented by the site collections, and the character of the site localities, was sufficiently interesting to warrant further work, and in February of 1957 I returned to the Middle Pecos area for about two weeks to attempt to locate more sites and conduct limited test excavations. The results of these two periods of work served as a basis for a short article on the Pecos Valley sequence (Jelinek, 1958), and, eventually, a dissertation on the cultural sequence of the Pecos Valley and the adjacent Llano Estacado (Jelinek, 1960). In the summer of 1960 I returned to the Middle Pecos Valley with a small field party from the University of Chicago, to undertake a more intensive survey and to explore the possibility of utilizing palynological and malacological evidence in the interpretation of cultural change in the valley. Despite the difficulties resulting from strong winds and unusually heavy precipitation (the July rainfall of 9.77 inches was the second highest monthly accumulation on record, and was approximately double the earlier *record* rainfall; the total June, July, and August rainfall equaled the all-time record of 13.10 inches set in 1933), we located an additional 53 sites in 1960, and conducted a series of test excavations on midden deposits and structures. Finally, in the late summer of 1965, I returned to the valley for a short time to conduct tests on a single site where the cultural position could not be resolved on the basis of the surface collections.

The work in 1956, 1957, and 1965 was sponsored by the University of Michigan Museum of Anthropology. The work in 1960 was made possible by a National Science Foundation grant (NSF-G13037), with supplemental aid from the Lichtstern Fund of the Department of Anthropology of the University of Chicago.

A large part of field work never appears in a formal report. However, several particular instances may convey some of the difficulties that were encountered in assembling the information for the report which follows. It is unlikely that I will forget the ice-encrusted mesquite bushes and drizzle of sleet through heavy mist which continued through much of the excavation of the structure at Site P4C in February of 1957. Nor will any of the 1960 field party fail to remember the clouds of mosquitoes that swarmed up into our ill-chosen camp on our first evening near the Bosque Redondo or the almost daily rains that seemed to pursue us wherever we traveled. The saga of the inflated rubber boat used on survey in the normally desert Pecos Valley during that summer will have to be told elsewhere. This was the area in which I learned (many times) that mesquite will puncture a six-ply tire and that four-wheel drive is not insurance against mud. Eventually, with sympathetic help from many local people, we did learn most of the things necessary for survival under the peculiar conditions of that summer, and profited considerably from the experience.

Published reports dealing with the archaeology of the Middle Pecos Valley, other than those mentioned above, are few and, in general, quite brief. Kidder's classic treatment of the Southwest (Kidder, 1924) assigns the Middle Pecos area to the Eastern Peripheral District, although the valley is not specifically mentioned. Mera (1931:2; 1938:13) mentions "campsites" in this area and later (1940:37) speaks of "extensions" of cultural activity from the southeastern New Mexican Sacramento Highlands as far east as the Pecos River. Renaud (1937) mentions a small sherd collection made in the vicinity of Fort Sumner. The most recent report on the area is that of Fenenga and Cummings (1956*a*:217-218), which mentions a number of "temporary" and "more permanent" camps north of the mouth of the Arroyo del Macho near Roswell, with brief artifact inventories.

Thus, in analyzing the materials gathered by the survey, I was interested in exploring the relationships of these materials to those from surrounding areas, and in creating a typology appropriate to the ceramics and projectile points, as the basis for a relative chronology. With the establishment of a chronological system it was possible to use the environmental evidence recovered in a further interpretation of the cultural events represented by the artifacts. In the course of this study it has not been possible to include all of the materials collected by the survey. In particular, chipped stone artifacts, other than projectile points and a few specialized tools, have not been treated, nor have other possible studies been made of the materials from which these artifacts were manufactured. I feel that studies of these artifacts and materials, as well as the flake debris from their manufacture, might well contribute additional information to our understanding of the cultural sequence in the valley. I have not included a typological study of the Navajo ceramics from the Bosque Redondo. Certainly this group of ceramics is the most securely dated in the Southwest, and should add to our information about Navajo activities in the Four-Corners area as already known from archaeological studies.

I am very much obligated to many people for their generous assistance and advice. Primarily and in particular, I would like to acknowledge the encouragement and support of James B. Griffin, Director of the Museum of Anthropology, University of Michigan, who also served as chairman of the doctoral committee which supervised the dissertation on this area in 1960. The other members of this committee, all of whom contributed of their experience to the dissertation study were: Pedro Armillas, Emerson F. Greenman, Claude W. Hibbard, John B. Rinaldo, and James N. Spuhler. The success of our field program was due in large part to the efforts of James M. Warnica of Portales, New Mexico, who gave generously of his time and extensive archaeological knowledge of the area. The collections which he and Gordon Brown, also of Portales, made for the survey added considerably to what we could learn of the area to the east of the valley. The many kindnesses of Mr. and Mrs. Jim Foley of Fort Sumner were deeply appreciated by all of us on the survey. Many local ranchers were most cooperative in aiding the survey; I would especially like to express my appreciation to Robert E. McKenzie, Ben Hall, Logan Barnhart, and Charles Lewis, and to Randolph Howard, the foreman of the McKenzie ranch. My assistant in 1956 was Peter Brechemin. In 1960 Leslie G. Freeman and Alan Kosse formed the field crew. All three have my deep appreciation for their work on the survey. A suggestion by Jack T. Hughes of the Panhandle-Plains Museum, Canyon, Texas, that the minimum stem diameter of points might be related to their function, initiated the projectile point study. Charles Eyman contributed his knowledge of computer programming in the projectile point analysis. Volney H. Jones and Richard A. Yarnell gave freely of their experience in identifying botanical materials. The pollen analysis by Paul S. Martin, and several discussions with him, have contributed very significantly to the understanding of environmental change. Robert J. Drake's analysis of the Pleistocene molluscs has expanded our knowledge of climate during the deposition of the earlier sediments. I would also like to express my appreciation to William H. Burt, Curator of Mammals, Museum of Zoology, University of Michigan, for permission to study specimens under his care. The friendly cooperation of the staff of the Laboratory of Anthropology, Santa Fe, New Mexico, on several occasions greatly aided the survey. In particular, Stewart Peckham and the late Stanley A. Stubbs aided in the identification of ceramics and made considerable experience available to me in discussions and letters. The fine secretarial work of Ina Mae Bull has greatly contributed to the final preparation of the report. It is customary for an author to acknowledge the support given by his wife in the preparation of reports on research; no routine acknowledgment could convey the contributions as editor and field assistant, or the encouragement that have been given by Eloise Jelinek under circumstances that were seldom easy for her.

I

GEOLOGICAL BACKGROUND

Origins of the Present Pecos Valley

The Pecos River and its tributaries form the second largest drainage system in New Mexico, and the course of this river is generally taken to mark the eastern frontier of the Southwest. This course follows a southeasterly direction from sources in the Sangre de Cristo Mountains of north central New Mexico to the vicinity of Fort Sumner; here it abruptly changes direction, going southward to about 40 miles north of the Texas-New Mexico border, where it again assumes a southeastward course to its confluence with the Rio Grande (Fig. 1). Through the Middle Basin of the Pecos Drainage (Parker and Paulsen, 1942: 23) the river flows between the eastern outwash plains of the southernmost ranges of the Rockies and the high plains surface of the Llano Estacado. Geological evidence suggests that these surfaces were once joined to form a continuous slope to the east, over which streams from the eastern Rockies drained into what is now west Texas, and continued in a southeastern direction to the Gulf of Mexico (Johnson, 1901, 1902). Evidence favoring a continuation of the southeastward drainage of the Pecos from the Fort Sumner area across the Llano Estacado is seen in the Blackwater Draw. This is a shallow depression, also referred to as the Portales Valley (Fiedler and Nye, 1933: 99), running slightly south of east from Krider to a few miles south of Muleshoe, Texas. Subsurface exposures in the Sanders Gravel Pit north of Portales reveal that this portion of the Draw is underlain by heavy deposits of coarse stream-laid gravel, suggesting that the Pecos may have flowed in this channel as recently as the Early Pleistocene: an estimate which is in accord with the structural evidence reviewed by Fiedler and Nye (ibid).

Before the Middle Pleistocene a series of solution cavities developed in the surface of the plain, proceeding in a northward direction from what is now Carlsbad, and gradually capturing the eastward drainage from the mountains. Eventually, this new stream, through continuing headward erosion, intersected and captured the drainage of the Pecos near Fort Sumner. Thus the present river channel from Fort Sumner to the south follows a

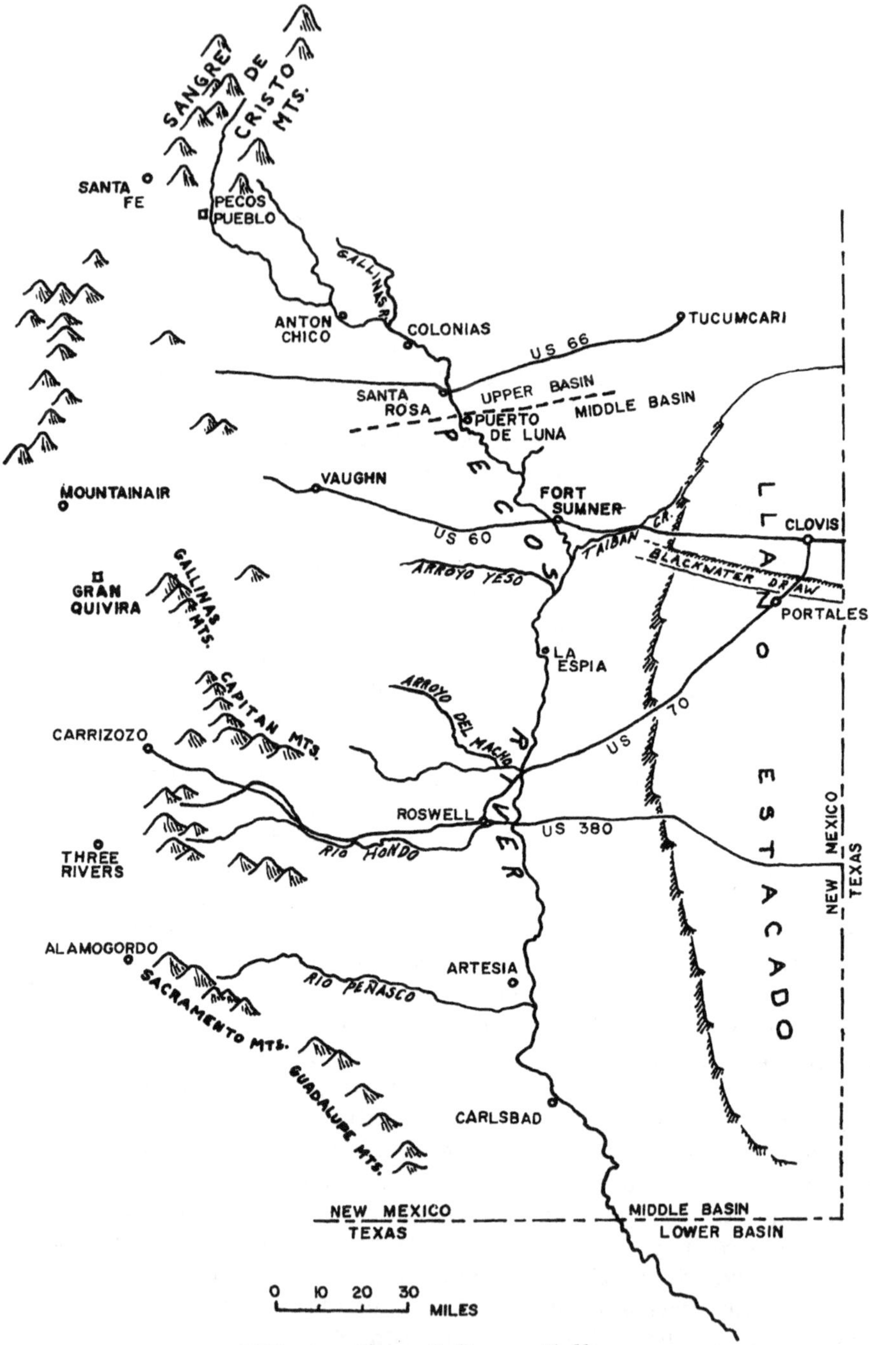

FIG. 1. Map of Pecos Valley.

series of small and large basins formed by solution of soluble subsurface rocks, chiefly in the Permian Chalk Bluff Formation (Harrington, 1957: 302; Morgan and Sayre, 1942: 37). The initial formation of the course of the river was succeeded by a sequence of alternating downcutting and aggradation which resulted in the formation of high pediments at the outer margins of the valley, and several terraces of alluvial materials flanking the river itself (Fig. 2).

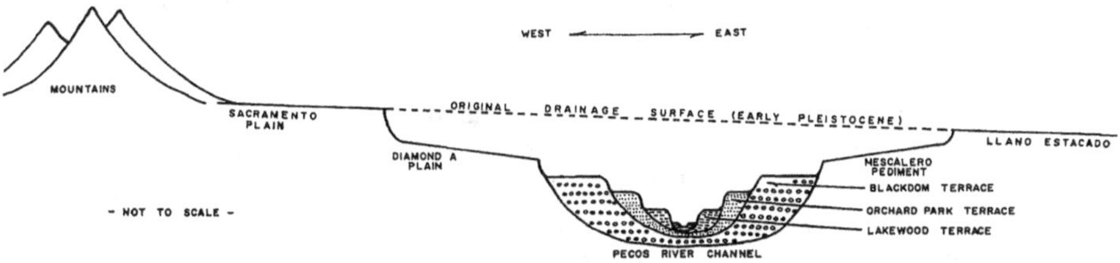

FIG. 2. Schematic cross section of the Middle Pecos Valley.

The Pleistocene and Post-Pleistocene Geological Sequence in the Middle Pecos Valley

The structural features of the valley produced by this erosion and deposition in the vicinity of Roswell, New Mexico have been described by Fiedler and Nye (1933), and correlations between deposits in the Fort Sumner and Roswell areas have been suggested by Morgan and Sayre (op. cit.), who also distinguish several additional features in the valley.

In brief, the described sequence includes three terraces which are adjacent to the river, and lie below an erosional pediment which was cut from the original drainage surface that extended from the mountains to the high plains. The eastern remnant of this surface, as previously mentioned, is the Llano Estacado; the western remnant, adjacent to the mountains, is the Sacramento Plain (Fiedler and Nye, op. cit.: 14). The pediment below this surface, representing the earliest cutting of the valley, on the west side of the river is designated the Diamond A Plain (ibid.), while on the east side it is referred to as the Mescalero Pediment (Morgan and Sayre, op. cit.: 35).

Fiedler and Nye distinguished 3 major terraces in the Roswell area. These were named (op. cit.: 10), from the oldest to youngest, Blackdom, Orchard Park, and Lakewood. The youngest of these deposits, the Lakewood Terrace, is described as a "smooth ancient flood plain in which the river has cut a narrow meandering channel" which varies in depth between 10 and 30 ft. "The Pecos no longer overflows this plain, even during the highest floods."[1] The presence of a high water table in the terrace, together with a high rate of evaporation, results in concentrations of alkali which render this surface unsuitable for cultivation (ibid.: 11). The materials composing the terrace are unconsolidated silts, sands, and gravels (ibid.: 107).

The Orchard Park Terrace lies 5 to 10 ft. above the surface of the Lakewood Terrace and 20 to 35 ft. above present stream channels. In the vicinity of Roswell it is a smooth grassy alluvial plain, little dissected by erosion (ibid.: 11). The sediments are chiefly loose to poorly consolidated sands and gravels, with pebbles averaging 1-2 in. in diameter and ranging up to 5-6 in. The sediments of this terrace are probably not more than 10 to 20 ft. thick (ibid.: 107-108). Nearly all of the irrigated farms near Roswell are on this surface (ibid.: 31), and this utilization has apparently suggested to Morgan and Sayre (op. cit.: 35) that the Orchard Park Terrace may be correlated with the cultivated surface of the floor of the Bosque Redondo south of Fort Sumner.

The oldest of the terraces, the Blackdom, is 30 to 50 ft. above the Orchard Park and 60 to 80 ft. above the present stream channel. Outliers of this terrace form low hills that rise above the Orchard Park surface (Fiedler and Nye, op. cit.: 12). These deposits, except near the surface, are usually fairly well cemented, forming hard conglomerates and sandstones. The pebbles in this terrace are somewhat larger than in the Orchard Park, averaging about 2 in. in diameter and ranging up to 1 ft. or more. Clay deposits are occasionally present, mostly "yellowish" to "reddish-brown," although some are "light to dark bluish-gray" (ibid.: 35). Each terrace surface is assumed to have at one time formed the floor of the valley, and the aggradation of each is separated from the preceding by a period of down-cutting.

The majority of pebbles in the Blackdom and Orchard Park terraces near Roswell are calcareous, derived from the local Chalk Bluff formation. There are lesser quantities of granitic

---

[1] Motts and Cushman (1964: 8) later disagreed with this qualification, stating, "Parts of this terrace (Lakewood) are inundated when the Pecos River is in high flood stage, and the terrace is commonly referred to as river-bottom land." Their further characterization, that "much of the terrace is covered by a lush growth of water-loving vegetation" because of the high water table, has important considerations in extending this classification north to the Fort Sumner area.

pebbles derived from mountains to the west, and quartzose pebbles from the north (ibid.: 108).

Our observations in the Fort Sumner area indicate that the depositional sequence there may be somewhat more complex than that near Roswell. The Fort Sumner sequence is most clearly seen in the northern-most sections of T1N, R26-27E (Fig. 3). Here (in Sec. 4, T1N, R26E), the apparent edge of the Diamond A Plain is approximately 2 miles west of the present Pecos channel, accentuated by a change in elevation of 80-90 ft. in a distance of 1/3 to 1/2 mile. The surface of the Blackdom terrace grades from an elevation of about 4000 ft. in the west to 3980 ft. in the east over a distance of 1-1/4 mi. and lies about 40 ft. above the next lower terrace, a narrow remnant between 1/4 and 1/3 mile wide at about 3950 ft. If this is the Orchard Park Terrace, that designation cannot be used for the cultivated surface of the Bosque Redondo, since that surface is between 10 and 20 ft. lower than this terrace (see p. 8). The floor of the Bosque Redondo corresponds to the next younger terrace in this sequence, which is clearly distinguished by a sharp drop in elevation amounting to about 15 ft. in a distance of about 200 ft. in the NW 1/4 sec. 2, T1N, R26E. This terrace corresponds in general physiographic features to the Lakewood Terrace, as originally described by Fiedler and Nye. It is of considerable interest to note the presence of remnants of small stream meanders in the S1/4 sec. 2, T1N, R26E, on the surface of this terrace on the E side of the Pecos, suggesting a more stable and slower-moving stream at the time this surface was deposited. However, these meanders may possibly represent the old mouth

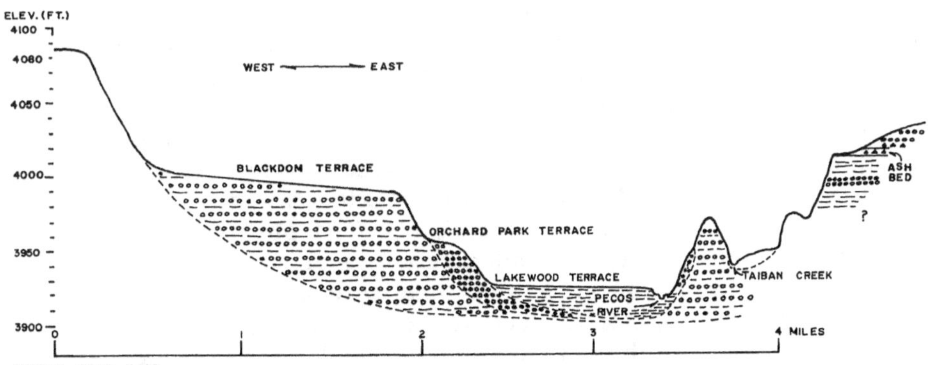

FIG. 3. Cross section of Pecos Valley sediments near Fort Sumner, New Mexico.

of Taiban Creek emptying into a now obliterated Pecos channel. Similar meanders, clearly remnants of the Pecos itself, are easily distinguishable on the surface of the Lakewood Terrace, on the east side of the present channel 4 to 5 miles north of US 70 near Roswell.

Below this terrace on the west bank of the river (actually the north side of a meander) in the S 1/2 sec. 2, T1N, R26E, there are two clearly distinguishable lower terraces above the present depositional and erosional stream channel (Terrace 1A). The upper of these (Terrace 1C) is about 6-8 ft. below the presumed Lakewood level, and the lower (Terrace 1B) is a few feet below that and adjacent to the present stream course.

Several additional geological features in this locality suggest a more complex Quaternary structure than hitherto described. The earliest of these is a bed of volcanic ash exposed on the east side of Taiban Creek in the SW 1/4, sec. 31, T2N, R27E (Locality U9), at an altitude of about 4010 ft. (about 90 ft. above the present Pecos channel). A deposit of pure ash between 3 and 4 ft. thick overlies a reddish compact silty alluvium apparently containing beds of consolidated sand and light gravels. The pure ash is overlain by a deposit of reworked ash mixed with reddish silt of approximately equivalent thickness, which is in turn overlain by a consolidated sand and gravel, a bed of sandy red silt, and another consolidated sand and gravel.

Finally, on the west bank of the Pecos in sec. 27, T2N, R26E, about 1 mi. north of the aforementioned localities, there are exposures of the Blackdom and Orchard Park terraces. These exposures show something of the complexity of the deposits, and tend to confirm the existence of these two separate terraces above the cultivated floor of the Bosque Redondo, as postulated on p. 9. In this portion of the valley the channel of the Pecos is at about 3935 ft. and the cultivated floor of the Bosque between 7 and 10 ft. higher.

The earliest materials in these exposures are gravels outcropping in a small ravine heading to the southwest, in the W 1/2 of the SW 1/4 of the NE 1/4 of the section, at an elevation between 3960 and 3970 ft. (Locality U8). The surface of these gravels is heavily oxidized and disconformably overlain by pond deposits of light yellowish gray sands with at least two distinct interbedded clay horizons. The top of these deposits grades into a buff alluvium, which is in turn overlain by a heavy deposit of terrace gravels. The thickness of the pond deposits at Locality U8 is about 3-1/2 ft.; the buff alluvium is at least of equivalent thickness, and the overlying gravels comprise the remainder of the section, which rises about 25 ft. above the top of the basal gravel to an elevation of about 3995 ft., 60 ft. above the river. Thus there appear to be two major periods of deposition for the Blackdom terrace in this locality.

Additional exposures of the pond deposits are apparent in erosional cuts on the west bank through most of section 27, particularly at Locality U4 (NE 1/4 of the NE 1/4 of the NW 1/4), and Locality U7 (NW 1/4 of the NE 1/4 of the SE 1/4). At the latter a total depth of over 5 ft. of pond sediments, exposed for a distance of about 15 ft. and containing three major calcareous clay horizons, is tilted down to the west at a declination of about 5°, presumably due to solution of underlying sediments. The elevation of these tilted beds at about 3960 ft. is approximately equivalent to the pond deposits of Locality U8.

Remains of small molluscs were in evidence at all three exposures of pond deposits and were collected for study. Table I gives the results of a preliminary analysis by Robert J. Drake of the Vancouver City Museum, Vancouver, British Columbia.

TABLE I

MOLLUSCA FROM BLACKDOM TERRACE POND DEPOSITS*

	Locality		
Type	U4	U8	U7
Pisidium casertanum (Poli)	10	-	-
Pisidium compressum Prime	23	25	-
Pisidium nitidum Jenyns	10	10	-
Valvata lewisi Currier	16	82	-
Marstonia crybetes (Leonard)?	-	-	14
Fossaria sp.?	-	-	1
Gyraulus circumstriatus (Tryon)	39	57	66
Promenetus exacuous (Say)	9	2	-
Helisoma sp.?	-	1	-
Physa sp.?	20	9	174
Limpet	1	-	-
Hawaiia sp.?	2	-	1
Vertigo sp.?	-	1	-

*Identified by R. J. Drake.

All forms described, except *Pisidium compressum*, are compatible with quiet pond or oxbow lake habitats. This species of *Pisidium* is described by Taylor as found only in "perennial water bodies with some current action, such as lakes, rivers, and creeks; it is never found in ponds, swamps, lagoons, or bogs" (Hibbard and Taylor, 1960: 78, H. B. Herrington, personal communication). The relatively shallow depth of deposits at localities U4 and U8, in comparison to U7, and their location in a northerly or up-stream direction from U7, suggests that some drainage may have been taking place from this direction, drainage perhaps sufficient to sustain *Pisidium compressum*, which is absent in U7. Three of the forms (*Promenetus exacuous*, *Gyraulus circumstriatus*, and *Valvata lewisi*) are climatically significant, since at present they are restricted to a more northerly habitat than the Pecos localities (Hibbard and Taylor 1960: 97, 107-108; Taylor 1960: 49); this would suggest cooler summers at the time of deposition. None of the reported species favors a warmer climate. One species, tentatively identified as *Marstonia crybetes* (originally described as *Amnicola crybetes*, Frye and Leonard, 1952: 150) is extinct, but has been reported from deposits of Pliocene and Early Pleistocene age in the Central Plains (Frye and Leonard, op. cit.; Taylor, 1960: 51). There now appears to be some evidence that the latest of these deposits, the David City Gravels, extends into the Kansan (C. W. Hibbard, personal communication). Frye and Leonard (op. cit.), suggest that this species was restricted to permanent or relatively silt-free waters.

The buff alluvium at U8, overlying the pond exposures, yielded badly fragmented bones and teeth of *Equus* and a large camel, brecciated with caliche. The horse teeth appear to be of moderate size. The best preserved specimen (missing the enamel on the buccal surface) is an upper right M2 or M3 from a young adult, and does not exhibit a mature wear pattern (Pl. IA). The maximum antero-posterior measurement is 27 mm. and the estimated length of the mature protocone is about 14 mm. A comparison of this specimen with a similar left upper molar which retains the medial and posterior buccal enamel suggests a total width of about 24 mm. during mature wear. A small pre-caballin fold is apparent on both teeth, with the post-protoconal valley preserved. It is virtually impossible to refer such fragmentary material to a particular species. The dimensions are most closely duplicated in a specimen ("112" A.M.N.H.) referred to *Equus excelsus* Leidy by Hay (1913: 592). Hibbard (1952: 13) considers this species to be "closely related - if not identical to" *Equus niobrarensis* Hay, to which he refers his material.

However, a specimen of *Equus complicatus* Leidy from Tule Canyon, Texas, figured by Gidley (1901: 132, Fig. 22), is also similar in both size and enamel pattern to the U8 material. *Equus complicatus* is reported from Kansan deposits in Oklahoma (Hibbard, 1958), and *E. niobrarensis* from the post-Kansan (Hibbard, 1952: 13) and Sangamon (Hibbard, 1958) in Kansas.

One fragmentary cheek-tooth of a large camel was recovered from locality U8. On the basis of the relatively thin enamel it is probably a form of *Camelops* rather than *Titanotylopus* (= *Gigantocamelus*). *Camelops* is present in North America from the Nebraskan through the Wisconsin while *Titanotylopus* is present from the Pliocene through the Kansan (Hibbard et. al., 1965: 513). Sediment from all of the pond localities, as well as the volcanic ash, was tested for pollen by Paul S. Martin at the Geochronological Laboratory of the University of Arizona. No pollen was preserved in these samples.

Another locality in this section which has yielded vertebrate remains is Site P41 on the Orchard Park terrace surface in the SW 1/4 of the NE 1/4 of the SE 1/4 of section 27. Here a buff alluvium similar in appearance to that of locality U8 has been cut away to form the surface of the terrace at an elevation slightly over 3960 ft.; this surface is strewn with caliche pebbles, many of which contain bone fragments. A badly broken segment of a right lower jaw containing portions of two teeth, as well as several isolated paracones, can be identified as *Equus*. The adjoining portion of the terrace to the east has been cut by the river, revealing an exposure of sands and gravels just below the surface of the terrace; these deposits are in a position equivalent to that of the pond deposits at U8, 1/2 mile to the north. Inasmuch as the heavy pond deposits of U7 lie only a few hundred feet to the north of this site, it would appear that this level of the Blackdom terrace has here been cut away and replaced by the gravels of the later Orchard Park terrace. The top of these gravels is over 15 ft. above the channel of the Pecos and over 10 ft. above the Lakewood surface on the east side of the river. Thus the sequence at the southern end of the Bosque Redondo appears to include the following events (Fig. 3):

(1) Deposition of the basal gravel of Locality U8: heavy river flow.
(2) Erosion of surface of basal gravel; dry conditions (?) or heavy moisture = downcutting.
(3) Formation of the pond deposits of Localities U4, U7, and U8; slow to stagnant river, stabilization of the flood-plain, cool summers.

(4) Deposition of the buff alluvium of Locality U8 and Site P41; disappearance of ponds, river flow probably intermittent, dryer conditions climaxed by the deposition of caliche cementing the bones of *Equus* and camel. Probably warm and dry.
(5) Deposition of the uppermost gravels of the Blackdom terrace; heavy, rapid to slow river flow.
(6) Stabilization of the surface of the Blackdom Terrace; slow river flow; warm conditions.
(7) Downcutting through Blackdom deposits; intermittent (?) rapid flow.
(8) Deposition of Orchard Park gravels overlying and adjacent to earlier Blackdom deposits on west side of river; heavy rapid to slow river flow.
(9) Stabilization of Orchard Park terrace surface; slow river flow.
(10) Downcutting through Orchard Park surface; rapid intermittent (?) flow.
(11) Deposition of the silts, sands and gravels of the Lakewood terrace; moderately heavy river flow - absence of pollen (see p. 13) indicates rapid deposition.
(12) Stabilization of surface of Lakewood deposits, forming floor of Bosque Redondo and other relatively broad alluvial plains in the valley to the south. Remains of meanders on this surface indicate Recent age (?). Slow river flow.
(13) Downcutting through Lakewood terrace with two or three periods of minor valley fill in deep-cut river channel; variable river flow.

In this sequence, the position of the volcanic ash deposit which is high on the east side of the river is unclear, since no stratigraphic association with sediments on the west side is in evidence. The elevation of this deposit, ca. 4010 ft., is higher than the top of the Blackdom terrace on the west side. This suggests, with the presence of the overlying sands and gravels, that the ash is earlier than the surface of the Blackdom gravels on the west bank. In the absence of evidence of Quaternary vulcanism closer than the Rio Grande (with the exception of a cinder cone and lava flow of relatively recent date at Carrizozo), it is tempting to equate the ash with the Pearlette Ash of the late Kansan on the Plains. If this deposit is Kansan and is separate from and earlier than the Blackdom gravels, all of the Blackdom deposits must be assigned to the Illinoian, and the pond and alluvial deposits regarded as interstadial; this would be supported by the presence of the northern varieties of molluscs in the ponds. The deposits of caliche in the buff alluvium argue for a prolonged arid interval, probably with hot summers and perhaps too extreme to have taken place during an interstadial. I therefore suggest that these deposits relate to the transition between the Kansan and Yarmouth, as indicated by the presence of *Marstonia crybetes*, and compatible with the known age of the other molluscs.[2] A correlation of the buff alluvium and its caliche deposits with the Yarmouth interglacial period would equate the upper Blackdom gravels with the Illinoian, and the upper Blackdom surface with the Sangamon.

This correlation finds support in fossil evidence from water-laid sands near the top of the Blackdom terrace, on the west side of the river fifteen miles south of Fort Sumner at Locality U6 (SW 1/4 of the SE 1/4 of the SW 1/4, sec. 4, T1S, R26E), where a badly eroded lower jaw of *Mammuthus imperator* (Leidy) was discovered (Plate I). The left molar was recovered and is now in the collections of the University of Michigan Museum of Paleontology (UMMP #44424). While this mammoth is reported from the Wisconsin (Hibbard, 1958: 20; 1955: 54), the possibility of a late Wisconsin date for this specimen, found in water-laid sands at the top of the highest terrace deposit, seems to be ruled out by the degree of downcutting in the valley adjacent to the locality. This indicates a prolonged interval following the deposition of the sands. In addition, all late Wisconsin mammoths from the Southwest which have been studied are *Mammuthus columbi* (Falconer). Specimens of this species have been reported both to the east (Sellards, 1952: 109), and to the southwest (Lance, 1959: 35), of the Middle Pecos area. While the U6 specimen of *M. imperator* was badly broken and apparently highly mineralized, it did not exhibit the heavy incrustations of caliche which occurred on the bone from the buff alluvium. Large heavily mineralized fragments of limb bone, apparently probiscidean, were collected on the surface near Locality U6, as were fragmentary teeth of an equid, none showing heavy caliche incrustations.

On the surface of Site P3, on the top of the Blackdom terrace about a mile north of Locality U6, there were abundant fragments of ivory, but no specifically identifiable materials were found.

---

[2]*Promenetus exacuous,* which Taylor believed only developed from *Promenetus kansasensis* during the Sangamon (Hibbard and Taylor, 1960: 107) has now been shown to range back into the Pliocene (Miller, 1966: 234-235).

If the top of the Blackdom terrace is Sangamon, then the subsequent downcutting and Orchard Park fill may be assigned to the Wisconsin. The downcutting through the Orchard Park terrace may have taken place during a major phase of melting of mountain glaciation in the late Wisconsin, and the subsequent aggradation would have then occurred in the terminal Wisconsin as stream loads were dropped due to decreasing flow. Following the Wisconsin the surface of the Lakewood terrace developed on top of these sediments, continuing as the flood plain of the Pecos until the last few hundred years. The clear remnants of meanders on this surface suggest not only that it was occupied by the river relatively recently, but that the character of the river was at that time quite different: a slow-moving narrow stream winding across the valley floor, probably resulting in a high water table and seasonal flooding.

It would appear most likely that the present channel of the river, cut into the Lakewood terrace, is the result of torrential headward erosion. It is clear from deposits in the southern portion of sec. 2, T1N, R26E, that two and possibly three periods of minor stability or aggradation have occurred during this period of erosion. The uppermost of these (Terrace 1C) is characterized by a cover of low vegetation in those portions farthest from the river, probably indicating deposition in the late prehistoric or early historic period; while the areas close to the river (Terrace 1B) are covered with salt-cedar (*Tamarix*), probably indicating a late historic deposition, which may have differed significantly in time from the areas of grass and mesquite vegetation. The lowest deposits above the present channel (Terrace 1A) have not been fully stabilized by vegetation, but appear to be developing a character similar to the *Tamarix*-covered level above. This level (1A) has undoubtedly been abandoned by the river only in the last few decades and is still part of the active flood-plain. It is likely that, without the interference of the Alamogordo Dam and the diversion dam north of Fort Sumner, the river in seasonal flood-stage would cover Terrace 1C; and possibly, would occasionally cover the lower portions of the Lakewood terrace, as appears to have taken place occasionally in the historic period (see p. 32).

Geological Factors of Concern to Prehistoric Man

The geological environment of the Middle Pecos area placed many limitations on the activities of prehistoric man. Permanent or semi-permanent settlements were restricted to the well-drained Blackdom and Orchard Park terrace surfaces, and are most frequently encountered where these surfaces are within a few hundred feet of the river. In the Fort Sumner area land suitable for cultivation would appear to have been largely confined to the Lakewood terrace surface, and possibly Terrace 1C (if it existed as a terrace in the prehistoric period). The narrow meandering river channel reflects moisture conditions favorable for cultivation by dry-farming, with probable seasonal soil renewal through flooding. In the Roswell area the salinity of the Lakewood Terrace may have been a barrier to cultivation if it was as extreme as it is at present. Certainly the increasing mineralization of the river water from this point south must have caused difficulties in obtaining both drinking water and water for cultivation.

Materials available in the geological deposits strongly influenced the course of several cultural activities. Sandstones of the Triassic Dockum Group, which outcrops beneath the Quaternary deposits south of Fort Sumner, provided slabs for the construction of wall bases and cyst linings. The same source was utilized for milling stones, both metates and manos. Occasionally mortar holes were ground into native sandstone outcrops in the vicinity of a site.

Virtually all of the material used for chipped stone tools appears to have been derived from the terrace gravels along the river. North of Roswell the terrace gravels are primarily of quartzose rocks, many of which are suitable for flaking. These include, in the order of their general abundance: quartzite, siltstone, agate, chalcedony, chert, and silicified wood. The only prominent exception to this stone source is in a small area just north of the Dunahoo Hills in the northern Bitter Lake Wildlife Refuge, where native outcrops of chert in the Permian Chalk Bluff Formation have been extensively utilized in stone-chipping.

Clays for ceramics would have been available both in terrace exposures and occasional exposures of the underlying Tertiary Ogalala beds. Most of the tempering materials for ceramics seem to have been derived from granitic rocks in the terrace deposits.

II

ENVIRONMENT AND ABORIGINAL POPULATION SEEN THROUGH THE HISTORICAL RECORD

Spanish Exploration

The first account of what is believed to be an exploration of the Pecos Valley in the vicinity of Fort Sumner is that of the Coronado expedition. It is related in the narrative of Castañeda that the army of Coronado, returning from the Plains under the command of Don Tristan de Arellano in early July, 1541, joined the river 30 leagues below the bridge that Coronado had constructed 4 days journey from Cicuye, or Pecos Pueblo (Winship, 1896: 510[3]). Prior to encountering the river they had visited several salt lakes, a feature so common on the northern Llano Estacado in the area of the Texas-New Mexico border as to be of little help in identifying the particular localities through which they passed. However, the distance given below Coronado's bridge is of considerable aid in calculating the point at which they joined the river. The relatively unencumbered party of Espejo, following the general course of the Pecos south out of Cicuye (Siqui) in 1583, in four days of travel (not including two days of rest or camp) covered a distance of 22 leagues; they camped on the sixth day of their journey "at a stream of water close to a small saline where we gathered salt to season the meat. We named this place La Salinilla. In this locality there are large holes of

[3]Winship's translation of Castañeda here is somewhat misleading. The phrase "*a quatro dias andados de camino dieron en un rio de gran corriente hondo que baxaba de hacia cicuy y a queste se puso nombre el rio de cicuye*" is translated by Winship (1896: 504) as "After four day's journey they came to a river with a large deep current, which flowed *down toward Cicuye* [emphasis mine] and they named this the Cicuye river." This would imply that they were upstream from the pueblo, a most unlikely route to the plains since it would lead them into increasingly rugged mountains. Instead the translation of Hammond and Rey (1940: 235), "After four day's march they came to a deep river carrying a large volume of water *from the direction of Cicuye*" [emphasis mine] is more accurate. It should also be noted that some authorities believe this river to have been the Canadian rather than the Pecos (Schroeder, 1962), a designation which to me appears inconsistent with the account of the return to Cicuye.

brackish water" (Hammond, 1929: 121). There is a place near the Pecos south of Pecos Pueblo where such features are encountered, and it is the only one for over 100 miles. It is about half way between Anton Chico and Santa Rosa; more exactly, about 8 miles down river from the settlement of Colonias, near the site of the present Walker Ranch, a distance which almost exactly matches that of the narrative. Because of the larger size and greater encumbrances (including livestock) of the Coronado expedition it is unlikely that they were able to travel this distance in four days, indicating that the generally accepted point of crossing in the Santa Rosa-Puerto de Luna area (Hammond and Ray, 1940: 235) is too far downstream by more than 25 miles. At present there are many fords across the river in the stretch from Anton Chico to the junction of the Gallinas and the Pecos, although the usefulness of these in spring is open to question; below this point there are no fords for a distance of about 10 miles. However, a crossing below the Gallinas would avoid a future crossing of that river, which up to this point lies to the east and roughly parallel to the Pecos (Fig. 4). The Gallinas is the last major stream to join the Pecos from the east; therefore, on an eastward journey it would have been of some advantage to go beyond its junction, but of no discernable advantage to follow the Pecos south of this point. These factors, plus the relative distance traveled by the Espejo party, tend to place the location of Coronado's bridge just north of Colonias. Estimates using this location would bring the returning army into the valley at the Bosque Redondo, south of Fort Sumner (calculating the league at about 2.8 miles to allow for distortion due to terrain and human error). This is in accord with the estimate of Williams (1959: 28), who has published a most interesting reconstruction of the eastern journey of the Coronado expedition, utilizing known distributions of resources mentioned in the account, as well as topographical features.

The earliest account of botanical resources in the valley is contained in the Castañeda narrative, which mentions that the banks of the river "are covered with a sort of rose bushes, the fruit of which tastes like muscatel grapes. They grow on little twigs about as high up as a man. It has the parsley leaf." (Winship, op. cit.). This would appear to be a wild currant of the genus *Ribes* (V. Jones, personal communication). In addition, Castañeda remarks on the presence of unripe grapes (or berries ?) and currants (?, *uino*), as well as wild marjoram (*oregano*). The fact that Coronado was obliged to construct a bridge to cross the river with livestock suggests that in the vicinity of

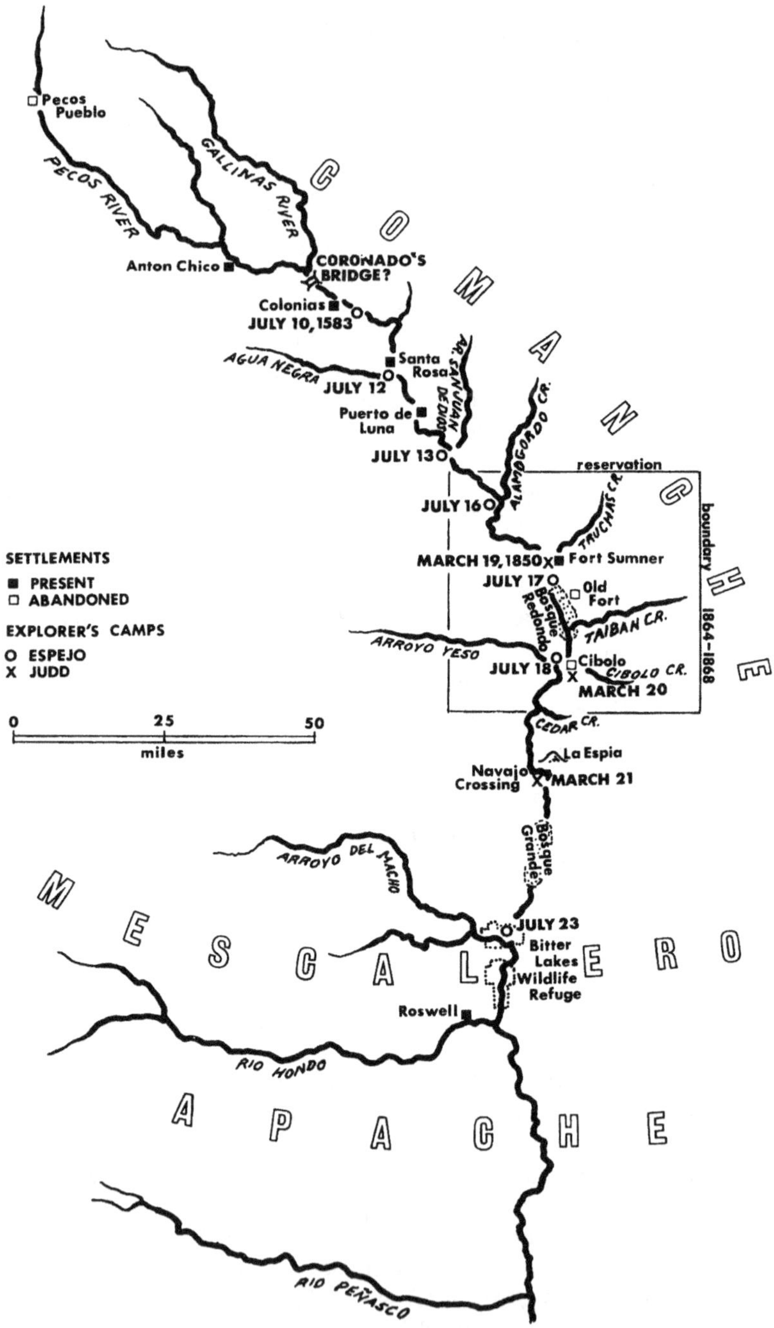

FIG. 4. Historic exploration in the Middle Pecos area.

Colonias it was characterized by high banks and, as is related by Castañeda, (in spring, at least) a deep, swift flow (Winship, op. cit.: 504).

Forty-two years after Coronado's army ascended the river, an expedition commanded by Antonio de Espejo descended the valley in July and August of 1583, following the river from Pecos Pueblo to the present Texas-New Mexico border. The journal of Diego Perez de Luxan (Hammond, 1929) contains a brief day-to-day account of this journey, from which a little information may be obtained on conditions in the valley in the late sixteenth century. The reconstruction given above of the first six days of travel would place the party about 10 miles upstream from Santa Rosa on the 10th of July. On the 12th they marched four leagues (c. 11 mi.) to "a stream with poplars" (cottonwoods ?). Luxan states that "This land is all very level, containing fine pastures and many waterholes," a description which coincides in topography and distance with an area about 1 mile south of Santa Rosa. Here they found "goad Sticks [lances] with which the Indians kill the cattle" (bison). On the 13th of July they marched six leagues (c. 17 mi.) and camped at the junction of the Pecos with a "fair-sized. . . . [stream] . . . . which runs from the east toward the west. This is likely to have been the Arroyo San Juan de Dios which is now an intermittent stream; however, it might well have been running in mid-July, a peak period for precipitation in this area. They left this locality on the 16th and marched 4 leagues (c. 11 mi.) to a place they called "El Rastro" (ibid.: 122), which can be translated either as "the trail" or "the slaughtering place." The distance would indicate a campsite near the junction of Alamogordo Creek and the Pecos. On July 17th, after a journey of 6 leagues (c. 17 mi.) they stopped at a place where "there were numerous mosquitos" (op. cit.). This could very well be the Bosque Redondo, south of Fort Sumner, which is still heavily infested with mosquitoes (especially at the south end) on summer evenings, and where a higher population of these insects would be expected than in the rest of the valley because of the broad level floor. The following day they marched six leagues (c. 17 mi.) to the site of "El Mesquital," so named because of the abundance of mesquite (op. cit.).[4] This camp was probably in the vicinity of 18 Mile Bend. Five days later and eighteen

[4]Although Kelley (1937) would place the first "El Mesquital" camp of Espejo's party about 32 miles south of Fort Sumner, the general schedule of natural features and distances described above, as well as the correlations which follow suggest that the 18 Mile Bend area is more likely.

leagues (c. 50 mi.) to the south, they encountered many springs emptying brackish water into the Pecos, and traveled through many *cienegas* in the next few days. This would appear to describe the Pecos in the vicinity of the two Bitter Lakes National Wildlife Refuge areas north and east of Roswell. Luxan later states that "in all this trip we did not find any cattle, nothing but many tracks." (op. cit.), indicating that perhaps during this relatively wet season the bison were relying on resources at some distance from the river; probably the grasslands of the Llano Estacado and the Sacramento Plain, where summer rainfall kept waterholes adequately supplied.

The only botanical information given in this portion of the narrative is the mention of abundant mesquite in the 18 Mile Bend area, demonstrating that this plant has probably been present since at least the late prehistoric period.

Neither the Coronado nor the Espejo expedition encountered any Indians in this portion of the valley, and it seems clear that there were no permanent settlements in the Middle Pecos area in the mid-sixteenth century.

This apparent lack of an indigenous population is supported by an account of the expedition of Gaspar Castaño de Sosa (Schroeder and Matson, 1965), who journeyed up the Pecos from the Rio Grande to Pecos Pueblo in October, November, and December of 1590, seven years after Espejo's descent. Although de Sosa sent out an advance party with specific instructions to find Indians, none were encountered south of Pecos Pueblo. Evidence of transient groups was discovered, however, including an obvious "trail," probably in the vicinity of the present Alamogordo Reservoir (ibid.: 71). This strongly suggests the feature that may have led the Espejo expedition to name their camp in the same area "El Rastro" (see above). The de Sosa account makes occasional mention of the use of mesquite and grass seed (*zacate*) for food while the expedition was traversing the northern Middle Pecos basin (ibid.: 70-72). No specific mention of the utilization of game in this area is reported; in fact, an account of the butchering of an ox to supply the advanced party, who had used up all the supplies they had taken along (ibid: 68), suggests that game was not easily accessible.

From this period until the beginning of the administration of this region by the United States in the late 1840's, there is little indication of the condition or the habitation of the northern Middle Pecos valley.

U. S. Military Exploration

In 1850 there was a military reconnaissance from Las Vegas to the Bosque Grande under Bvt. Capt. Henry B. Judd of the U. S. Third Artillery. This reconnaissance resulted in a map which conveys some information about natural conditions as well as a number of Spanish names for topographic features which have since dropped from use (National Archives Record Group 77, U. S. 148). At Judd's fifth camp (March 19, 1850), at the head of the Bosque Redondo on the site of the present town of Fort Sumner, he reported the wood plentiful and the water bad. This is the first occasion on which bad water (probably high in gypsum) was reported south of Las Vegas; from this point on down the river, only bad water is reported. This camp is located on a stream called "Las Carretas," apparently the present Arroyo de Añil. Wood was also reported in good supply at the sixth camp (March 20) at the mouth of a stream called "Alamos Mochas," which topographically fits the present Cibolo (or Buffalo) Creek. The campsite on the south bank of the mouth of the creek was the location of the small settlement of Cibolo later in the nineteenth century. Most of the area between these camps is apparently included under the designation "Bosque Redondo," noted as having "Rich Bottom Land" and shown as forested only on the west bank of the river, a depiction which is certainly in error on the basis of later records. The rugged terrain in the vicinity of 18 Mile Draw on the east bank of the river is noted as "not practical for wagons," a circumstance which at present continues to apply to most motor vehicles. The party encountered "water in holes" on Cedar Creek (unnamed on the map), about seven miles east of its junction with the Pecos, and made its seventh camp on March 21 at Navajo Crossing near Crow Canyon. Here wood seems not to have been especially abundant and the water continued bad. In a letter written on March 30, Judd reported that this ford was used by Navajos from west of the Rio Grande, who would travel north to the Bosque Redondo to run off sheep (Schroeder and Matson, 1965: 71). This would imply that Mexican sheepherders were already established in this region by the mid-1800's, as do the Spanish names applied to relatively minor topographic features at the time of the reconnaissance. The eighth camp (March 22) was at the south end of the Bosque Grande, another area of "rich bottom land" shown as forested only on the east bank of the river. The Judd map appears to indicate a somewhat sketchy reconnaissance in several respects. Such major tributaries as Taiban Creek, on the east side, and virtually all tributaries on the west side (including Arroyo Yeso, Arroyo de la Mora, Wylie Draw and Higgins Creek) are not noted; bends in the river are apparently portrayed only conventionally, with the exception of the large bend above Navajo Crossing; and finally, probably due to circumstances less easily controlled, the parallels of 34° and 33° 30' are drawn between ten and twelve miles too far to the north. It appears, however, to be the first attempt at an accurate topographic portrayal and description of the area of our study.

The 1851 report of J. S. Calhoun, then U. S. Indian Agent in Santa Fe, indicates (p. 197) that the Bosque Redondo was a locality favored by Comanches and Apaches (p. 195). In the same year a license was issued for an Indian "trading post" (probably to the *Comancheros*), in the Bosque (Frazer, 1965), though no subsequent accounts mention the presence of such an establishment.

In testimony before a congressional committee meeting at Fort Sumner in the Bosque Redondo in 1865, James M. Giddings revealed that the northern Middle Pecos Valley was not entirely without settlement in the 1850's (U. S. Congress Joint Special Committee, 1867: 342-343). He states that:

> [I] first came here in 1835, returned in 1836, came back again in 1840, and have remained here ever since [probably referring to New Mexico]. I have lived on the Pecos some three or four miles [thirty or forty (?) see p. 31] from here since 1853. I have kept a ranch, cattle, and sheep, and have been farming. . . . I have had from eight to thirty-three families in my house or fortification. . . . This reservation has been very little used as pasturage grounds by the Mexicans on account of its proximity to the Comanches and other Indians.

Regarding natural conditions his testimony furnished the following:

> The grasses on the reservation [a forty mile square around the Bosque Redondo with old Fort Sumner at the center] outside of the lands capable of irrigation are very fine and nutritious, much better than the grasses of the latter. Cattle, sheep, horses and mules keep in good condition all winter without hay, from the natural pasturage. On the lands of the reservation, each section of land one mile square would sustain, summer and winter, one hundred head of cattle. . . . This reservation would maintain one sheep to the acre, winter and summer, more than one million sheep in all. There is mesquite all over the reservation; it is the very best kind of fuel. There are some bottoms here on the river subject to overflow, when if once ploughed and stock kept out, will spring up to cottonwood very thick. . . [implying that *Tamarix*, the salt cedar, was not present in any quantity in this area in 1865].

Louis Kennon, a physician apparently formerly attached to the army, in testimony before the same committee (ibid.: 334), stated that in 1854 or 1855 Major (later General) Carleton thought the Bosque a suitable place for a "four-company post;" however, Captain (later Confederate General) Ewell, a year or two later, felt that the supply of wood in the Bosque would be exhausted within four or five years by such a post.

The 1854 report of Calhoun's successor, D. Merriwether, who was also Governor of New Mexico, mentions that the territory of the Mescalero Apache included "both sides of the Pecos . . . from the northern boundary of Texas to about the thirty-fourth parallel of latitude" (p. 171). He remarks that "that portion of the valley of the Pecos occupied by the Mescaleros contains some of the most desirable lands for agricultural purposes within New Mexico;" however, he also states that "Game is comparatively scarce in their country . . ." (op. cit.). This is in some contrast to the report of Pope (1854: 65), who mentions a "considerable quantity of deer, antelope, and partridges" between Delaware Creek and the mouth of the Peñasco in 1854.

In 1855 the northern and middle Pecos valley was visited on several occasions by military expeditions sent out against the Mescalero. The journal of James Bennett, a dragoon, who participated in these excursions (Brooks and Reeve, 1948), includes several references to the character of the river and the country. An entry for January 1, 1855 describes conditions below Anton Chico: "Traveled 20 miles yesterday along the Rio Pecos, which is a deep, muddy stream with very high banks. Today went 22 more miles and camped in a beautiful walnut grove [probably between Santa Rosa and Puerto de Luna] . . . This is now a very fine country, with the stream lined with walnut groves. Passed at least 6000 sheep." (op. cit.: 59). The next entry is several days later, on January 4: "Down the river all day yesterday [3rd]. Found it increasing in size. No more timber to be seen. Today left Rio Pecos and went toward the Sierra Blanca range. At dark struck Rio Ruidoso [actually the Rio Hondo below the junction of the Ruidoso and the Bonito], a very pretty mountain stream emptying into Rio Pecos" (op. cit.: 60). Between August 24 and 26 of the same year he traveled down the Pecos between the mouth of the Rio Hondo and the Peñasco, remarking that "The soil is filled with vermin. Thousands of rattlesnakes, tarantulas, and centipedes are running over the ground throughout this region. . . It is dry barren soil. The banks are so high and steep that we can hardly find a place to water our animals. The water in the Pecos is quite brackish, not good water." (ibid.: 75-76). These observations are evidence that the river was well entrenched in the Lakewood terrace by the mid-nineteenth century, and that conditions of salinity were similar to those at present. The fact that "no more timber" was seen on the last day of travel before leaving the river and joining the Hondo would place this journey south of Bosque Grande, in keeping with the distances of 20 to 22 miles per day mentioned earlier. While the description of the fauna appears somewhat exaggerated, it gives an impression of the contrast between the pleasant mountain area of the Bonito and Hondo and the relatively barren valley of the Pecos.

The Bosque Redondo Reservation Period

In one of the most tragic episodes in the history of the Southwest, thousands of Navajo and Apache Indians were confined by the military authorities at the Bosque Redondo in the mid-1860's. One effect of this confinement was a serious disruption of natural conditions in the northern Middle Pecos Valley. The report of a board of officers appointed to select the exact site of the Fort Sumner reservation at the Bosque Redondo in November of 1862 anticipated many of the difficulties which were to be encountered at this post (Bailey, 1964: 147):

> The advantages of the site and its immediate vicinity are that the ground is above the land of the highest floods; it commands a view of the plain for two or three miles in every direction; it is convenient to water and cottonwood, and the grazing in the vicinity is good.
>
> It has the following disadvantages: it is remote from the depot of supplies, and from the neighborhoods that supply forage. Building material will have to be brought from a great distance. The water of the Pecos contains much unhealthy mineral matter. A large part of the surrounding valley is subject to inundation by the spring floods.

The board then recommended that the Fort be built at the junction of the Pecos and the Aqua Negra, about forty miles to the north, where both wood and fresh water were abundant and other disadvantages lessened.

It is interesting, in this regard, to follow the description of the Bosque Redondo by John C. Cremony (1868), who visited the area at the time of the selection of the site in late 1862 and remained to work with the Apache until early in 1864. At one point he described the Bosque Redondo (op. cit.: 200) as a wooded area "16 miles long, by 1/2 mile wide at most, and not thick anywhere," while elsewhere (p. 218) he states, "the Pecos for 25 miles about the Bosque Redondo is fringed for 1/2 mile in depth, on both sides, with gigantic cottonwood trees." In terms of wildlife, he states (op. cit.):

> The cottonwoods and the dense undergrowth of shrubbery, which produced many kinds of wild berries, and large fields of wild sunflowers, abounding with nutritious seeds renders the Bosque Redondo a favorite abode with wild turkeys which existed there in great numbers and were exceedingly fat and fine flavored. . . . My Apache friends kept my larder lavishly supplied with turkeys, grouse, deer, bear and antelope hams and a species of very superior turtle [probably soft shell] which is abundant in that part of the Pecos river.

Beavers were also frequently encountered and mention is made of a large beaver dam six miles below old Fort Sumner (p. 226). Carnivores were also encountered, including "catamounts" (probably *Lynx rufus*), "California lions," and "panthers" (probably *Felis concolor*), "grizzly bears and even jaguars were by no means uncommon" (p. 219). On the grasslands above the valley he describes a hunt in which in a short time 110 mounted Apache surrounded and killed 87 antelope (p. 204).

Hunting parties from the post encountered hostile Apache, Navajo and Comanche; the Bosque is specifically mentioned as the former favorite hunting ground of the Comanche, who gradually withdrew in the face of the increasing military pressure and swelling population of Apache and Navajo (p. 219). Although the nearest town was Anton Chico, 90 miles upstream, use of the Bosque area for grazing sheep is attested by the presence of an "old Mexican sheep corral," built of wood, on the future site of the fort. This locality was chosen because it was approachable through an open space in the woods, near water, and covered with excellent pasture (p. 199). While Cremony notes the potential scarcity of wood in his initial description of this locality, it is possible that this observation was influenced by events subsequent to his early impressions but prior to the writing of his report.

The description of a fight between a mountain lion and a brown bear in a "rocky canyon" about 400 yards downstream from this point (p. 225) suggests a locale several miles further south, where the river is confined between high outcrops of the Dockum group; perhaps in some details Cremony's memory was not always accurate. At no point does Cremony mention that the river water was especially unpalatable; in this respect he is virtually unique among 19th century chroniclers.

In the spring of 1863 about 400 Mescalero Apache from the Sacramento mountains had been settled at the Bosque Redondo and began work on cultivated and irrigated fields over an area of about 150 acres, using draft oxen and ploughs (Labadi, 1864: 425). Considerable difficulty with mesquite roots was encountered in the cultivation. Much of the work had to be done with shovels and hoes, and only about 70 men and women participated; nevertheless, the harvest yielded about 1500 bushels of corn, 20 fanegas [1 fanega = 1.6 bushel (Hammond and Rey, 1940: 399)] of beans, not including those consumed green, and 1000 pumpkins and squashes. Labadi remarked that the "excellent quality of the soil, a never-failing supply of water for domestic and irrigating purposes, a remarkably salubrious and temperate climate, the abundance of game, and its remoteness from the settlements tend to render the Bosque Redondo the very best place in the whole territory for an Indian reservation." (op. cit.: 427).

There is a record of the report of a representative of the Surveyor General's Office in Santa Fe (Clark, 1865), based on a personal reconnaissance seven to eight miles above and below the fort, in March, 1863. He estimated the alluvial land of the Bosque Redondo at 4000 acres, and the maximum area of arable land in the proposed reservation, consisting of a 40-mile square with Fort Sumner at the center, at 6000 acres. These observations are qualified by the following statement:

> It is, of course, well known to you [Michael Steck, Superintendent of Indian Affairs in New Mexico] that there is no arable land in the square above described, except that which can be irrigated by the waters of the Pecos River. There is good grazing on the mesas on both sides of the river, but no timber, and very little water for a considerable distance from the Bosque.

A letter from Steck to the Commissioner of Indian Affairs (Steck, 1865) makes clear the isolated position of the Bosque area with respect to other settlements and terrain habitable in the 1860's:

> East and west of the Bosque no settlement can be made for the distance of seventy-five miles, being arid plains. North, the nearest settlement is forty-five miles [Puerto de Luna?]; and south it is not probable that permanent settlement will ever be made, as the salt plains in that direction render the water of the Pecos River unfit for use.

Labadi had earlier remarked (op. cit.: 426) that the nearest mountains "cannot be reached in less than two days and nights of rapid travel."

Both the personnel of the Military establishment in New Mexico and the Office of Indian Affairs found that this position of isolation appeared to offer ideal conditions for the confinement of troublesome Indians. A basic disagreement between these groups concerned the number and origin of the Indians to be confined; the Indian Affairs faction favored the restriction of the proposed reservation to Mescalero and Jicarilla Apache, numbering perhaps 3000 (Labadi, 1865: 203), while the military, championed by Brig. Gen. James H. Carleton, proposed to send both Apaches and Navajos to the Bosque (Carleton, 1864: 110). Since the Navajo at that time were estimated to number about 15,000 (Labadi, op. cit.), and possessed considerable livestock, it seemed clear to the Indian Affairs Office that the resources of the Bosque Redondo were insufficient for their support, no matter how desirable the isolation of the area. However, in September of 1863 Carleton, apparently on his own initiative, sent the first 51 of an eventual 8-9000 Navajos to confinement at Fort Sumner. In his letter reporting this action to Brig. Gen. Lorenzo Thomas, the Adjutant-General (Carleton, op. cit.), he offered the view which later became a slogan of his faction, "*you can feed them cheaper than you can fight them.*" (emphasis his). The consequences of this action were disastrous for the Navajo and the Mescalero Apache. The effects of the disruption of natural conditions in the Bosque Redondo are still in evidence.

The story of this "concentration" of the Navajo has recently been well presented by Bailey (1964). The situation at the Bosque can be pieced together from Bailey's account and from reports and documents of the time. By October of 1864, over 7000 Navajos had been captured and sent to Fort Sumner (Steck, 1865: 183). This influx into the reservation, which in January of that year had been set aside by President Lincoln for the Apache Indians (Usher, 1865), caused considerable difficulty for the Mescalero, whose fields were largely robbed of their produce by the hungry Navajo. The remaining corn crop was almost entirely destroyed by insects (Labadi, 1865: 203). Early in 1865, a report by Capt. Francis McCabe (1896: 525) of the 1st New Mexico Cavalry stated that:

> Game is found in abundance some miles from the river and killed by the Indians. . . . The cottonwood, hackberry, and trees of a smaller growth line the banks of the Pecos at this point and at various points along the course of the stream. The ground mesquite. . .forms a very pleasant article of fuel. . . . There is an almost unlimited supply of this species of fuel extending over many miles in each direction from the post.

In September 1865 the Indian Superintendent for New Mexico reported that 3500 acres had been planted "in corn, wheat, beans, pumpkins, melons, &c., the result of which has exceeded their expectations (however, see Norton, 1867: 43), except the loss of a portion of their wheat during harvest by the continual heavy rains." (Delgado, 1866: 161).[5] This cultivation was made possible through the use of an irrigation ditch (*acequia*), about seven miles long, constructed by Apache and Navajo labor under the direction of Labadi during the preceeding year. Labadi was removed as Indian Agent at Fort Sumner in March, 1865 ostensibly after protesting that the Navajo were being given rations of meat from diseased cattle and from horses and mules (Labadi, 1866: 173), but more probably because of illegal appropriation of government property (Bailey, op. cit.: 200-201). After Labadi's transfer, the Indians at the Bosque Redondo were under the direct control of the Military Department of New Mexico, although eventually other agents were appointed by the Office of Indian Affairs.

A Congressional Committee appointed to investigate the conditions at the Bosque Redondo reservation in 1865 received considerable conflicting testimony regarding the quality of the reservation and its potential for success (U. S. Congress Joint Special Committee, 1867). The testimony of Percy Ayers, a former enlisted man, stationed at the Bosque for two months in the winter of 1863 is among the most negative as to the natural conditions of the area (ibid.: 335):

> In the vicinity of Fort Sumner the water is wretched; my whole company and the horses suffered from it. At the time I was there, there was very little water, and of very bad quality; it operated on man and beast like salts. The effect differed with different individuals; some were affected a few days with looseness of the bowels; with others, it was permanent during their stay. This was between the months of January and March. . . . At that time the water ran in a very small stream, but was principally in holes. Aside from the question of water I do not think the Bosque a suitable place for a reservation. There is a great scarcity of wood. The only facilities the Indians had for obtaining wood was by digging the mesquite roots. . . . I consider the water at Fort Sumner as unhealthy, a salt stream running into the Pecos north of the Fort.

In contrast to this is the testimony of Capt. Henry B. Bristol (ibid.: 344):

---

[5]The heaviest annual rainfall recorded in Fort Sumner is that for 1865, in which 27.27 inches were measured; almost double the mean annual rainfall (Bernard, 1942: 9).

As to the health of this post I can say with confidence that it is very healthy. There is as little sickness as at any post I was ever stationed at. The water has never affected me nor any other person I know of, except two new-comers, who said that it slightly relaxed their bowels for a day or two.

Perhaps the most extreme view in this regard was that of George Guyther, Surgeon of the 1st New Mexico Cavalry, who endorsed the healthfulness of the Bosque for several somewhat peculiar reasons (ibid.: 338):

From my knowledge of the health of this post, as my experience has enabled me to acquire, I consider it the healthiest place I ever lived in. It is particularly healthy because of its locality upon an open plain. Its freedom from stagnant waters [see Ayers above], the ability to prevent liquor at the post, and the power to enforce hygienic laws, are the forces which combine to produce the healthy condition of this locality. . . . There are, at all seasons of the year, strong winds blowing from various quarters, and these winds prevent the accumulation of mephitic vapors. The water, I have no hesitation in saying, has never proved detrimental at this post.

He proceeded to discuss the benefits of the Pecos water, to which he ascribed cures leading him to "regard the post as a '*Santarium*' [sic, emphasis his]." During four months of the year when the water was "low and clear" he found it "largely impregnated with salts," chiefly calcium sulfate and sodium sulfate. "During the remaining eight months the water is supplied from the melting snows and rains of the upper country, which makes it of the finest character" (op. cit.).

Another surgeon, Charles L. Warner, in charge of the Indian Hospital, also noted the difference between the character of the water when high and low (ibid.: 342):

When the river is high it comes down principally from the mountains, from rains and melting snows, but when low it partakes more of the waters of the Aqua Negra.[6]

[6]The Aqua Negra is mentioned in the statement of James M. Giddings (U. S. Congress Joint Special Committee, 1867: 342) as the somewhat mineralized stream used in irrigating his crops; he also mentions the presence of springs below the Aqua Negra which run into the Pecos. While he states that he lived on the Pecos some "three or four miles" from the place at which he was giving testimony (Fort Sumner), since 1853, it would have been difficult for him to irrigate from the Aqua Negra, some forty miles upstream. Perhaps the testimony should have been reported "thirty or forty" miles from Fort Sumner, placing Giddings' ranch on the Aqua Negra Grant just south of Santa Rosa.

The indifference felt by many New Mexicans to the plight of the Navajos at the Bosque Redondo in 1865 is clear in the testimony of Miguel Piño taken at Santa Fe (Ibid.: 336):

> Am a native of New Mexico; have resided in Santa Fe forty-four years; am mayor of the city; am a farmer by occupation. During all my lifetime the relations have been almost all the time hostile between the Navajoes and the people of New Mexico. My opinion the way to have a permanent peace is, to have the Indians placed on a reservation; I am not acquainted with the country around the Bosque Redondo, nor with the country formerly occupied by the Navajoes. I think the Indians are well off at the Bosque Redondo if there are enough troops to restrain them.

Piño neglects to mention that a great part of the hostility of the Navajos resulted from raids for slaves by New Mexicans.

On the night of November 3, 1865 all but nine of the 335 Mescalero Apache who remained on the reservation deserted and their lands were given to Navajos (Dodd, 1867: 149). If at that time the Mescalero were still where Cremony reported them in January, 1864, about three miles south of the fort on the east bank of the river (Cremony, 1868: 234),[7] these lands were at the very southern extreme of present cultivation in the valley and at the lowest elevation of the Lakewood terrace surface in that portion of the Bosque. Dodd mentions (op. cit.) that in August of 1866 heavy rains caused the Pecos to suddenly overflow these fields; this caused considerable damage to crops, washed away dwellings and implements, and drowned a woman and four children.

The 1866 report of J. K. Graves (1867), Special Indian Agent for New Mexico, was optimistic concerning the permanent settlement of the Navajos at the Bosque Redondo, while discounting some of the difficulties already obvious to the "anti-Bosque" adherents. He states (p. 136): "There is a fine growth of young cottonwoods coming forward, which will eventually furnish fuel. Mesquit [sic.] root is now plenty for fuel, and other kinds at a distance of twenty-five miles, which can be cut and floated down the river." This implies that most of the cottonwood forest in the vicinity of the Bosque had already been destroyed. The water is described as "good, though sometimes brackish." The 1866

[7] I have been unable to discover any basis for the statement by Coolidge and Coolidge (1930: 26) that the Navajo were kept on the west side of the river and the Mescalero on the east side. It does appear that the Navajo preferred the west side since they felt that "they do not die there so much." They were permitted to build houses on that side if they wished to (U. S. Congress Joint Special Committee, 1867: 355).

report of Col. Norton (1867: 146-147), Superintendent of Indian Affairs for New Mexico is somewhat less enthusiastic:

> These Indians have now been settled on this reservation for over three years, and it is now high time that they should be self-supporting, at least so far as the need of grain for bread is concerned. But the fact is lamentably true that not one-fifth of the amount required was raised last year, and the crop this year is no better than last, which failure is, in my opinion attributable to the want of skill and proper attention in the management of the labor and in irrigating the lands at proper times and in a proper manner, and not to the poverty of the soil nor scarcity of water for the purposes of irrigation.

By the following year (1867), however, Norton seems to have been of a different opinion (Norton, 1868: 190):

> The soil is cold, and the alkali in the water destroys it. The corn crop this year is a total failure. Last year 3,000 bushels only was raised on 3,000 acres, and the year before last six thousand bushels, continually growing worse instead of better. The self-sustaining properties of the soil are all gone. The Indians now dig up muskite [sic] root for wood, and carry it upon their galled and lacerated backs for 12 miles. . . . The water is black and brackish, scarcely bearable to the taste, and said by the Indians to be unhealthy, because one-fourth of their population have been swept off by disease, which they attribute mainly to the effects of the water. What a beautiful selection is this for a reservation. It has cost the government millions of dollars, and the sooner it is abandoned and the Indians removed the better.

The report for that year from Theodore H. Dodd, the Indian Agent at Fort Sumner emphasized the problem of fuel (Dodd, 1868: 201):

> The scarcity of timber and wood is the greatest objection to the reservation at the Bosque Redondo.
>
> During the severe cold weather last winter the Indians suffered a great deal for want of wood, as they were compelled to go six to twelve miles to procure mesquit [sic] roots and then dig and pack them on their backs to their homes. When the Navajoes were first located on the reservation four years ago, mesquit roots were comparatively plenty near the post of Fort Sumner, but now they have been consumed, and the Indians will be compelled to go further every year to procure them.
>
> . . . Cedar wood for the garrison at Fort Sumner is hauled for 20 to 30 miles, and is not very abundant at that distance.
>
> Timber and lumber for building purposes is transported from the Capitan Mountains and the vicinity of Fort Union, a distance of about 100 miles from Fort Sumner.

The repeated failure of the corn crop at the Bosque was due to a pest mentioned as the "army worm" or "cut-worm," whose method of destruction is described best by Carleton (1867: 229):

> As I understand it, the butterfly or moth, which lays the egg that produces this worm, lays that egg in the moist silk of the growing ear. . . . If I am correctly informed, once you destroy a thread of that silk before impregnation takes place, no kernel of corn will grow at the point where that thread had root upon the ear. . . . The moth that lays the egg looks like a small butterfly.

The effect of the worm is mentioned by McCleave (1867: 312): "The appearance of the corn in the field is excellent, but the cursed insects seem to devour all the grain in the ear."[8]

By 1868, following the publication of the report of the congressional investigation of 1865, continuing depletion of fuel resources, and additional failures in agriculture, the government was ready to abandon the enterprise and return the Navajo to a reservation in their former habitat. The report of an agent for the New Mexico Superintendency of the Office of Indian Affairs for that year briefly presents several aspects of the closing phases of the Bosque Redondo reservation (Davis, 1868: 161):

> . . . it has proved a total failure. It was certainly a very unfortunate selection for a reserve; no wood, unproductive soil, and very unhealthy water, and the Indians were so much dissatisfied they planted no grain last spring [1868], and I verily believe they were making preparations to leave as the Apaches did. . . . they are now located upon a reservation in their old country, west of the Rio Grande, and are living peacably, happy, and contented.

The Post-Reservation Period

With the departure of the Navajo and the gradual subjugation of the Comanche and Kiowa on the plains to the east, the northern Middle Pecos Valley was open to grazing of cattle and sheep. Intensive sheep-ranching continued until the late 1920's, when the

---

[8]This description indicates that the insect was the corn earworm, *Heliothis zea* (Boddie), which has been described as the worst pest of corn in the United States (Metcalf and Flint, 1962: 498). Although the present distribution of this species is worldwide, the fact that it was first described in 1793 from specimens probably taken in the West Indies and its favoring of New World plants, such as corn and tomatoes, suggests that it is native to the western hemisphere. The first report of its observation as a pest (on cotton), however, was not made until 1821, and in 1841 it was first mentioned as attacking corn in the southern United States (Little and Martin, 1942: 41). These relatively late observations suggest that its role as an agricultural pest may not extend back into the prehistoric period.

lower prices of Australian wool lowered the profits of the eastern New Mexico ranchers. Since that time grazing has been largely confined to cattle, which subsist at present on a still depleted range. The range deterioration of this area in 1940 was estimated between 11% and 50%, with deterioration in the area below the 18 Mile Bend of over 26% (U. S. National Resources Planning Board, 1942 - hereafter cited as USNRPB: Pl. 31). The estimated annual capacity of the range at that time varied from 9 to 15 head per section; a considerable decrease from Gidding's 1865 estimate of 100 head. Possibly Giddings exaggerated; he was apparently a Pro-Bosque adherent who felt that the Navajo were an excellent buffer against the Kiowa and Comanche (U. S. Congress Joint Special Committee, 1867: 343).

Farming activities in the northern Middle Pecos area, following the removal of the Navajo, are summarized by McMains and Hill (1942: 137-138). The main irrigation canal was used for a few years and abandoned. In 1898 only insignificant irrigation was being carried out along the river between Roswell and Puerto de Luna. In 1903 construction began on the present irrigation system, which serves most of the floor of the Bosque on the east side of the river north of Taiban Creek.

Present Conditions in the Northern Middle Pecos Valley

In general biotic classification, the area of our study is included in the western edge of the Kansan province (Dice, 1943: 39). Bailey (1913) places the valley of the Pecos in the Lower Sonoran life zone as far north as Santa Rosa, but qualifies this assignment considerably. In general, he describes the Pecos Valley as the "least arid of the Lower Sonoran Valleys in New Mexico" (ibid.: 12). In addition, "the Lower Sonoran Zone in the Pecos Valley . . . includes some mixed areas [with Upper Sonoran], especially along the edges and in the narrow northern strip extending along the river between Roswell and Santa Rosa, where only traces of the zone are found on hot slopes in the form of dwarf mesquite and occasional bushes of small-leaved sumac. . ." and a few other forms (ibid.: 13).

The valley is bordered on either side by Bailey's Great Plains division of the Upper Sonoran zone (ibid.: 25); broad grassy slopes, with stands of piñon pine and juniper in favored areas at higher elevations.

Climatic conditions are summarized in Figure 5. At Fort Sumner over 80% of the annual precipitation normally falls in

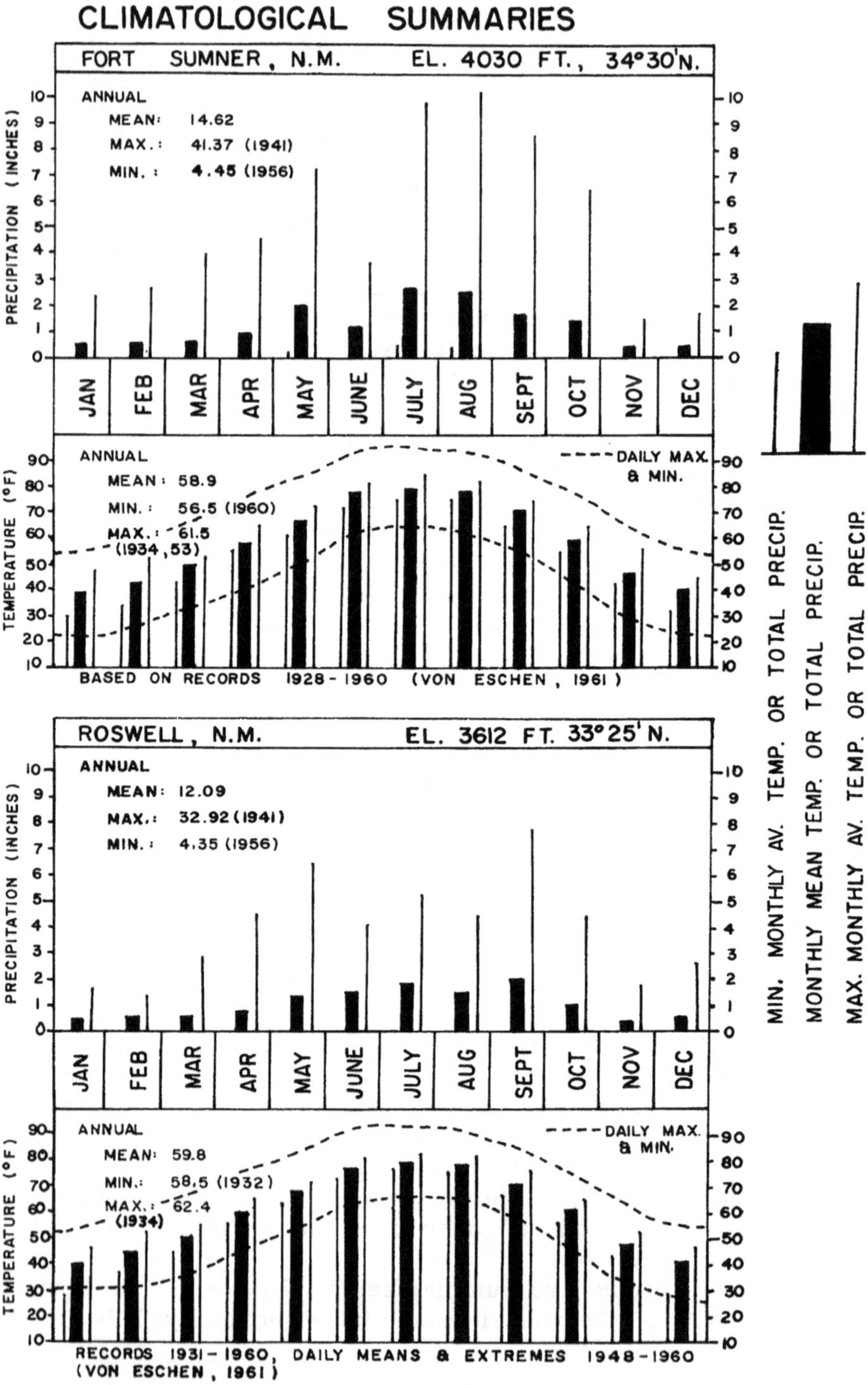

FIG. 5. Climatic data from two stations in the Middle Pecos Valley.

the six months from May through October (Von Eschen, 1961: 29); at Roswell over two-thirds of the precipitation occurs in this period (ibid.: 51). The growing season in this area is somewhat over six months, from mid-April to late October. In Trewartha's modification of the Koppen climatic classification (Espenshade, 1960: 8-9), the Middle Pecos area falls into the category of a relatively cool sub-tropical steppe (BS^{h}).

The potential vegetation in the area, as described by Küchler (1964), is seen in Figure 6. In this projection the valley proper from the Alamogordo reservoir south to about 18 Mile Bend shares the Grama-Buffalo Grassland cover which characterizes the Llano Estacado to the east and south. A few miles to the west of this portion of the valley a transition is seen into a Grama-Galeta Steppe; this includes scattered woody vegetation, such as *Artemisia,* in addition to grasses, and is restricted to northern New Mexico and Arizona. To the south, between 18 Mile Bend and the Bosque Grande, the river is bordered by a narrow band of Saltbrush-Greasewood shrubby vegetation. This is replaced by a Creosote Bush-Tarbush shrub-dominated zone to the south, extending as far south as Artesia. The Middle Pecos basin marks the easternmost occurrence of the Grama-Galeta Steppe, Saltbrush-Greasewood, and Creosote Bush-Tarbush groups. The major distribution of the Saltbrush-Greasewood group lies far to the north and west, through the Great Basin, while the Creosote Bush-Tarbush association characterizes most of the valleys of southern New Mexico and southeastern Arizona. Similarly, in its northern reaches the Middle Pecos forms the western boundary of the Grama-Buffalo Grass plains. The two outliers of Shinnery near Taiban Creek are characteristic of the semi-arid scrub vegetation of the Canadian Valley of northeastern New Mexico and the Texas Panhandle, and thus relate to the adjacent High Plains Grama-Buffalo Grass vegetation.

The present vegetation of the valley differs from Küchler's scheme chiefly in the presence of mesquite as the dominant shrub throughout the well-drained areas of the terraces bordering the river, and in the presence of Salt Cedar (*Tamarix*) in old channels immediately adjacent to the river. The only arboreal vegetation south of the Bosque Redondo other than occasional cottonwoods in a well-watered area of the valley is a scattered stand of Juniper on the north-facing exposures of the drainage of Cedar Creek. All of the grasses have been extensively depleted by overgrazing to such an extent that areas almost completely barren of vegetation are frequently encountered between the mesquite on the Blackdom and Orchard Park terraces.

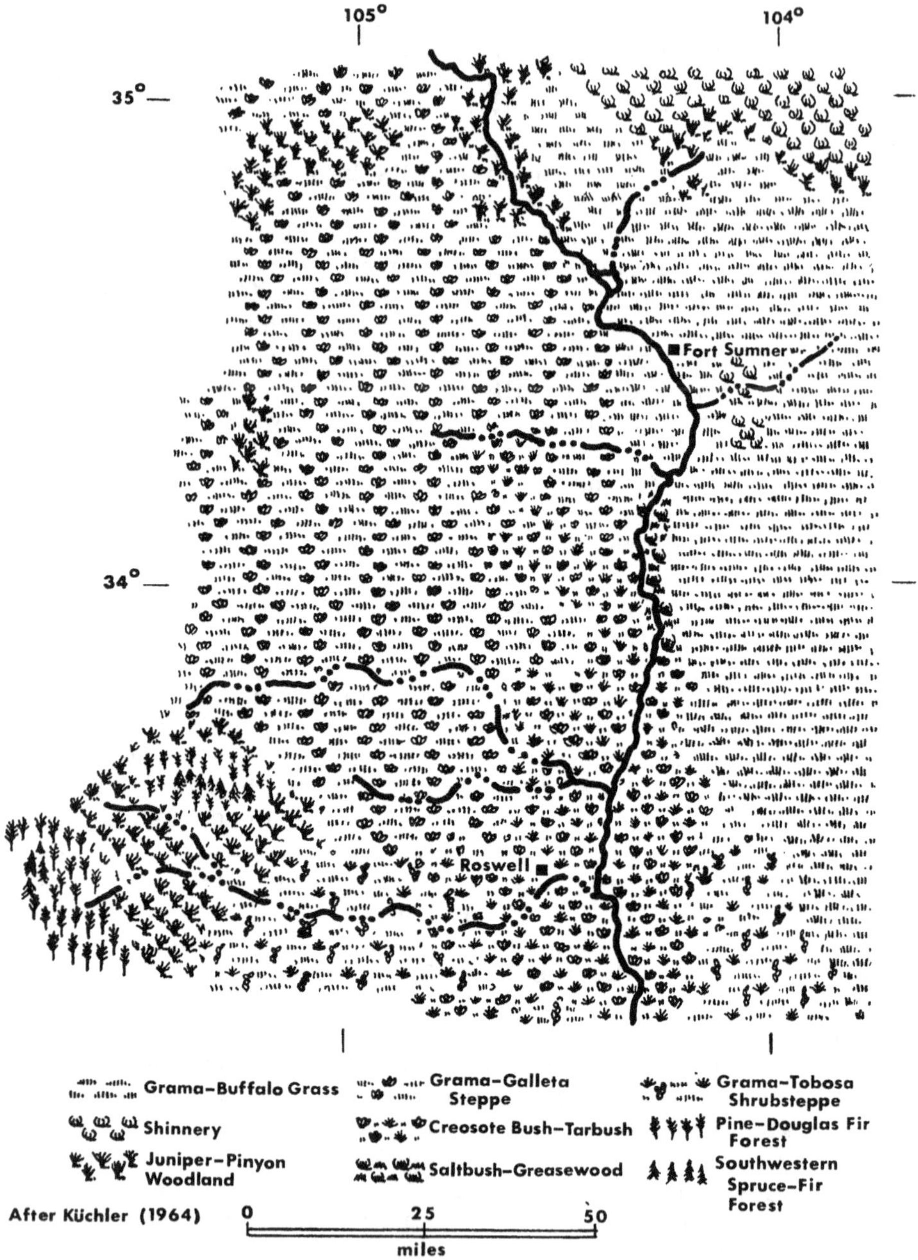

FIG. 6. Potential natural vegetation of the Middle Pecos Valley.

By most classifications of environment, then, the Middle Pecos Valley appears to fall on the eastern margin of the Southwest and is closely linked to the High Plains. It is also clear that within the Middle Valley it is possible to distinguish two natural zones. One, lying north of the Bosque Grande, can be associated with patterns characteristic of valleys of the northern Southwest (sometimes designated "Upper Sonoran"), while the other is more characteristic of valleys of the southern Southwest ("Lower Sonoran").

Factors of Historically Reported Natural Environment Likely to Have Affected Prehistoric Settlement in the Middle Pecos Valley

The most obvious natural resource affecting aboriginal occupation of the Middle Pecos Valley is water. The most apparent water source is the river itself, which according to historic references maintained some flow throughout the year. In addition, the beds of several tributary drainages contain rocky hollows in which water is available most of the year (e.g. Cibolo Creek and Yeso Creek). There are also several springs scattered along the Mescalero Pediment about 5-10 miles east of the river, which are either actively flowing at present or, from the presence of luxuriant vegetation, promise water a short depth below the surface. Rainfall probably increased the flow of local tributaries during the summer in the prehistoric period, while melting snows of the Sangre de Cristo and other areas of the Northern Valley were the source of the spring floods mentioned in historic accounts. It is probable that a confined mature drainage, such as that suggested by aerial photos of the area near Taiban Creek and south of Bosque Grande (see preceeding Chapter), would be subject to overflow of the valley bottom during spring floods, which would also leave deposits of fine silt. In such a drainage the water table would be maintained at a fairly shallow level by absorption from the slow-moving meandering stream. While summer rains might produce occasional torrential flooding, it is likely that with good ground cover this effect was less frequent than at present, and the effects of the rain would have been largely beneficial to vegetation in the valley bottom. Assuming the presence of all or a major portion of these factors, it is likely that under normal conditions the water sources of the valley could have supported some form of primitive cultivation.

Carter (1945: 92) suggests that there are no climatic factors limiting the practice of primitive agriculture in this area.

The descriptions of wild plant and animal foods indicate that game was present in some abundance near the river, and in lesser quantities on the grasslands bordering the valley. It would appear that a strong contrast existed between specific forms in these two habitats, with deer, wild turkey, and large carnivores most apparent in the valley bottoms, and antelope and bison dominant on the surrounding grasslands. In addition, it is probably safe to say that the jackrabbit (*Lepus*) was most abundant in the latter habitat and the cottontail (*Sylvilagus*) in the former. The ornate box turtle (*Terrapene ornata*) was probably present throughout the area, while the soft-shelled turtle (probably *Amyda mutica*, observed by the field party in 1960) was present in the immediate vicinity of the river. Fish and shellfish were either absent or of so little importance that no mention is made of them in the historic records.

Wild plant foods mentioned specifically in historic documents include wild currants, mesquite, grass seeds, and wild sunflower seeds. Prickly pear (*Opuntia*) may be inferred to have been present in the southern Middle Valley. Undoubtedly numbers of edible plants escaped the notice of historic chroniclers.

Thus it would appear that the Middle Pecos Valley may have offered a favorable setting for a limited aboriginal population, either subsisting entirely on collected resources or relying in part on those produced by limited cultivation on the valley flood plain. Sedentary communities may not have been possible (without irrigation) in the late prehistoric period because of changes in natural conditions which took place sometime before the sixteenth century; this seems attested by the lack of native inhabitants mentioned in the early historic accounts. By the late historic period sedentary settlements would have been impossible because of the predatory Comanche, Kiowa, and Apache.

III

RESULTS OF THE SURVEY: DISTRIBUTION OF SITES IN THE MIDDLE PECOS VALLEY

The maximum extent of the surveys of 1956 and 1960 ranged from the vicinity of the Alamogordo Reservoir in the north to the southern extreme of the Bitter Lakes Wildlife Refuge, directly east of Roswell in the south. While the survey was largely confined to the vicinity of the river, several sites on tributary streams were sampled, as were localities in the vicinity of springs and draws to the east of the river on the Mescalero Pediment. In addition, our collections from these latter sites were supplemented by those of amateur archaeologists from the Portales area, in particular James Warnica and Gordon Brown.

With the limited facilities, manpower, and time of both seasons, and the unfavorable weather conditions of the 1960 season (when almost twice the previous *record* rainfall was recorded in July [Von Eschen, 1961: 30]) an intensive survey of the entire valley between these extremes was not possible. Therefore, as a compromise, a few areas were sampled intensively, while only sporadic checks were made for site materials along several extended sections of the valley. Those areas which were examined most thoroughly include: (1) The west side of the Bosque Redondo from about two miles south of Fort Sumner to about two miles south of the mouth of Taiban Creek, (2) Both sides of the river in the vicinity of the 18 Mile Bend as far south as 18 Mile Draw, and about four miles north of the Bend, and (3) The west side of the river in the vicinity of Cedar Creek and the LX Ranch. Major survey areas are delineated in Figure 7.

A total of 64 sites were located by the survey, ranging in extent from scatters of about a hundred flakes or sherds to extensive exposures of cultural material and architectural remains. Finds of isolated artifacts or a very few flakes or sherds were not given site designations in this survey. The numbering system used for designating sites was initiated in 1956, when sites on the Llano Estacado as well as in the Pecos Valley were being studied, and when collections made by Warnica and Brown were being incorporated into the data. At this time I felt it necessary to distinguish between sites in the valley (numbers preceeded by the letter "P"), sites on the Llano (preceeded by "L"), site

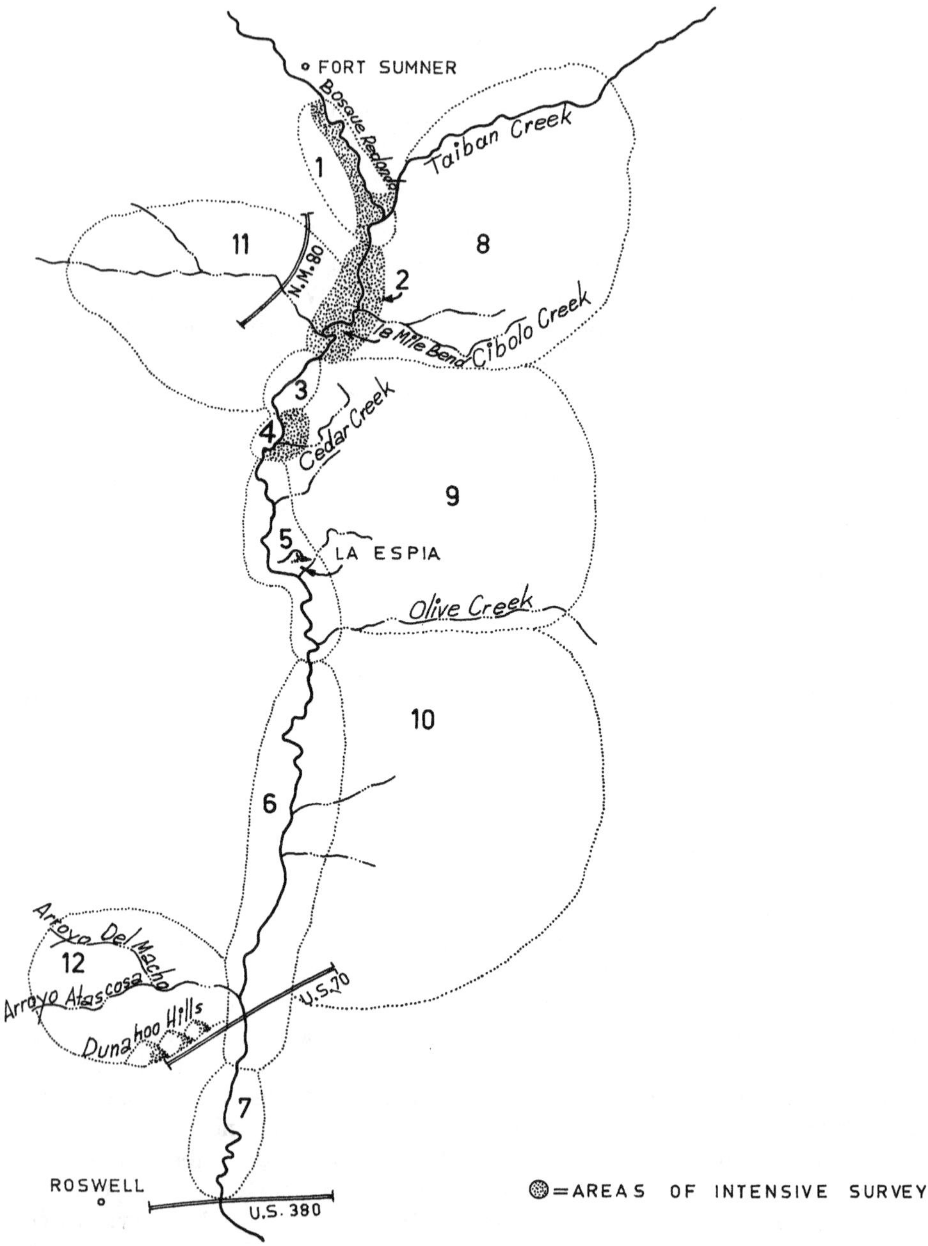

FIG. 7. Major survey areas.

collections by Warnica (preceeded by "W") and collections by Brown (preceeded by "B"). During the first seasons nine sites were located in the Valley and designated P1 through P9 from north to south. The 55 succeeding sites located in the 1960 season were numbered from P10 to P64 in the order of discovery.

Soon after our initial investigations in the valley in 1956 it became apparent that particular topographic localities were favored for settlement, while others were neglected. Specifically, promontories or flat-topped hills of the Orchard Park and Blackdom terraces, adjacent to present or ancient channels of the river, were the localities favored for most extensive sedentary occupation. The largest of these sites were adjacent to relatively broad expanses of valley bottom. A few sites were found on the Lakewood Terrace, more frequently in the southern portion of the survey than in the north. In addition, the apparent sources of permanent water on the Mescalero Pediment were points of concentration of large quantities of artifact material, although few definite architectural remains were observed in these localities.

I have classified the sites into the following general categories:

A. Scatters of less than 100 sherds and/or flakes with little or no indication of permanent architecture
B. Concentrations of several hundred flakes and/or sherds and occasional indications of permanent architecture
C. Concentrations of several thousand flakes and/or sherds with little or no indication of permanent architecture
D. Concentrations of several thousand flakes and/or sherds with frequent indications of permanent architecture.

For purposes of presentation here, the sites of each type are grouped geographically according to the areas defined in Figure 8. The distribution of the sites visited by the survey, plus three of Warnica's sites, is seen in Table II. Table III presents a list of the sites in numerical sequence, showing general category (A, B, C, or D) and terrace location, geographical area and size of surface collections.

TABLE II
GEOGRAPHICAL DISTRIBUTION OF SITE TYPES

Area / Type:	A	B	C	D	Total
1.	6	4	2	1	13
2.	1	8	2	3	14
3.	-	6	-	-	6
4.	1	2	-	1	4
5.	4	5	-	1	10
6.	-	1	2	-	3
7.	-	2	-	-	2
8.	1	1	2	-	4
9.	-	2	1	-	3
10.	-	-	2	-	2
11.	-	1	1	-	2
12.	1	2	2	-	5
Total	14	34	14	6	68

TABLE III
LIST OF SITES: LOCATION, TERRACE, AND CONTENT OF SURFACE COLLECTIONS (1956-1960)

Site No.	Area	Type	Terrace*	Stone Count**	Sherd Count
P1	1	C	B	Flakes	1233
P2	2	B	B		251
P3	2	B	B		417
P4	2	D	B	not	8057
P5	11	C	Yeso Creek		1
P6	5	A	B		0
P7	6	C	O	counted	1540
P8	6	C	O		1375
P9	6	B	L		704
P10	2	B	B	567	420

TABLE III (Continued)

Site No.	Area	Type	Terrace*	Stone Count**	Sherd Count
P11	5	B	L	132	6
P12	5	D	O	335	523
P13	1	D	L	228	361
P14	1	C	B/O	454	0
P15	2	B	B	231	36
P16	2	B	O	87	60
P17	2	C	O	319	612
P18	2	Buried Hearth	L	0	0
P19	2	D	L	Historic Village	
P20	2	B	B	856	518
P21	2	C	O	79	489
P22	2	B	B	664	48
P23	2	B	B	129	175
P24	2	D	B	254	370
P25	3	B	O (?)	281	556
P26	8	C	Cibolo Creek	474	1168
P27	4	B	B	359	0
P28	4	B	O	356	39
P29	4	D	B	673	1730
P30	4	A	B	96	23
P31	5	B	B	178	150
P32	5	A	B	77	8
P33	5	A	O	82	3
P34	5	B	O	163	48
P35	5	A	O	11	7
P36	5	B	L	542	236
P37	1	A	B	58	62
P38	1	B	O	584	904
P39	1	B	O	284	267
P40	1	A	L	68	67
P41	1	A	O	114	79
P42	1	A	O	96	79

TABLE III (Continued)

Site No.	Area	Type	Terrace*	Stone Count**	Sherd Count
P43	1	B	L	289	136
P44	1	B	O	341	286
P45	1	A	O	43	41
P46	2	A	B	21	6
P47	2	A	B	119	0
P48	3	B	O	290	92
P49	3	B	B	39	15
P50	3	B	B	26	48
P51	3	B	B	60	95
P52	9	B	MP	132	93
P53	8	A	MP	39	4
P54	8	B	MP	210	44
P55	8	C	MP	1890	3431
P56	7	B	O	284	255
P57	12	B	AA	180	29
P58	12	B	AA	335	390
P59	12	B	AA	942	3
P60	12	A	AA	11	49
P61	12	C	AA	1664	7
P62	1	A	B	2	51
P63	7	B	O	129	116
P64	3	B	B	72	42
W7	11	B (?)	Conejos Creek	Flakes	101
W9	10	C	MP		589
W42	9	C	MP	not	209
L6	10	C	MP	counted	1224
L8	9	B	MP		109

* B = Blackdom
O = Orchard Park
L = Lakewood
MP = Mescalero Pediment
AA = Arroyo Atascosa

** Includes flakes and implements, except projectile points.

IV

MIDDLE PECOS VALLEY CERAMICS

Typology

In order to present the artifact materials in a meaningful frame of reference which includes their chronological as well as spatial relationships, a discussion of ceramic typology and the chronological implications of ceramic distribution are presented first, followed by discussions of the typology and distribution of other artifact materials as they relate to the ceramic sequence.

Two basic categories are obvious in the classification of the Middle Pecos ceramics: the brownwares and the graywares. Both are related to previously described ceramics from eastern New Mexico; the brownware to Jornada Brown of Southern New Mexico Mogollon origin, and the graywares to Chupadero Black on White of southern Anasazi origin. I was able to distinguish consistent and chronologically significant typological differences within each of these previously homogeneous types and therefore have expanded the typological description of each, following the ceramic systems suggested by Wheat, Gifford and Wasley (1958).

The Jornada Brownware System

Jornada Brown

History

This is the first brownware described from the southeastern New Mexico area (Mera, 1943). The original type description (op. cit.: 12) is extremely broad, much more so than Jennings' (1940) previous description of the Jornada ware from the type site (LA 2000) assigned by Mera. Lehmer's description of an El Paso Brownware (1948: 94) does not seem sufficiently different to distinguish El Paso from Jornada Brown and the two are here (as in Fenenga, 1956a: 232) considered as the same type. The original type description is largely retained here, with minor modification.

Area

Southeastern New Mexico, south of the vicinity of Gran Quivira between the Rio Grande and Pecos rivers, extending an unknown distance into northern Mexico.

Type Site

LA 2000 on the Peñasco River, about 40 miles west of Hope, New Mexico.

Derivation

Alma Plain (?).

Paste

Tan to black, frequent black core. Hardness varies considerably, although some correlation with the amount of temper is present. Fracture is generally slightly to very friable.

Temper

Generally metamorphic or granitic derivatives which have been crushed or ground. Angular fragments of feldspar are most common, with secondary fragments of quartz and infrequent particles of mica. Size of particles varies from over 3 mm. to microscopic; most obvious particles were .5-.8 mm. and are abundant to very abundant (140-210 per cm^2).

Construction

Coiled.

Walls

4-9 mm., average of 6-7 mm.

Finish

Frequently polished over a hand-smoothed exterior on ollas. Some tool-smoothed finish without polishing. Interiors hand- or tool-smoothed. Only largest fragments of temper protruded through polished surfaces, but many medium to large fragments are usually apparent on smoothed surfaces.

Forms

Ollas and bowls with direct rims, also seed jars. Olla rims extend in a smooth curve above shoulder about 4-6 cm. Infrequent olla specimens exhibit thickened "disc" base characteristic of Chupadero wares. There is some evidence that this is a late development.

Decoration

Rare decoration with red paint. Bowls either have overall interior wash, overlapping exterior about 1/2 inch, or broad-line interior decoration. Some polychrome decoration with black and red pigments.

Variants

Jornada Polychrome, Jornada Red on Brown, Coarse Jornada Brown (similar to Jornada Brown but fragments of quartz and feldspar temper much coarser and frequently dragged on surface).

References

Jennings, 1940: 5-6; "unnamed brown ware" and "plain brown ware." Mera, 1943: 12.

Middle Pecos Micaceous Brown

History

New type, mentioned by Fenenga and Cummings (1956a: 217) and Peckham (1957: 57).

Area

The valley of the Pecos River in the vicinity of the Bosque Redondo (Fort Sumner) and south an undetermined distance beyond the mouth of Yeso Creek, but north of the mouth of the Arroyo del Macho.

Type Site

P4b, immediately northwest of the 18 Mile Bend of the Pecos River.

Derivation

Jornada Brown.

Paste

Tan to black with frequent black core. Hardness fairly constant, with fracture usually quite friable.

Temper

Crushed granitic and metamorphic derivatives, with very small flakes of mica abundantly distributed through the paste and concentrated on the wall surfaces. Some magnetite is always present; frequently it is in quantities sufficient to demonstrate by pulling a sherd off balance with a magnet. Rock particles vary from about 1.5 mm. to microscopic, with the average range of the larger particles about .5 to .8 mm. They vary in abundance from about 120 to 175 per cm^2.

Walls

2.5 to 9.0 mm.; average 6-7 mm.

Finish

Tool-smoothed interior and exterior; marks of the smoothing tool obvious on vessel surfaces. Mica is only element of temper apparent on vessel walls and just beneath surface, suggesting floating.

Form

Ollas and bowls. Rims direct and somewhat less attenuated or extended than in Jornada ollas, resulting in a shorter neck. Very rare bowl sherds with coiled basketry impressions on exteriors. These sherds may perhaps represent a phase of training in pottery construction.

Decoration

Broad red line or overall red wash on bowl interiors not infrequent. Rare red decoration on olla exteriors. Rare bowls with vivid heavy red slip on interior (Meadowsweet red [Maerz & Paul, 1930]).

Variants

Middle Pecos Micaceous Red on Brown.

Roswell Brown

History

New type. Formerly designated as "Polished Brown" by J. Holden (1952, p. 101; personal communication, 1958).

Area

The valley of the Pecos River in the vicinity of Roswell, New Mexico, and the valley of the Hondo River as far west as Ruidoso, New Mexico.

Type Site

P9, about 1/2 mile south of the U. S. 70 crossing of the Pecos River, on the Orchard Park terrace.

Derivation

Jornada Brown.

Paste

Tan to black with most frequent shade a dark tan. Black fire-clouding and black core frequent. Hardness similar to Middle Pecos Micaceous Brown, with somewhat less friable fracture.

Temper

Crushed granitic derivatives, with a predominance of weathered granite (quartz and feldspar). Little or no mica or magnetite.

Particle size is either coarse or very fine with few intermediate pieces. The large particles range from about 1.0 to 3.0 mm. and the smaller ones from about .2 to .5 mm. The large particles are scattered infrequently through the paste and the small particles are profuse (over 450 per cm^2.). The weathered granite particles are occasionally oxidized to orange-red; these red specks in the temper form one of the characteristics of the type.

Walls

5-10 mm., average about 6 mm.

Finish

Tool-smoothed and polished on interiors of bowls and exteriors of ollas. Polish on bowl interiors extremely well executed. Fine finish of polished surfaces suggests floating. Largest fragments of temper occasionally protrude through vessel walls.

Form

Ollas and bowls. Rims most commonly flattened or slightly flattened. Direct rims occur rarely. There appears to be a trend from direct rims on the older sites to squared rims on the later sites. A few rounded olla rims exhibit a slightly rolled exterior edge. Ollas appear to have the wide mouth and neck described for Jornada Brown.

Decoration

Bowls are not infrequently decorated with broad red lines on the interior surfaces. These lines are always vertical or at a greater than 45° angle to the rim and usually measure from 10 to 12 mm. in diameter with spaces of 7 mm. to 14 mm. between lines. Rims of these decorated bowls are always painted red. There also appear to have been some bowls decorated with an overall red interior wash.

Variants

Roswell Red on Brown, Roswell Corrugated (Brown Corrugated ware with Roswell paste).

McKenzie Brown

History

New type.

Area

Same as Middle Pecos Micaceous Brown.

Type Site

P4c, immediately northwest of the 18 Mile Bend of the Pecos River.

Derivation

Middle Pecos Micaceous Brown (?).

Paste

Tan to black. Almost always a heavy black core, with the characteristic wall color a blackened tan. Fractured and weathered surfaces quite friable.

Temper

The most obvious elements in the temper are fragments of crushed quartz, the largest of which seldom have a diameter of over 1 mm., the average ranging from .2 to .5 mm. These fragments are abundant to profuse in the paste (about 300 per cm^2.) and are accompanied by sparse large rounded quartz grains and by abundant small fragments of mica (muscovite), biotite, and feldspar.

Walls

3-9 mm., average about 6 mm.

Finish

Hand or tool-smoothed with some polishing of exteriors of all vessels, and interiors of bowls. Thin layer of fine clay on surfaces suggests floating.

Form

Ollas and bowls. One sherd of a seed jar rim. Most bowl bases and some olla bases are the "pancake" type similar to Chupadero. Several bowls have unmodified coils on exterior or top coil left unmodified. Olla rim sherds exhibit extremely short-necked vessel shape, with rim curving up from shoulder in about an inch. Some olla rims are rolled. Most bowl and olla rims are direct.

Decoration

Bowls are infrequently decorated with an overall red interior of the vivid hue mentioned as occurring on rare Middle Pecos Micaceous bowls. A single decorated olla sherd had thick highly polished deep red exterior slip. One small jar was decorated with leather-hard incised lines parallel to rim in the manner of certain eastern Texas ceramics.

Variants

McKenzie Red on Brown.

South Pecos Brown

History

New type. Probably includes some material classified by Mera as Carlsbad Brown in the site files of the Laboratory of Anthropology, Santa Fe.

Area

The valley of the Pecos River for an unknown distance south of Roswell, New Mexico, possibly as far as the Texas border.

Type Site

L10, on the outwash slope below the scarp of the Llano Estacado in the Mescalero Sands area about 12 miles south of U. S. 385.

Derivation

Jornada Brown (?).

Paste

Tan to blackish tan, orange, and rarely pink. A gray core frequent, but a black core rare. Quite hard, with fractures not very friable.

Temper

Predominantly crushed feldspar combined with some magnetite, apparently derived from a weathered granite. Mica and quartz rare to absent. The feldspar fragments are angular and quite coarse ranging up to 2 mm. or more in diameter with most fragments about 1 mm. in diameter. They are relatively sparsely scattered through the paste, seldom more than 75 per cm^2.

Walls

4-7 mm., average about 5 mm.

Finish

Hand and tool-smoothed. Occasionally polished, particularly bowl interiors. Temper frequently protrudes through surface and is surrounded by radial cracks.

Form

Ollas, bowls and occasional seed jars. Rims generally direct and frequently gently tapering. Some beveled rims occur, with bevel on exterior surface on both bowls and ollas. Height of olla rims similar to Jornada Brown.

Decoration

Infrequent decoration in broad red lines or solid red interior on bowls. Paint a deep maroon color. Rare red decoration on olla exterior. It appears on the basis of the weathering seen that overall red interior decoration may be earlier than broad-line on bowls, as suggested by Mera for the red-on-brown wares in the Mogollon-Three Rivers series (Mera, 1943).

Variants

South Pecos Red on Brown.

The Chupadero Black on White System

Chupadero Black on White

History

This was the first native reduced-fired ware to be reported from the southeastern New Mexico area (Mera, 1931). The original type description is rather vague, with emphasis mainly on vessel form, finish, and design. Hawley's redescription (1950) is somewhat more detailed and is followed here.

Area

The south central portion of New Mexico, bordered on the east by the Pecos River, on the west by the Rio Grande, on the north by the southern Salines in Torrance County, and on the south probably by the White Sands area of the Tularosa Basin and by the valley of the Hondo River. The southern boundary is difficult to delineate, since the ware was apparently traded in this direction to a considerable extent.

Type Site

An unnamed site on the Chupadero Mesa about eight miles south of the Pueblo of Tabira.

Derivation

Socorro Black on White, Red Mesa Black on White (?), Crosby Black on Gray.

Paste

Varies from white to dark gray, seldom exhibiting a dark core. Quite hard, with linear fracture which is not friable.

Temper

Ground black and white rock fragments and quartz. Also frequent mixture with sherd temper. Fragments of stone temper quite fine, largest about .5 mm. in diameter. Temper relatively abundant, but widely variable in abundance.

Construction

Coiled.

Walls

c. 6 mm.

Finish

Bowl interiors and olla exteriors covered with thin uneven slip or wash and polished slip frequently cracked. Some surfaces appear to be floated. Bowl exteriors roughened or striated, or coils occasionally left unaltered; olla interiors striated. Temper occasionally protrudes through lighter areas of slip or wash and float (?).

Forms

Ollas and bowls. Ollas globular with thickened disc base and vertical neck with flared rim. Lugs almost always present and usually two- or three-strand. Bowls both regularly curved and of truncated funnel shape with flat bottom and disc base.

Decoration

Slipped, washed, or floated (?) surfaces decorated with heavy mineral (iron) paint. The most common design motifs are opposing angular solid and hatched elements and broad and thin lines. Draftsmanship varies from competent to careless.

Variants

Casa Colorada Black on White (same as Chupadero Black on White but bowl exteriors and olla interiors are smoothed).

References

Mera, 1931; Mera, 1935: 29; Hawley, 1950: 67; Smiley, Stubbs, and Bannister, 1953: 58.

Crosby Black on Gray

History

New type.

Area

The valley of the Pecos River from the vicinity of Roswell, New Mexico, north to the Bosque Redondo.

Type Site

P9, about 1/2 mile south of the U. S. 70 crossing of the Pecos River, on the Lakewood terrace.

Derivation

Socorro Black on White (?).

Paste

Light to dark gray, infrequent darker core. Fracture varies from linear to slightly friable. Hardness varies widely.

Temper

Similar to Chupadero except sherd temper rare to absent. Occasional sherds have yellowish-white fragments in temper which effervesce strongly with dilute hydrochloric acid (limestone?). Also occasional sherds have carbonized elements in temper.

Construction

Coiled.

Walls

4 to 8 mm., average 6-7 mm.

Finish

High polish over thin gray slip or floated surface on interior of bowls and exterior of ollas. Bowl exteriors vary from slipped and polished to smoothed. Olla interiors occasionally smoothed but generally striated.

Form

Bowls and ollas. One seed jar rim. All vessels appear to have had direct rims; flared rims absent. Some thickening of vessel bases but disc base rare to absent. Funnel-shaped bowl with flat bottom present. Single and double strand lugs. Coiled basketry impression on bowl exteriors present but rare—see interpretation under Middle Pecos Micaceous.

Decoration

Exterior of ollas and interior of bowls painted with thin mineral paint (iron) which is frequently oxidized to red-brown. Motifs include small solid pendant triangles, crude hatching, thin parallel lines in pendant triangle arrangements, and large triangular and rectangular solid elements connected by thin lines. Draftsmanship crude to competent. Some evidence that thin paint is a remnant of an absorbed original heavy application.

Middle Pecos Black on White

History

New type.

Area

Same as Middle Pecos Micaceous Brownware.

Type Site

P4c (see McKenzie Brownware).

Derivation

Crosby Black on Gray, Chupadero Black on White (?), Red Mesa Black on White (?), Socorro Black on White (?).

Paste

Light to dark gray with occasional streak of darker core. Yellowish tinge common. Fracture somewhat friable. Paste noticeably softer than in Chupadero Black on White.

Temper

Variable amounts of crushed dark rock, clear quartz, opaque quartz and sherd. Tends to be more sparse than in Chupadero. Yellow-white temper fragments which effervesce in dilute hydrochloric acid present in about 50% of the sherds.

Walls

3 to 8 mm., average about 6.5 mm.

Finish

Bowl interiors and olla exteriors covered with extremely irregular thin white slip. Early bowl exteriors are slipped and the slipped surface of all vessels frequently shows evidence of polishing prior to the application of the slip. Later examples of ollas have striated interiors and bowls have roughened exteriors. Interior of late bowls frequently roughened or striated then superficially smoothed before slip applied.

Form

Bowls and ollas. Olla rims sometimes flattened as in Chupadero Black on White, but most frequently direct. Bowl rims frequently somewhat flattened but normally direct. Infrequent examples of flared bowl rims. Coiled basketry impressions on bowl exteriors occasionally encountered. Lugs include single, double, and triple strand as well as small "canteen" lugs.

Decoration

Slipped surface decorated in thin to heavy black mineral paint. Slip is almost never crackled, as it frequently is in Chupadero Black on White in the southern Middle Pecos Valley. Most frequent motifs include hatched elements with heavy lines paralleling their borders, opposed hatched and solid angular elements, and solid angular elements connected by thin lines.

Hatching is generally fairly well executed with lines ranging 1 to 1.5 mm. in diameter. Broad lines average about 8-9 mm. and interstices between hatched lines average slightly wider than the lines themselves. Some curvilinear motifs are known, including two examples of heavy curved and interlocking lines. A single sherd depicts what appears to be a coiled snake in the bottom of a bowl—the only life form thus far discovered in ceramic decoration in the Middle Pecos Valley. Sherds are highly vulnerable to weathering, with slip frequently becoming chalky, painted designs obliterated or assuming a "fugitive" appearance, and sherd edges noticeably smoothed.

Temporal Distribution of Intrusive Ceramics

Small quantities of sherds of external origin were found in most of the larger sherd collections from the Middle Pecos. The known temporal distribution of these materials offered frequent clues regarding the approximate chronological position of our samples. The following types were present:

ANASAZI ORIGIN

Basketmaker III - Pueblo I
- Lino Gray (Hawley, 1950: 21)[9]
- Kiatuthlanna Black on White (Hawley, 1950: 27-28)

Pueblo II
- Red Mesa Black on White (Hawley, 1939: 52-53)

Pueblo II - III
- Wingate Black on Red (Colton and Hargrave, 1937: 118-119)
- Cebolleta Black on White (Dittert and Ruppé, 1951: 120)

Pueblo III
- Kwahe'e Black on White (Mera, 1935: 5-6)
- Los Lunas Smudged (Mera, 1935: 28-29)
- Pitoche Rubbed-Ribbed (Mera, 1935: 29)
- St. Johns Polychrome (Hawley, 1950: 49)
- Santa Fe Black on White (Hawley, 1950: 68-69)
- Socorro Black on White (Mera, 1935: 27)

Pueblo IV
- Rio Grande Glaze Wares

---

[9]Citations are not necessarily those of the original description, but are those which appear to most accurately delineate the type.

MOGOLLON ORIGIN

Period Indeterminate
Alma Plain (Haury, 1936: 32-34)

Mogollon 5 (after Wheat, 1955: 11)
Broadline Red on Terra Cotta (Mera and Stallings, 1931: 2-4; Mera, 1943: 13). Classified as San Andres Red-on-Terra-Cotta by McCluney (1962)
El Paso Polychrome (Stallings, 1931)
Jornada Corrugated
Lincoln Black on Red (Mera and Stallings, 1931: 5-7)
Mimbres Black on White (Hawley, 1950: 62-63)
Playas Red Incised (Hawley, 1950: 61)
Reserve Black on White (Martin and Rinaldo, 1950: 502-503)
Three Rivers Red on Terra Cotta (Hawley, 1950: 65-66)

Seriation of the Ceramic Collections

Ceramics provided the basic element in establishing a chronological sequence of cultural phases in the Middle Pecos Valley survey and, in fact, the "cultural" phases designated throughout are primarily ceramic groupings. The full cultural significance of these changes in the local ceramic styles will not be understood until more detailed studies are carried out on other aspects of the archaeological remains in the valley, such as architecture.

The sherd count of ceramic types in the 29 site or component collections of over 100 prehistoric sherds from the Valley proper is seen in Table IV; Table V lists the same data for samples under 100 sherds. On a few sites distinct components are areally separated. These components are isolated in the table by letters following the site numeral, e.g. P4A, P4B and P4C. The only exception to this usage is Site P12A which appears to be distinct from Site P12.

Sherd samples were both weighed and counted. In keeping with traditional methods of presentation the tabulations for each site are presented by count. However, the comparison of samples was done by weight in the expectation that differences due to the random factors of breakage could be better controlled. A modest test of the advantage of the use of measures of weight was conducted on ten pairs of site samples described in the original study (Jelinek, 1960: 147). The indices of likeness of weighed samples were compared with the indices of likeness of counted samples for the five most closely related pairs of samples and

TABLE IV

SHERD COUNTS FOR SAMPLES OF OVER 100 SHERDS

	BROWNWARE																	BLACK ON WHITE																
SITE	MICACEOUS	ROSWELL	JORNADA	S. PECOS	ALMA	LATE ROSWELL	McKENZIE	CORRUGATED	EL PASO	EL PASO POLY.	BROADLINE R/TC	THREE RIVS. R/TC	LOS LUNAS SM.	PITOCHE RUB.RIB.	WINGATE B/R	ST. JOHNS POLY.	OTHER	LINO GRAY	RED MESA	LOCAL? P II	CROSBY B/G	M. PECOS	CHUPADERO	ERODED CHUPAD.	RESERVE	CEBOLLETA	SOCORRO	SANTA FE	KWAHE'E	MIMBRES	OTHER	GLAZEWARE	NAVAJO	TOTAL
P-1	247	167	234	17	21		180								1		9			2	63	243	12			1							36	1233
2	57	35	59	5	6												1		4		58	18	5		1		2							251
3	187	9	87	23				20									1		3		29	45	1								6	6		417
4A	229	28	556	138	39														52															1042
4AB	644	90	224	86	25						3								16	1	18	13			2	3	3				3			1131
4B	1127	192	190	22	13		14				8						9		42	1	646	195	33		3	23	19	2			14			2553
4C	48	1	271		8		517						10	5			2		5	21	175	2120	76					3	24?		45			3331
7	87	544	174	30	36		64	1		1	19	3	1				4		1		61	150	360			3					1			1540
8	4	276	203	87	47		41				23	5					16		1		61	73	533								5			1375
9	5	400	9	15	13												12				238		8			4								704
10	95	17	12	15	5			?			-						6		8	1	30	15	1				2	1	1?	1	3	28		248
10B	102	9	7	10	5												13		2?	1	3	6						1?			1	12		172
12	291	31	63	18	11	14		1									5				62	14	8				1			1	3			523
13	272	4	14		3				1								9				48	7						1?			2			361
17	375	11	43	45	4												1		3	2	74	32				18	2				2			612
20	26		480	7	5?																													518
21	75	54	65	3	2		45	2									5		2	2	106	110	14					2			2			489
23	74	15	31	27	9												1		10	8														175
24	185	27	31	9	13		3										1		5		54	35	3		1?						1			370
25	96	130	34		17	4	55										1				64	82	13					1?			9			556
29	1003	221	148	114	111	10			6								15		35		27	22	3			10				2	3			1730
31		15	8		6	2	2	42								1	1				16	43	12				2?							150
36		93	11	100	7												24	1																236
38	84	21	48	1	8		5	2												1	50	28	3	4			1						299	904
39	149	13	20	1	5		2												3?	2	44	13	8	4							3			267
43	9			3	2	1	1		3?								2					23	87	5										136
44B	126	5	12	5	3														1		32	7		2	1?	1?								195
56		32	90	112	15																	1	3	2										255
58	5	92	83	106	6	8	1				1						4				6	4	61				1				12			390
63		4	60	50	2																													116

the five least closely related pairs. This comparison can be seen in Table VI. In only one case does the ranking of the likeness differ for the two techniques and this difference is sufficiently minor to suggest that, in general, the two techniques convey the same kind of information. However, an examination of the table will show that of the five highly similar pairs, four are shown to be more similar under the index of likeness for weighed samples. Conversely, among the five least similar pairs, all are shown to be less similar under the index of likeness for weighed samples. This suggests that the kinds of relationships in which we are interested are shown in greater contrast in weighed samples than in counted samples. The major difference between the two techniques can best be explained by the influence of random breakage on the counted samples, which might tend to obscure the relationships. The weighed sherds are treated, in effect, as a single sherd of varying size for each type.

The arrangement of the ceramic collections in a succession of phases was accomplished through the use of several techniques.

TABLE V

SHERD COUNTS FOR SAMPLES OF UNDER 100 SHERDS

	BROWNWARE										BLACK ON WHITE													
SITE	MICACEOUS	ROSWELL	JORNADA	S. PECOS	ALMA	LATE ROSWELL	McKENZIE	CORRUGATED	THREE RIVS. R/TC	OTHER	LINO GRAY	RED MESA	LOCAL? P II	CROSBY B/G	M. PECOS	CHUPADERO	ERODED CHUPAD.	KIATUTHLANNA	RESERVE	CEBOLLETA	OTHER	GLAZEWARE	NAVAJO	TOTAL
P-10A	4			4	1									1				2			1			13
11														1								5		6
12A	3		24																					27
15	8		17	6	1					2	2?													36
16	8	9	13	2	2									15	8	3								60
22	5		4	5							4										1	16		36
22A																					1	11		12
28	5	3	22	5										3	1									39
30	13	2	2								2				4									23
32	3		4	1																				8
33	1							1	1															3
34	8	4	25	1	3	3		1						1?	2									48
35					4											3								7
37	2		1			1	2	5						8	36	1	6							62
40																							67	67
41															1								78	79
42	41	2	1	2	1			1		1				10	1		1						18	79
44A	30	12?	26	11	10							2												91
45	21	5	3	3	6							1		1									1	41
46				4	1					1														6
48	5	5	6			1?	2					4	2	11	35	9	3			1	1	7		92
49	5	1	7									1			1									15
50	27	2	3									1	1	10	3		1							48
51	55	2	16	6	13							3												95
57			13												5									18
57A			6	1																				7
57B			1											1		2								4
59																3								3
60		7	22						4						3	13								49
61		6	1																					7
62		1																					50	51
64									1						34	7								42

In my initial study of the materials from the 1956 and 1957 collections I attempted a Brainerd-Robinson matrix ordering (Brainerd, 1951) of the samples from the various components of Site P4 (A, AB, B, and C) and Site 2, since these appeared to be the only collections approximating single components in the relatively restricted geographical area of the Northern Middle Pecos Valley (Jelinek, 1960: 155-157). The disadvantages of the Brainerd-Robinson technique were particularly obvious in the Pecos Valley study because of the type of geographical distribution represented by the collections. As is obvious, the indices of likeness used in this method reflect similarities based upon two kinds of cultural proximity; proximity in time and proximity

TABLE VI

COMPARISON OF INDICES OF LIKENESS BY COUNT AND WEIGHT

Sample Pair	Index by Weight	Index by Count
P3-P4AB	155.2	153.6
P2-P4B	153.1	148.2
P7-P8	149.8	147.3
P3-P4B	138.0	144.8
P1-P2	131.3	104.3
P4AB-P4C	25.4	27.5
P4AB-P9	23.5	32.2
P4A-P4C	18.4	19.8
P9-P4C	16.9	19.7
P4A-P9	12.1	17.3

in space. Our collections were made over a sufficiently extended portion of the valley to introduce both kinds of differences into the data and as a result it was impossible to construct a meaningful matrix of all single-component sites from both the northern and southern site areas. In order to clarify the relationships between the sites, as represented by these indices of likeness, I constructed diagrams in which the approximate numerical distance between samples was represented graphically (Fig. 8). This representation did give some indication of the separation of a northern and southern tradition, but it was not useful in chronological ordering except in the general sense of clustering those collections which were most similar and placing those least similar at greater distances from each other. This resulted in a somewhat linear arrangement of each tradition, ranging from one age extreme to the other. Eventually I settled on a chronological arrangement based upon the ordering of the Site P4 components, reinforced by trade ceramics and interpolation of the mixed-component samples of other sites in the north. In the south I utilized the apparent chronological distinctions between Sites P8 and P9, with the supporting evidence of the mixed components at Sites P7 and L10. This chronological scheme established the order of appearance of the basic native ceramic types in the Middle Valley, which in turn made it possible to determine the approximate chronological position of samples gathered in 1960 using the cumulative graph (Jelinek, 1962). On the basis

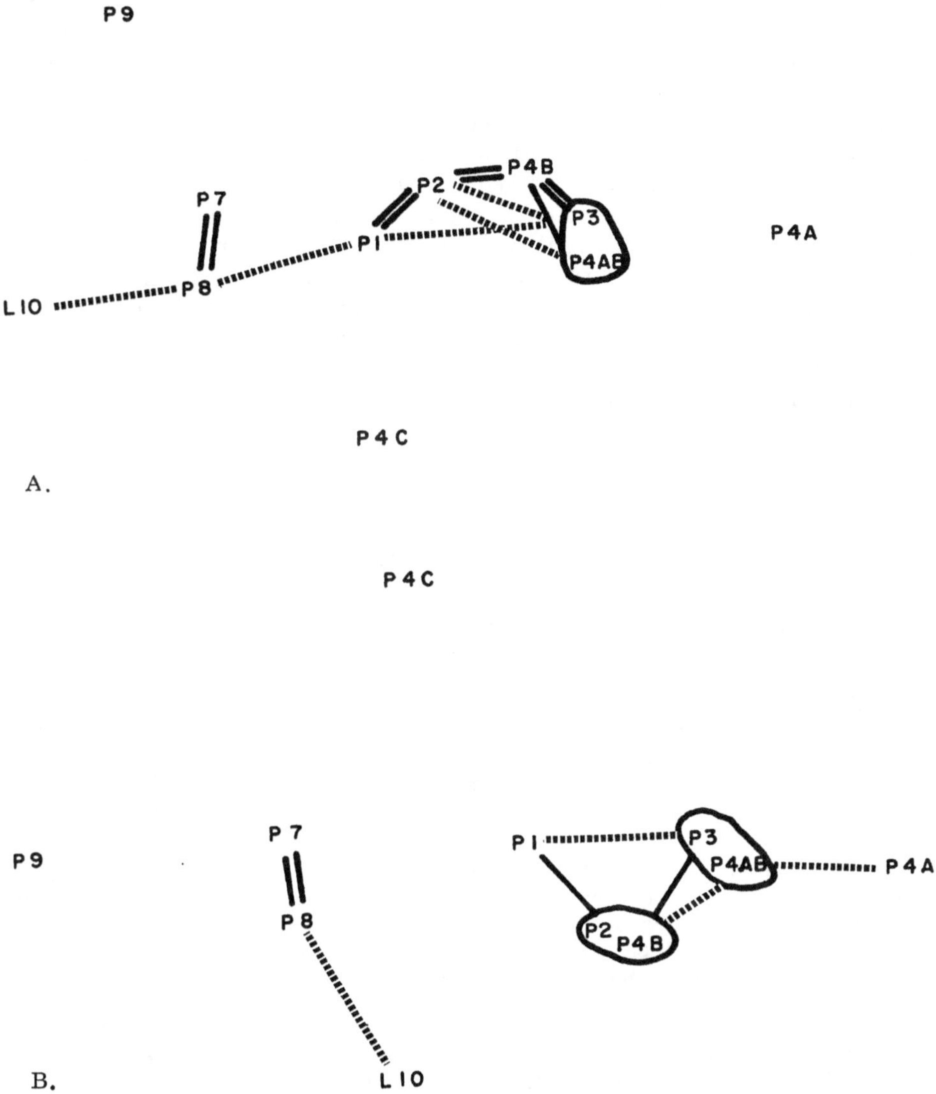

FIG. 8. Graphic representation of relationships shown by Brainerd-Robinson indices of likeness. Circled samples are most closely related; intensity of line indicates other relationships. A. indices based on count; B. indices based on weight.

of this cumulative graph ordering, a bar-graph diagram was constructed from the larger samples to indicate the preponderance of the best represented ceramic types in the Northern Middle Pecos Valley sequence (Fig. 9). Within this sequence it is possible to isolate groups of relatively uniform composition which represent ceramic phases. I have assigned the names used in the initial designation of cultural phases (Jelinek, 1960) to these ceramic phases, with the additional modification of a separation of an early and late manifestation of each. This results in six phases in the Northern Valley: Early 18 Mile, Late 18 Mile, Early Mesita Negra, Late Mesita Negra, Early McKenzie and Late McKenzie. For convenience in handling the data all prehistoric material following the Late McKenzie Phase was lumped as "Post-McKenzie" and treated as a phase. The particular characteristics of each of the ceramic phases are as follows:

Early 18 Mile.—Brownware accounts for virtually the entire ceramic sample. Jornada Brown is the dominant type and Middle Pecos Micaceous Brown is of secondary importance. South Pecos Brown and Alma Brown are both present in small quantities and are probably intrusives. Sites included in this phase are: P12A, P15, P20, P22, P32, P36, and P46.

Late 18 Mile.—While this phase is characterized by a heavy predominance of brownware, it is marked by the first appearance of reduced-fired pottery in the form of Red Mesa Black on White. The small quantity of this type (seldom over 10%) suggests that it is intrusive, as does the character of the paste. The dominant brownware in this phase appears to shift from Jornada, in the earlier period, to Micaceous in the later period. South Pecos Brown is well represented as is Alma Brown. Roswell Brown appears in the Northern Valley for the first time during this phase. Sites included in this phase are: P4A, P10A, P23, P44A, and P51.

Early Mesita Negra.—The earliest examples of native reduced-fired ceramics appear in this phase. Two types are represented; Crosby Black on Gray and Middle Pecos Black on White, both early examples of Chupadero ware. Red Mesa continues to occur, but in smaller quantity than in the Late 18 Mile Phase. The dominant ceramic type is Middle Pecos Micaceous Brownware, with Jornada, South Pecos, Alma, and Roswell Brown present in small amounts. A few sherds of Chupadero Black on White occur in the context of this phase. Sites included in this phase are: P3, P4AB, P12, P13, P17, P29, P30, P44B, P45, and P49.

Late Mesita Negra.—This phase is marked by a dominance of Crosby Black on Gray over Middle Pecos Black on White, which previously occurred in almost equal quantities. Middle Pecos B/W continues to occur in quantities under 10%, while Crosby B/G may comprise over 30% of the sample. During this phase Chupadero B/W begins to occur regularly in small amounts and Red Mesa B/W also continues to occur in small quantities, perhaps as salvaged sherds. The most striking feature of the brownware distribution is the marked deterioration in importance of

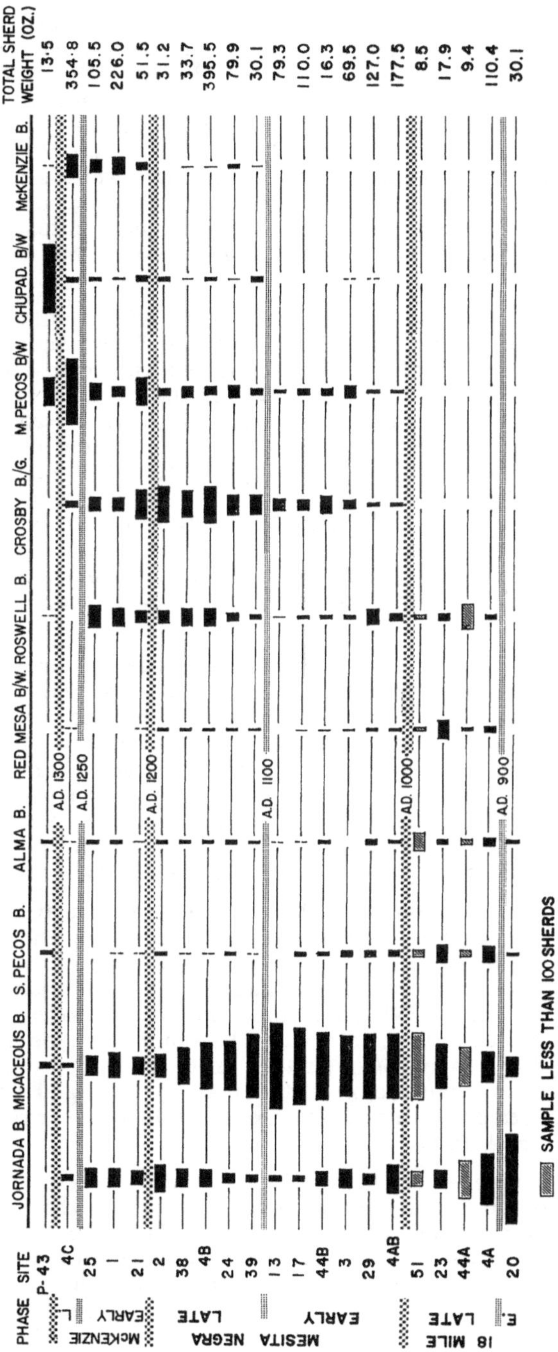

FIG. 9. Popularity of most abundant ceramic types in the northern Middle Pecos Valley; percentages by weight.

Middle Pecos Micaceous Brown during this phase, and a relatively small resurgence in the quantity of Jornada Brown. This last factor may reflect the nature of the classification of Jornada Brown, which as used here includes all of the relatively coarse-tempered brownware which was not assigned to one of the other types. Roswell Brown is more important than in preceding phases, averaging about 10%. South Pecos Brown continues to occur, but in somewhat smaller quantity, while Alma Brown also continues in small amounts. McKenzie Brownware occurs in this phase for the first time, always in very small quantity. Sites included in this phase are: P2, P4B, P16, P24, P28, P34, P38, P39, P42, P48, and P50.

Early McKenzie.—This phase is marked by the virtual disappearance of two earlier types—Red Mesa Black on White and South Pecos Brownware. Jornada Brown and Middle Pecos Micaceous occur in about equal amounts and together comprise less than 40% of the total, a smaller quantity than at any previous time in the sequence. Alma Brown continues in small quantity. Roswell Brown occurs in greatest quantity in the Northern Middle Valley in this phase; up to 20%. McKenzie Brown becomes an important element of the brownware tradition and is present in quantities between 5 and 15%. Middle Pecos B/W continues to form about 10% of the sample and Crosby B/G is reduced to about the same quantity. Chupadero B/W continues to occur in about the same quantity as in the preceding phase. Sites included in this phase are: P1, P21, and P25.

Late McKenzie.—The definition of this phase is based largely on the collection of over 3300 sherds from component C of Site P4. In this sample Middle Pecos Black on White is the dominant pottery type, accounting for almost 60% of the sample. McKenzie Brown is the next most important type at about 20%, while Jornada Brown, Micaceous Brown, Crosby B/G and Chupadero B/W are all present in about the same small quantities (2-5%) and may, to some degree, represent salvage of earlier vessels or sherds. Roswell Brown was not represented in the sample. Sites included in this phase are: P4C, P31, P37, and P64.

Post-McKenzie.—Sherds from Post-McKenzie sites are quite varied and frequently include examples of Rio Grande Glazewares and corrugated brownwares. The largest sample of this period, from Site P43, does not include either of these wares; it suggests, through the presence of 23% of Late Middle Pecos B/W, that some continuity exists with the Northern Middle Valley ceramic tradition. The dominant type in this sample is Chupadero B/W (over 60%) and is probably intrusive, suggesting that the Middle Pecos types represented may be salvaged specimens. Sites from which collections primarily represent this phase are: P10C, P11, P22A, P33, P35, and P43.

Bosque Redondo Phase.—This term has been used to designate the materials attributed to the concentration of the Navajo at the Bosque Redondo Reservation during the historic period. The distribution of the ceramics is confined to sites on the west side of the valley from a few miles south of the town of Fort Sumner to near the mouth of Taiban Creek. The pottery of this phase is mostly Navajo Utility Ware, although a few sherds of bowls decorated in fugitive red and black paint also occur. Sites with large proportions of Navajo sherds are: P38, P40, P41, and P62.

Ceramic Phases in the Southern Middle Pecos Valley

We did relatively little work in the area of the Middle Valley near Roswell in the 1960 season and as a result the earlier definitions of ceramic distinctions are retained with little modification. These include the recognition of two distinct phases:

Crosby Phase.—This phase, based on Site P9, is distinguished by the predominance of Roswell Brown (about 55%) and Crosby Black on Gray (about 40%). Small amounts of South Pecos, Alma, Jornada, Chupadero and Middle Pecos Micaceous occurred in that order of frequency.

The occurrence of a pre-Crosby phase in this area is suggested by collections from Sites P56 and P63, which contain large quantities of South Pecos Brownware and Jornada Brownware, and relatively small quantities of Roswell Brown and Alma Brown. The sites appear to represent temporary camps, however, and in addition the presence of a few sherds of Chupadero B/W and one of Middle Pecos B/W at P56 suggests that their existence as representatives of a distinct phase is questionable.

Roswell Phase.—Sites of this period are characterized by a continuation of Roswell Brown as the dominant brownware, with almost equivalent quantities of Jornada Brown also present. South Pecos Brownware forms over 5% of the sample and the dominant intrusive brownware is McKenzie Brown, suggesting equivalence with the Late McKenzie Phase in the north. Chupadero B/W, which forms about 30% of the sample, is the most abundant pottery type on the site, and its dominance as a black on white ware suggests an increasing popularity of reduced-fired wares parallel to the Late McKenzie Phase, where Middle Pecos B/W is the dominant ceramic type. Middle Pecos Black on White and Crosby B/G occur as minority types (about 5% each).

The Distribution of Intrusive Ceramics in the Middle Pecos Sequence

The intrusive ceramics in the Middle Pecos Valley provided one of the few means of relating the local sequence to the prehistoric sequence in adjacent areas and to establish absolute chronologies. These ceramics will be treated by phase.

Early 18 Mile.—Seven sherds which appear to be Lino Gray have been recovered from sites assigned to this phase. No intrusive decorated sherds were recovered. A single sherd of Middle Pecoc Micaceous Brown with a red wash on the exterior was found at Site P20 and is the only decorated specimen in the collections from this phase. Among the brownwares, South Pecos and Alma are presumed to be intrusive and are represented in small quantities in the collection from Site P20 and P15 and by about 1/3 of the brownware sample from Site P22.

Late 18 Mile.—All collections but one assigned to this phase contain small quantities of Red Mesa B/W, which, as stated earlier, is believed to have been manufactured outside of the Pecos Valley area, on the basis of different tempering and finishing techniques than are encountered in the local ceramic tradition. The single exception to this distribution is in the collection from component A of Site P10, which contains two sherds assigned to Kiatuthlanna Black on White, on the basis of design and sandy paste. The varying amounts of Roswell, South Pecos and Alma Brown represented in Late 18 Mile site samples are assumed to be intrusive.

Early Mesita Negra.—The most abundant intrusive decorated pottery on sites of this phase is Red Mesa B/W, which is found on all but two sites, P13 and P30. On the latter site two sherds similar to Lino Gray are the only intrusive materials. Site P13 is the youngest site in this phase in the seriation pattern and was not included in the Late Mesita Negra series only because of the absence of Chupadero B/W and McKenzie Brownware. The only intrusive decorated sherd noted for the site is a doubtful example of Santa Fe Black on White, which is characteristically associated with Late Mesita Negra and following phases. Cebolleta B/W occurs on about half of the sites in the phase, and on all sites with samples exceeding 100 sherds except P13. Other decorated sherds occasionally represented in this phase are: Socorro B/W, Mimbres B/W, Reserve B/W, and Broadline Red on Terra Cotta. Brownwares include continuing examples of South Pecos, Alma, and Roswell, as well as several examples of a paste indistinguishable from that of El Paso Polychrome in the Sacramento Highlands, and here distinguished as El Paso Brown. It might be noted that the only site in this phase from which South Pecos Brown was not recovered was P13.

Late Mesita Negra.—The most frequent decorated intrusive in this phase is Chupadero B/W. Sherds of Red Mesa B/W, perhaps from earlier horizons, are frequently encountered and occasional examples of Socorro B/W, Cebolleta B/W, Santa Fe B/W and Broadline R/TC are present. South Pecos Brown continues to occur in very small amounts, which may represent vessels manufactured in earlier phases. The relatively constant amount of Alma Plain may, in part, represent sherds of the relatively fine paste Broadline R/TC without pigment in evidence.

Early McKenzie.—Relatively few intrusive sherds are present in the three site collections assigned to this phase. The dominant intrusive type is Chupadero B/W, represented by about a dozen sherds in each of the collections. Three sherds of Santa Fe B/W, two of Red Mesa, and one each of Cebolleta and Wingate B/R-St. Johns Polychrome comprise the remainder of the decorated intrusives. Intrusive brownwares include South Pecos and Alma in small amounts, with the South Pecos probably representing relics of earlier phases and the Alma including some unpainted red on terra-cotta fragments. The relatively high proportion of Roswell Brown (almost 20% on two sites) suggests that some of this type may have been manufactured locally, or that an extremely strong exchange system was in effect between the northern and southern Middle Valley during this phase.

Late McKenzie.—Textured brownware sherds are present for the first time in quantity among the intrusive wares in this last sedentary phase. While it is possible that some of these are of local manufacture (e.g. McKenzie and Jornada Corrugated), it is clear that Los Lunas Smudged and Pitoche Rubbed-Ribbed are intrusive from the central Rio Grande area. The most abundant intrusive in this phase is Chupadero B/W. Two dozen sherds from Site P4C, perhaps from one vessel, were identified as possibly of Kwahe'e B/W by the late Stanley Stubbs. It is possible that these sherds at P4C, as well as those of Red Mesa B/W and local Pueblo II, represent a small earlier occupation or materials salvaged or retained from occupations on the adjacent earlier components of Site P4. Other trade sherds assigned to sites of this phase are of Socorro B/W, Santa Fe B/W and a very few examples of late Roswell Brown.

Post-McKenzie Phase.—All sherds from sites in this group are presumed to be intrusive.

Crosby.—In this southern Middle Valley phase only one pottery type, Cebolleta B/W, clearly comes from outside of the Pecos Valley. Intrusive sherds from cultural groups within the valley include small quantities of Middle Pecos Micaceous and South Pecos Brown. The few sherds of Alma Brown and Chupadero B/W may be either of valley or extra-valley origin.

Roswell.—Sites P7 and P8, which represent this phase, each yielded one sherd of Red Mesa B/W, which probably relates to earlier horizons, as may the three sherds of Cebolleta B/W from Site P7. It is possible that a Crosby occupation was also present at this site, although the small quantity of Crosby B/G does not favor this. Broadline Red on Terra Cotta is strongly represented on both sites and Three Rivers R/TC occurs in smaller quantities. One sherd each of El Paso Polychrome, Los Lunas Smudged, and brown indented corrugated ware were found on Site P7. Intrusives from the northern Middle Valley were more strongly represented at P7 than at P8, a distribution that might be predicted on the basis of the more northerly location of the former site. In both sites Micaceous Brown and McKenzie are represented, although only four sherds of the former occur at Site P8, in contrast to 87 at P7. This, again, may indicate an earlier occupation at P7. Several other factors of distribution suggest a geographic influence, including the higher ratios of South Pecos Brown and Alma Brown in the more southerly Site P8 and the lower ratio of McKenzie Brown in the same site.

Distribution of Particular Techniques of Local Ceramic Manufacture

Use of Red Decoration on Brownwares

The earliest example of this technique is the single sherd of a red-washed Micaceous olla from Site P20 in the Early 18 Mile

Phase. Two bowl fragments of Jornada Brown with red slip were found at Site P44A, and three of South Pecos Brown at P23 in the Late 18 Mile Phase. The greatest number of examples of this treatment in that phase is from Site P4A, where 12 bowl sherds with red slip were recovered; six of Jornada, four of South Pecos, two of Roswell, and one of Micaceous Brown.

In the succeeding Early Mesita Negra Phase the distribution suggests a ratio of about five or six to one in favor of red-slipped bowl sherds over ollas for Jornada, Micaceous, South Pecos and Roswell Brown. This phase marks the first appearance of decoration with broad lines rather than an overall color. One olla sherd of South Pecos and three bowl sherds of Roswell Brown exhibit this treatment. Two bowl sherds of Alma Brown with broadline decoration in red may be referred to as possible examples of Mogollon Red on Brown, since the paste appears distinct from Broadline Red on Terra Cotta.

In the Late Mesita Negra Phase examples of red-decorated ollas are even less frequent than in the preceding phase; they are confined to one sherd of Roswell and two sherds of Jornada Brown. All three appear to be red-slipped. Broadline decoration in this phase is limited to bowls of Jornada (2 sherds), Roswell (4 sherds), and South Pecos Brown (4 sherds). Decorated examples of Middle Pecos Micaceous Brown are confined to red slipped or red washed bowls (22 sherds) as are McKenzie Brown (9 sherds) and Alma Brown (4 sherds). Six Roswell bowl sherds have overall red interior decoration, as do 13 Jornada and one South Pecos bowl sherds.

In Early McKenzie Phase collections red decorated olla sherds are similarly rare, confined to one example each of Micaceous and Jornada Brown. Broadline decoration is found on Roswell Brown; seven of 16 decorated bowl sherds show this motif, coupled in one instance with the use of a stepped triangle. The only other instance of broadline red decoration in this phase is on the interior of a bowl with paste suggesting Broadline R/TC and of roughened exterior similar to Chupadero B/W. The three sherds present in the collection appear distinct from oxidized Chupadero and remain unclassified. Bowl sherds with red interior slip or wash are the most common form of decorated brownware. In addition to the examples of this type of decoration already mentioned, there are 20 sherds of Micaceous, five of Jornada, two of South Pecos, and 16 of McKenzie Brown. The McKenzie sherds are particularly noteworthy because of the characteristic vivid hue of the red slip, reminiscent of the fluorescent red used in current advertising. While this kind of slip appears rarely on Micaceous vessels (see type description), it is quite frequent on McKenzie Brown.

All sherds in this category from the Late McKenzie Phase were collected from Site P4C. As might be expected in view of the composition of the brownware collections from this site, the sherds are predominantly McKenzie Brown. Of 24 bowl sherds of this type, all but three or four have an overall red slip. The remaining few sherds appear to have been decorated in a broadline design. Clearer examples of broadline decoration are found on five of the six decorated Jornada sherds. Three Micaceous Brown bowl sherds are decorated with red slip.

In the southern valley broadline red decoration is found on bowls of Roswell Brown in the Crosby Phase at Site P9. Two distinct line widths were observed on the few examples studied, one of 10-12 mm. and a smaller width of about 4 mm. In the following Roswell Phase, Roswell Red on Brown remains the dominant decorated brownware, with almost 50 sherds from P7 and P8. Four specimens are broadline and one is decorated with a fineline design reminiscent of Three Rivers R/TC. One bowl each of McKenzie and Micaceous Brown had red slip decoration, and nine sherds of South Pecos Brown also had red slip or wash decoration.

Rim Form

The terminology for most rim forms found in the collections is illustrated in Fig. 10. In the analysis this terminology is coupled with that for the wall form adjacent to the rim shown in Figure 11.

A total of 262 rims were examined from site collections of Early 18 Mile through Late McKenzie Phases from the Northern Middle Pecos Valley. Within this sample it is possible to see

FIG. 10. *Rim Forms*. *A* Direct, *B* Tapered Direct, *C* Rounded Direct, *D* Rounded, *E* Squared, *F* Rounded exterior, *G* Beveled Exterior, *H* Beveled Interior, *I* Thickened Exterior, *J* Thickened, *K* Rolled Exterior, *L* Coil Exterior, *M* Angled Flared, *N* Curved Flared.

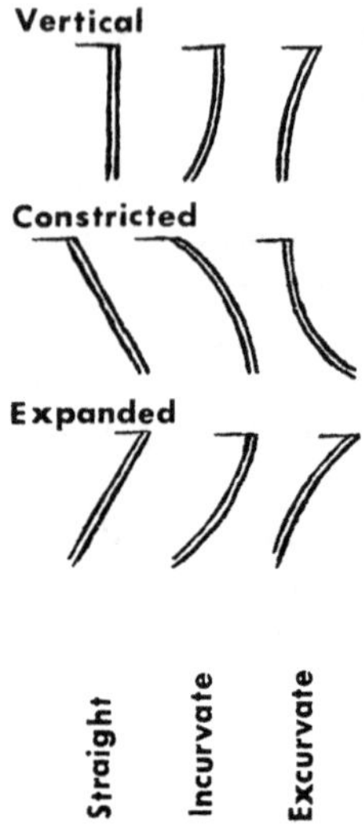

FIG. 11. Wall form adjacent to the rim.

trends in preferences in both rim form (Table VII) and wall form adjacent to the rim (Table VIII). The latter, of course, reflects vessel shape and in the absence of any complete vessels from the area is one of the most valuable indicators of this cultural feature.

A marked decline in direct rims is obvious from the early to late periods. While these forms account for over 90% of the rims in the Early 18 Mile Phase, by the McKenzie Phases they represent no more than about 20%. The absence of simple rounded and squared rims in the 18 Mile Phases also appears significant. Other significant distributions are the relatively high incidence of rounded exterior rims in the middle of the sequence, particularly in the Late Mesita Negra Phase; the high frequency of externally bevelled rims in the Early McKenzie Phase; and the increasing occurrence of curved flared rims toward the close of the sequence.

Vessel form, as reflected in the wall form of the rim sherds, also shows some significant trends. Neckless jars ("hole-mouth" or "seed jars") are most popular in the earliest phase and occur only sporadically after that time. Incurvate vertical bowl forms reach their greatest popularity in the Late Mesita Negra and Early McKenzie Phases. Constricted excurvate necked ollas have two periods of popularity, the Early Mesita Negra Phase and the Late McKenzie Phase.

TABLE VII

DISTRIBUTION OF RIM SHERDS BY PHASE

Rim Form	Early 18 Mile	Late 18 Mile	Early Mesita Negra	Late Mesita Negra	Early McKenzie	Late McKenzie	Total
A	7	8	26	3	6	-	50
B	1	1	-	-	2	-	4
C	15	4	16	10	5	3	53
D	-	-	13	8	8	2	31
E	-	-	8	5	12	-	25
F	2	3	16	13	7	1	42
G	-	1	4	1	10	1	17
H	-	-	8	-	1	-	9
I	-	-	-	-	1	-	1
J	-	1	1	-	-	-	2
K	-	-	2	1	4	1	8
L	-	-	1	1	1	2	5
M	-	-	-	-	2	-	2
N	-	-	1	3	6	3	13
Total	25	18	96	45	65	13	262

Within these two classes of form it is possible to see two kinds of significance in cultural relationships. The rim forms can be expected to reflect stylistic differences and to change through time in the same fashion as other elements of style. The wall form of the vessel reflects stylistic change to some degree, since the shape of each kind of vessel is influenced by style; however, it also is dependent upon the kind of vessels involved, and thus also reveals functional patterns in ceramic usage. As a test of this hypothesis indices of likeness were computed for all pairs of phases for both rim form and wall form. The best ordered matrix of the indices for rim form indicates an ordering paralleling that of the chronological ordering of the phases (Table IX). Only one sign change, between the Early and Late McKenzie Phase samples, is out of order in this matrix. The ordering indicates the presence of a significant relationship between the development of rim forms and other aspects of ceramic typology.

TABLE VIII

DISTRIBUTION OF WALL FORM ON RIM SHERDS BY PHASE

Wall Form	Early 18 Mile	Late 18 Mile	Early Mesita Negra	Late Mesita Negra	Early McKenzie	Late McKenzie	Total
1	5	4	12	3	-	1	25
2	1	4	14	18	32	3	72
3	-	1	2	-	-	-	3
4	1	-	7	4	2	1	15
5	14	1	3	3	-	1	22
6	4	4	42	10	15	6	81
7	-	-	1	-	-	-	1
8	-	-	1	-	6	-	7
9	-	-	-	-	-	-	-
Indeterminate	-	4	14	7	10	1	36
Total	25	18	96	45	65	13	262

TABLE IX

MATRIX ORDERING OF RIM FORMS

	1.	2.	3.	4.	5.	6.
1. Early 18 Mile	X					
2. Late 18 Mile	124.2	X				
3. Early Mesita Negra	103.7	131.1	X			
4. Late Mesita Negra	73.8	95.4	136.3	X		
5. Early McKenzie	66.0	72.6	116.5	124.4	X	
6. Late McKenzie	61.5	70.7	92.4	117.1	104.5	X

A matrix ordering of wall form by phase shows no significance in the arrangement in Table X. This grouping suggests that the Late 18 Mile to Late Mesita Negra and Late McKenzie Phases are more similar to each other, as regards vessel shape, than any of this group is to Early Mesita Negra or Early McKenzie (with the exception of the close relationship of Late

TABLE X

MATRIX ORDERING OF WALL FORMS BY PHASE

	1.	2.	3.	4.	5.	6.
1. Early 18 Mile	X					
2. Late 18 Mile	91.2	X				
3. Early Mesita Negra	79.3	138.3	X			
4. Late Mesita Negra	74.8	144.4	137.1	X		
5. Early McKenzie	46.3	119.5	112.8	161.5	X	
6. Late McKenzie	78.7	152.3	168.2	158.1	113.8	X

Mesita Negra and Early McKenzie). It appears that the high number of neckless jars is responsible for the isolation of the Early 18 Mile Phase in this ordering. The similarity between Late Mesita Negra and Early McKenzie is based upon relatively equal proportions of vertical incurvate walls (bowls), constricted excurvate walls (ollas), and indeterminate forms. Other similarities are based on a more general balance of relationships. It seems likely that the factors which determine the isolation of the Early 18 Mile Phase and the similarity between the Late Mesita Negra and Early McKenzie Phases are questions of style in vessel manufacture rather than functional predominance of bowls or ollas. The relationship between these two forms as seen in the decorated reduced-fired wares is treated below.

The particular associations of rim form and vessel wall with individual pottery types were examined, but the quantity of variation with respect to the small size of the sample was such that little specific significance can be attached to any particular combination. In the Early Mesita Negra, Late Mesita Negra, and Early McKenzie Phases, there are a relatively high proportion of rounded exterior rim sherds on vertical incurvate walls, indicating a preference for this particular style of bowl form. The Early Mesita Negra Phase is unique in the relatively high number of direct rims associated with the constricted excurvate olla wall form. In none of these associations does there appear to be a preference for any particular pottery type beyond that which would be expected on the basis of the general distribution of types within each phase.

It seems clear from the analysis undertaken here that changes in the attributes of rim form in this sample provide corroborating evidence for the ceramic style changes outlined in the section on seriation. The shape of the vessel walls as seen in sherds adjacent to the rim, appears to be related to factors which do not have chronological significance in this sample.

Rim forms from the southern Middle Valley were not treated in this analysis due to the small sample from that area. It is my impression that the sequence of rim form parallels that of the northern area.

Bowl and Olla Sherds Among Distribution of Reduced-Fired Ceramics

This study was restricted to reduced-fired ceramics because of the ease of determining bowl and olla sherds among this group, as opposed to the brownwares, where infrequent decoration was the only clue to the type of vessel from which body sherds had been derived. Since sherds were not weighed by vessel form, but only by type, this comparison is based upon sherd count.

The counts of bowl and olla sherds are given below:

TABLE XI

COUNTS OF BOWL AND OLLA SHERDS BY PHASE

Phase	Bowls No.	%	Ollas No.	%	Total
Late 18 Mile	46	(61.3)	29	(38.7)	75
Early Mesita Negra	231	(40.2)	344	(59.8)	575
Late Mesita Negra	372	(28.4)	939	(71.6)	1311
Early McKenzie	139	(23.2)	461	(76.8)	600
Late McKenzie	647	(26.1)	1835	(73.9)	2482

These ratios include all bowls and ollas in surface collections from sites in the Northern Valley falling within the phases listed. They are taken to reflect patterns of usage of the two major vessel forms of reduced-fired wares. The major trend apparent in the table is a gradual increase in the number of reduced-fired olla sherds relative to bowl sherds from the earlier to the later portion of the sequence. A relatively stable ratio of slightly under 30% of bowl sherds, which appears to have been reached by the Late Mesita Negra Phase, persisted through the final sedentary occupation.

In order to explore more fully the patterns of local ceramic manufacture I separated the data for all sherds[10] of Crosby Black on Gray and Middle Pecos Black on White, and examined the trends within each of these forms, as well as in the combination of the two types for each phase. The results of these comparisons are as follows:

TABLE XII

COUNTS OF BOWL AND OLLA SHERDS FOR NATIVE GRAY WARES BY PHASE

Phase	Bowls No.	%	Ollas No.	%	Total
Crosby Black on Gray					
Early Mesita Negra	42	(17.4)	200	(82.6)	242
Late Mesita Negra	165	(19.5)	679	(80.5)	844
Early McKenzie	55	(20.2)	217	(79.8)	272
Late McKenzie	36	(18.0)	163	(82.0)	199
Middle Pecos Black on White					
Early Mesita Negra	42	(51.8)	39	(48.2)	81
Late Mesita Negra	118	(38.3)	190	(61.7)	308
Early McKenzie	93	(26.9)	253	(73.1)	346
Late McKenzie	505	(21.8)	1805	(78.2)	2310
Crosby B/G and Middle Pecos B/W					
Early Mesita Negra	84	(26.0)	239	(74.0)	323
Late Mesita Negra	283	(24.6)	869	(75.4)	1152
Early McKenzie	148	(24.7)	450	(75.3)	598
Late McKenzie	541	(21.5)	1968	(78.5)	2509

The table shows a remarkably constant ratio of bowls and ollas of native grayware throughout the sequence, indicating that the changes in vessel form seen in the preceding table are not due to native wares, but are dependent upon ratios of intrusive wares (e.g. Red Mesa B/W, Reserve B/W, Cebolleta B/W, Socorro B/W, Santa Fe B/W, etc.) which were included in that table. The table above demonstrates that the ratio of Crosby B/G bowl

[10]Includes sherds from excavations conducted prior to 1960 on Site P4.

to olla sherds remains approximately constant at 20% bowls and 80% ollas throughout the period of manufacture of this type. The ratio of Middle Pecos B/W bowl to olla sherds, however, seems to indicate that this white-slipped ware was initially treated as a functional equivalent of the intrusive graywares and only gradually approximated the ratio of Crosby B/G. An examination of the intrusive wares indicates that, with the exception of Chupadero B/W, a very high ratio of the sherds of the reduced-fired wares are from bowls. The high ratio of bowls to ollas in the early 18 Mile Phase results from the fact that 90 to 100% of the graywares in this phase are intrusive. The 10% difference is dependent upon whether 8 sherds of unidentified type of general Pueblo II character are native or intrusive. In succeeding phases the ratio of intrusive to native reduced-fired ceramics gradually declines; about 24% of these sherds are intrusive in the Early Mesita Negra Phase, 13% in the Late Mesita Negra, 6% in the Early McKenzie, and less than 5% in the Late McKenzie Phase. (This assumes that the Red Mesa and Pueblo II sherds in the collection from Site P4C are relics of a pre-Late McKenzie occupation.) This decline in the ratio of intrusive graywares thus appears to be largely responsible for the decline in the ratio of bowls to ollas in the reduced-fired ceramics from the Northern Valley.

In summary, the data indicate that there is only a slight change in the ratio of bowl to olla sherds among native reduced-fired sherds in the Northern Middle Pecos Valley. This change was toward a greater number of olla sherds, which may merely indicate that ollas increased slightly in size relative to bowls. This change in native ceramics is accounted for entirely within one type, Middle Pecos Black on White, since the ratio of these sherds among samples of Crosby Black on Gray is constant for all phases in which the type occurs. A relatively large number of bowls of intrusive wares were in use in the earlier phases. This usage gradually declined through time.

Extent of Decoration on Reduced-Fired Ceramics

Reduced-fired bowl and olla sherds which were sufficiently well preserved to indicate the presence or absence of painted decoration on the slipped or smoothed surface were tabulated to determine meaningful temporal relationships in the use of decoration. The number and per cent of decorated sherds of bowls and ollas from the Northern Valley are listed by phase in the following table:

TABLE XIII

RATIOS OF DECORATED REDUCED-FIRED BOWL AND OLLA SHERDS BY PHASE

Phase	Bowls No.	% Dec.	Ollas No.	% Dec.	Total No.	Decorated % of T.
Late 18 Mile	32	(69.6)	16	(55.2)	48	(64.0)
Early Mesita Negra	132	(57.1)	118	(34.3)	250	(43.5)
Late Mesita Negra	231	(62.0)	241	(25.7)	472	(36.0)
Early McKenzie	97	(69.8)	164	(35.6)	261	(43.5)
Late McKenzie	472	(73.0)	792	(43.2)	1264	(51.6)

In all categories on the table there appears to be a decline in relative abundance of decorated sherds in the Early to Late Mesita Negra Phases, followed by an increase which continues through the Early and Late McKenzie Phases. Since a large percentage of the earlier reduced-fired wares are intrusive (see p. 64), the corresponding ratios for samples of native wares are of interest in determining the effect of these "trade wares" on the table above. The ratios for native wares are listed in Table XIV. It is apparent from Table XIV that within the total sample there was a gradual increase through time in the amount of the vessel surface which was decorated. Within each specific category, however, this increase is not always present. In particular, the distribution of the ratios of decorated olla sherds of Middle Pecos Black on White suggests the same decline in decoration during the Late Mesita Negra Phase that was observed in the table summarizing all grayware sherds. This decline may indicate that the white-slipped Middle Pecos B/W ollas followed the decorative style of the intrusive wares in the earlier portion of the sequence. While there is a slight decline in quantity of decoration of Crosby B/G ollas from Early Mesita Negra through Early McKenzie, it is not as pronounced as the decline in the Middle Pecos B/W ollas. The heavy increase in ratio of decorated sherds of Crosby B/G in the Late McKenzie Phase suggests a definite style change in that period. The marked increase in ratio of decorated sherds in all categories except Crosby B/G ollas in the Early McKenzie Phase suggests that the initial evidence for this kind of style change in both of the native decorated graywares can be assigned to this period. The difference in the magnitude of decline in ratio of decorated sherds in the total sample of native graywares (Table XIV) as opposed to all

TABLE XIV

RATIOS OF DECORATED NATIVE REDUCED-FIRED BOWL AND OLLA SHERDS

Phase	Bowls No.	% Dec.	Ollas No.	% Dec.	Total No.	Decorated % of T.
			Crosby Black on Gray			
Early Mesita Negra	18	(42.8)	50	(25.0)	68	(28.1)
Late Mesita Negra	70	(42.5)	146	(21.5)	216	(25.6)
Early McKenzie	35	(68.6)	38	(17.5)	73	(26.9)
Late McKenzie	30	(83.3)	74	(45.4)	104	(52.2)
			Middle Pecos Black on White			
Early Mesita Negra	17	(40.5)	24	(61.5)	41	(50.6)
Late Mesita Negra	68	(57.6)	64	(33.7)	132	(42.9)
Early McKenzie	66	(71.0)	107	(42.3)	173	(50.0)
Late McKenzie	330	(65.4)	791	(43.8)	1121	(48.6)
			Crosby B/G and Middle Pecos B/W			
Early Mesita Negra	35	(41.7)	74	(31.0)	109	(33.8)
Late Mesita Negra	138	(48.7)	210	(34.2)	348	(30.2)
Early McKenzie	101	(68.2)	145	(30.8)	246	(41.1)
Late McKenzie	360	(66.6)	865	(44.0)	1225	(48.8)

graywares (Table XIII) appears to indicate that the intrusive wares are largely responsible for the relative abundance of decorated sherds in the earlier phases.

Sherd Size

A comparative study of sherd size was made to investigate whether the assumption of a relatively randomizing effect on comparative sherd counts by breakage could be supported. I also hoped to substantiate a hypothesis advanced earlier (Jelinek, 1960: 43-44, 60) that the earlier ceramics in surface collections tend to be broken into smaller sherds.

A comparison of sherd size, indicated by quantity of sherds per ounce, for the most abundant ceramic types in collections of over 100 sherds from the Northern Valley is presented in

Table XV. The sites are arranged in chronological order, with the oldest at the bottom and the youngest at the top. Only samples of over 20 sherds are shown.

It is apparent that there is no relationship between specific sherd size and the chronological position of the sample, or between sherd size and ceramic type, in the comparison of individual site samples. This indicates that factors other than chronological position and ceramic type are responsible for the differences observed. The nature of the kinds of variables which intervene is suggested by the most likely explanation for the small sherd size of the sample from Site P20: the site is located adjacent to an abandoned stone sheep corral, and it is

TABLE XV

SHERD SIZE (SHERDS/OUNCE) OF MAJOR CERAMIC TYPES BY SITE

Site	Jornada Brown	Micaceous Brown	Roswell Brown	McKenzie Brown	Crosby B/G	M. Pecos B/W	All Sherds
P4C	11.4	6.0	-	7.1	9.2	10.1	9.3
P25	4.4	5.0	6.2	5.0	5.2	5.0	5.3
P1	8.4	7.1	8.0	7.0	7.1	7.1	7.6
P21	11.2	10.1	10.4	13.6	8.5	9.1	9.5
P2	8.2	8.8	10.0	-	-	-	8.0
P38	8.6	7.6	4.4	-	7.0	8.7	7.4
P4B	6.2	7.0	7.8	-	5.1	7.2	6.5
P24	4.5	5.4	4.7	-	3.7	3.9	4.6
P39	9.1	8.7	-	-	8.3	-	8.9
P13	-	4.4	-	-	4.5	-	4.6
P17	10.0	5.0	-	-	6.9	4.7	5.7
P44B	-	12.9	-	-	12.8	-	12.0
P3	7.9	5.1	-	-	4.8	6.2	6.0
P29	14.6	13.6	13.5	-	8.7	11.0	12.3
P4AB	4.9	6.2	8.2	-	-	-	6.3
P51	-	10.8	-	-	-	-	11.2
P23	11.5	10.4	-	-	-	-	9.7
P44A	8.4	9.4	-	-	-	-	9.7
P4A	11.3	7.6	11.2	-	-	-	9.3
P20	19.8	5.1	-	-	-	-	17.21

reasonable to suppose that the trampling of the stock over the site resulted in increased breakage of the sherds. The relatively large size of some sherds suggests later disturbances, such as erosion or rodent activity subsequent to the use of the corral.

In order to better assess the possible regularities in relative sizes of the sherds by type and through time, the values for each site were scaled to an equivalent of 20 sherds per ounce for the total number of sherds in the site collection. While many extremes of size difference were reduced in this test, the common scale also failed to indicate regularities due to chronology or type.

In an attempt to cancel out some of the apparently random variables affecting the difference in size of sherds between sites, I combined all sherds from site samples in each of the sedentary phases and calculated sherd size by type for each phase (Table XVI A). Then, in order to examine the relative size of the sherds for each type, I re-scaled the values to a common standard of 10 sherds per ounce for the total number of sherds per phase (Table XVI B).

Red Mesa Black on White is the only ceramic type likely to have been imported into the valley during a single phase (Late 18 Mile); if this is so, the ratios of sherd size of this type in part B of the table tend to support the hypothesis of smaller sherd size for older sherds in each collection. A generally similar trend is seen in the equalized ratios of South Pecos Brownware, whose import into the Northern Valley seems to be largely restricted to the earlier phases. The less marked decrease in relative sherd size for Crosby Black on Gray perhaps indicates that as the manufacture of this type continued, greater quantities of accumulated older sherds contributed to a smaller relative size in later horizons. Perhaps the relatively smaller sherds of McKenzie Brown and Chupadero Black on White in earlier phases indicate continuing fragmentation of sherds of these types through time; although why this effect should be confined to these two types, and why the results of fragmentation of these types should differ from other contemporary types, is open to question. No particular chronological relationships are apparent in the sequence of equalized sherd size for Jornada, Micaceous, Alma, or Roswell Brown.

A similar equalization to 10 sherds per ounce *by type*, in order to compare ratios within phases, revealed no particularly remarkable relationships. It was noted, however, that sherds of Jornada, Roswell, South Pecos Brown and Red Mesa Black on

TABLE XVI

A. SHERD SIZE EXPRESSED IN SHERDS/OUNCE FOR MAJOR CERAMIC TYPES BY PHASE

Phase	Jornada Brown	Micaceous Brown	S. Pecos Brown	Alma Brown	Roswell Brown	McKenzie Brown	Red Mesa B/W	Crosby B/G	M. Pecos B/W	Chupadero B/W	All Sherds
Early 18 Mile	14.9	*6.0*	10.3	*11.8*	10.8	-	-	-	-	-	12.4
Late 18 Mile	11.2	8.6	10.2	6.0	10.0	-	9.1	-	-	-	9.6
Early Mesita Negra	6.6	6.9	11.6	13.2	8.9	-	9.3	6.0	6.4	*9.2*	7.2
Late Mesita Negra	7.2	7.0	*6.8*	10.0	7.4	*8.1*	8.7	5.1	6.7	6.8	6.6
Early McKenzie	7.5	6.8	*10.0*	*5.9*	7.6	7.0	*10.0*	7.0	6.9	*7.3*	7.1
Late McKenzie	11.4	6.1	-	*10.8*	*4.1*	7.1	*16.7*	9.5	9.9	9.0	9.3
All Sherds	8.9	7.0	10.3	9.0	8.0	7.1	9.1	6.8	8.8	7.8	7.7
Number of Sherds	2943	5652	678	354	1302	892	201	1686	3031	212	16963

B. SHERD SIZE SCALED TO 10 SHERDS/OUNCE FOR THE TOTAL NUMBER OF SHERDS IN EACH PHASE

Phase	Jornada Brown	Micaceous Brown	S. Pecos Brown	Alma Brown	Roswell Brown	McKenzie Brown	Red Mesa B/W	Crosby B/G	M. Pecos B/W	Chupadero B/W
Early 18 Mile	12.0	*4.9*	8.3	*9.5*	8.7	-	-	-	-	-
Late 18 Mile	11.7	9.0	10.6	6.3	10.4	-	9.5	-	-	-
Early Mesita Negra	9.2	9.6	16.1	18.3	12.4	-	12.9	8.3	8.9	*12.9*
Late Mesita Negra	10.9	10.6	*10.3*	15.2	11.2	*12.3*	13.2	7.7	10.2	10.3
Early McKenzie	10.6	9.6	*14.1*	*8.3*	10.7	11.4	*14.1*	9.9	9.7	*10.3*
Late McKenzie	12.1	6.6	-	*11.6*	*4.4*	7.6	*17.9*	10.2	10.6	9.7
All Sherds	11.5	9.1	13.4	11.7	10.4	9.2	11.8	8.8	11.4	10.1

(Italics indicate samples of less than 50 sherds.)

White, tended to be smaller in size in most phases than were sherds of Micaceous and McKenzie Brown, Crosby Black on Gray, and Middle Pecos and Chupadero Black on White. This may indicate a general pattern of smaller sherd size in earlier types.

In summary, the examination of relationships of sherd size appears to indicate that the fragmentation of ceramics is not governed to any significant degree by predictable factors of composition (i.e. type) or time, but is instead the result of random hazards at each depositional locality. These findings support the conclusions on p. 60, that more accurate comparisons of sherd materials can be made by weight than by count, since the uncontrolled variation caused by fragmentation is eliminated when sherd weights are compared. The hypothesis that older sherds on a site are broken into smaller fragments can be supported only by a very small portion of our data, perhaps because most types in the Middle Pecos Valley continued to be manufactured through several phases. In the one instance of reasonable certainty of confinement of an intrusive type (Red Mesa B/W) to a single phase (Late 18 Mile), the progressive decrease in sherd size through succeeding phases seems to support the hypothesis.

Collections from Sites on the Mescalero Pediment

Several ceramic sites were found scattered along the western margin of the Mescalero Pediment, a few miles to the east of the Pecos River. These sites were usually located in sandy areas in the vicinity of small trees or other vegetation which suggests relatively favorable local water resources. These sites exhibited medium to heavy concentrations of sherds on the surface, but had little trace of structural features other than clusters of fire-cracked rock.

The sherd counts for eight of these sites are given in Table XVII. The time range of the Mescalero Scarp sites appears to be restricted to the interval from the Early Mesita Negra Phase through the Late McKenzie Phase. Collections were made from separate concentrations on two of the sites in an effort to determine whether separate components were present. The six collections from Site P55 exhibited no significant differences and are therefore combined in the table. Only two of the four collections from Site P26 were similar enough to indicate that they belonged in the same phase (samples 038 and 039); therefore, three separate groups of sherds from this site are

TABLE XVII

SHERD COUNTS OF COLLECTIONS FROM SITES ON THE MESCALERO PEDIMENT

Type	P26 (036)	(037)	(038-039)	P52	P54	P55	L6	L10	W9	W42
Micaceous Br.	55	5	157	26	11	1340	530	50	101	23
Roswell Br.	42	-	184	-	10	221	219	189	193	40
Jornada Br.	27	3	223	2	4	1012	276	232	52	11
S. Pecos Br.	2	-	15	7	10	160	122	355	89	-
Alma Br.	2	1	13	38	5	86	34	46	18	-
McKenzie Br.	6	-	126	6	-	20	-	3	5	54
Corrugated Br.	-	9	2	-	-	11	1	1	5	-
Crosby B/G	22	6	105	3	-	113	11	11	24	10
M. Pecos B/W	10	6	122	11	5	101	19	24	55	52
Chupadero B/W	-	-	10	-	-	23	-	161	29	3
Eroded Chupadero	14	3	67	-	-	221	-	-	-	-
Other	3	4	24	-	4	123	12	58	18	16
Total	183	37	948	93	44	3431	1224	1130	589	209

presented in the table. Sites P26, P52, P54, and P55 are located adjacent to the Northern Middle Valley. Sites L6 and W42 are east of the area intermediate between the Northern and Southern Middle Valley sites, and Sites L10 and W9 are east of the Southern Middle Valley sites.

P54 and P55 appear to be the earliest of the northern sites; P55 in particular appears to be identical to Early Mesita Negra sites in the valley. This equation is substantiated by the presence of intrusive sherds of Red Mesa B/W (13), Cebolleta B/W (8), Socorro B/W (1), and Mimbres B/W (3). Two sherds assumed to be Lino Gray were also collected, suggesting, with the Red Mesa B/W, that the earliest occupation was in the 18 Mile Phase. Four sherds of Pueblo IV utility ware and the McKenzie sherds suggest that the area was also visited in later periods. The lack of late native ceramics suggests an Early Mesita Negra affinity for Site P54; there were no intrusive sherds in the sample from this site. From Site P26, sample 036 appears to represent an occupation transitional between Early and Late Mesita Negra, as evidenced by the high proportions of Micaceous Brown and Crosby B/G. The only intrusive sherds in this collection are a single example each of Red Mesa B/W and Reserve B/W, both more characteristic of an Early Mesita Negra period. Samples 038 and 039 from this site appear characteristic of the Early McKenzie Phase; however, the South Pecos Brown sherds indicate remnants of an earlier occupation. The only intrusive sherds are five examples of Socorro B/W, a type associated most frequently with Late Mesita Negra occupations in the Northern Middle Valley. Sample 037 almost certainly represents a Late McKenzie or immediate post-McKenzie occupation, since the nine corrugated sherds are made with a McKenzie paste. The single intrusive sherd in this collection is Rio Grande Glazeware, suggesting a post-McKenzie occupation.

The two sites in the area intermediate between the Northern and Southern Middle Valley appear to represent a similar time range. Site L6 is similar to Early Mesita Negra in the northern area. The high percentage of South Pecos Brown might be expected from the geographical location. Twelve of the thirteen intrusive sherds are a hard white ware without surviving decoration. The character of the paste suggests examples of Red Mesa B/W from the Northern Middle Valley and they are tentatively assigned to that type. The single remaining intrusive sherd is similar to Pueblo IV utility ware and may represent a brief occupation in the post-McKenzie period. The Site W42 collection appears to represent a Late McKenzie occupation.

The intrusive sherds in this collection include examples of Pueblo IV Utility Ware (12), El Paso Polychrome (1), and Three Rivers R/TC (3).

The chronological position of the two southern sites is somewhat more difficult to assess because of the relative lack of comparable material from that area and the position of Site L10 well to the south of the other sites. The very high proportion of South Pecos Brown on Site L10 and the relatively high proportion on W9 appear to be directly proportional to the geographic location of the two sites. Intrusive sherds from L10 suggest occupation over a considerable period of time. They include one example each of Red Mesa B/W, Reserve B/W, Socorro B/W, and Rio Grande Glaze I Red. Two sherds of El Paso Polychrome, 14 of Broadline and 13 of Three Rivers R/TC indicate patterns of contact to the west, as do six sherds of Mimbres B/W. A single sherd of Mimbres B/W occurs at Site W9, with seven intrusive sherds of Broadline R/TC. The presence of a few sherds of McKenzie Brownware on each site suggests an occupation in the Roswell Phase, as does the high porportion of Chupadero B/W at L10. The ceramics at W9 were apparently subjected to a strong northern influence, shown in the high proportions of Micaceous Brown and Middle Pecos B/W. The former is indicative of an occupation contemporaneous with the Crosby Phase in the valley, and the latter with the Roswell Phase. Perhaps the best that can be said for these samples is that they represent mixed occupations with the latest sedentary phases of valley occupation most strongly represented.

In summary, the sites on the Mescalero Pediment show an eastward extension of the ceramic phases outlined for the Middle Pecos Valley from Early Mesita Negra through the Late McKenzie period, with indications of short-term occupations continuing into the post-McKenzie period.

V

MIDDLE PECOS VALLEY LITHIC MATERIALS

Chipped Stone

The chipped stone other than projectile points has not been studied intensively, although an attempt was made to collect a random sample of flakes and tools from each site, relative in quantity to ceramics. The projectile points were subjected to several quantitative techniques of analysis which indicate meaningful changes through time in this implement form. Since these changes appear to represent *trends* in the development of Post-Archaic projectile point forms I have devised a typology which incorporates only the changes which appear to be meaningful in a temporal or obvious functional sense. The typology of the remainder of the chipped stone material is more or less traditional.

Projectile Points

Approximately 330 whole or fragmentary projectile points and notched or stemmed knives were recovered by the survey, exclusive of broken tips. Of these, 5 are apparently Paleo-Indian; 48, which are either of distinctive form or from sites yielding no ceramics, are presumed to be Archaic; and the remainder are from later periods.

The Paleo-Indian points, represented by 5 bases (Pl. VII), appear to be exclusively lanceolate and unfluted, although 2 (A and D), show long basal thinning flakes on one surface. All have marked evidence of basal and lateral grinding. Four of the 5 were recovered from sites containing predominantly ceramic-period materials, while the fifth (E) was found on the surface of the Blackdom terrace to the west of the river a few miles south of Fort Sumner. A and B are from Site P28 in area 4, C is from P7 in area 6, and D is from P24 in area 2. A single channel flake characteristic of the Folsom technique was found on Site P7.

As can be seen in Plate VII, the point bases vary in form, suggesting diverse cultural origins. It is apparent that neither the maximum width nor thickness of any of the points survives on the fragments in our collection. However, for possible comparison with other specimens the dimensions for these fragments are presented in Table XVIII.

TABLE XVIII

DIMENSIONS OF PALEO-INDIAN PROJECTILE POINTS

Point	Maximum Length	Maximum Width	Maximum Thickness	Basal Width	Material
A	24.7	26.5	6.6	19.3	Dark gray chert
B	18.7	20.2	4.2	16.8	Light gray chert
C	24.0	25.0	7.0	17.5	Tan quartzite
D	17.5	20.5	5.3	18.6	Tecovas jasper
E	19.1	24.5	3.7	21.0	White quartzite

(All measurements in mm.)

The post-Paleo-Indian projectile points are chiefly stemmed and notched forms and these attributes provide several additional variables for comparison. The metric comparisons are based on measurements of length, maximum width, maximum thickness, minimum diameter of stem, distance from base to minimum stem diameter and distance from tip to minimum stem diameter (Fig. 12). I believe that, in addition to stylistic preference, these dimensions tend to reflect functional differences in hafting which were meaningful to the manufacturers of the points. The following formal attributes were also observed:

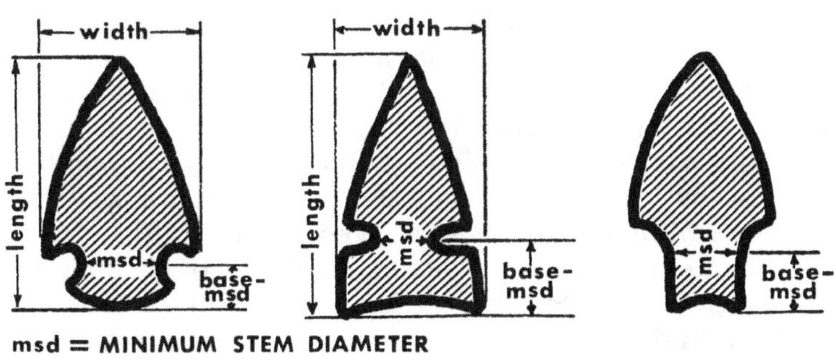

FIG. 12. Projectile point measurements.

1. Blade shape
2. Presence or absence of serration
3. Barb form
4. Number of notches
5. Position and direction of notches
6. Shape of notches
7. Shape of base
8. Shape of stem

The points were studied, both as a group and in restricted temporal phases based on association with ceramics.

Observations Considering the Total Population of Projectile Points

In a two-tailed test for *r*, significant correlations were observed between almost all metric observations; the only exceptions were the relationship between minimum stem diameter (*msd*) and length, and between thickness and the distance from base to *msd* (*b-msd*). Inasmuch as the shapes of all projectile points are similar in a general sense the probability significance of particular numerical values of correlation may be open to question. For this reason I have concentrated in this interpretation only on those values which fall beyond the .001 level of significance and lumped these under the category of "high correlations." Occasionally correlations significant at the .01 and .05 level are mentioned as "significant." High correlations among the metric attributes were observed between *msd* and *b-msd*, between width and thickness, and between length and distance from tip to *msd* (*t-msd*) or blade length. Since the very high correlation of blade length with total length is in part self-evident, the significance of this correlation is questionable.

Between metric and non-metric attributes, high correlations were present between *b-msd*, and notch depth and notch shape, as well as between *t-msd* and notch and barb shape; among non-metric attributes, notch direction, notch depth, notch shape, and barb shape are all linked to one another by high correlations. This suggests that a single variable is present as a determinant of notch form which might be observed in the future by recording a single non-metric observation, such as barb shape. In addition, the obviously related variables of stem shape and notch direction show high correlation. The only remaining high correlation is between barb shape and base shape.

Scatter diagrams were plotted for the thickness-width correlations and for *msd*- to *b-msd* correlations in an attempt to determine whether clusters were present along the axis of the correlation which might be indicative of functional or temporal differences within the sample.

The clearest cluster which appears to be indicative of function is found in the relationship between width and thickness (Fig. 13). Here the heavy cluster between a width of 10 to 20 mm. and a thickness of 2 to 4 mm. appears to indicate the normal range for arrow points; this is opposed to the larger dimensions which, on the basis of temporal factors and form, appear to reflect the size preferences for dart points and knives. The coincidence of the distribution of late triangular side-notched points with the cluster of other arrow points is interesting in the light of the position of these point forms in the correlation of *msd* and *b-msd* (Fig. 14). Here the late triangular side-notched forms fall between the large Archaic points and the smaller points of the Archaic and post-Archaic period; these again appear to represent two functionally distinct groups, dart points and knives on the one hand and arrow points on the other. The intermediate status of the triangular side-notched forms appears to reflect a broader and longer hafting element than that which characterizes the earlier arrow point forms. The relationship of blade length to total length (not illustrated) shows the same general separation by size of apparent arrow points and those intended for darts or as knives. In this relationship, however, the Archaic and earliest ceramic period points tend to cluster toward the large-size end of the distribution, while most of the later points are smaller in form, perhaps indicating a chronologically significant trend.

The distribution of the triangular side-notched points in the last two of these correlations is sufficiently distinctive to indicate that, in terms of size and dimensions of hafting elements, we seem to be dealing with three different groups of points; the large dart points and knives, the smaller arrow points of form generally similar to the dart points, and the triangular side-notched arrow points.

For purposes of a more detailed descriptive typology the sample of points seemed too small for a meaningful separation by statistical analysis and I have instead relied upon the more traditional method of classification by silhouette. In a general sense I have attempted to indicate size differences in this classification, but no absolute metric data is included.

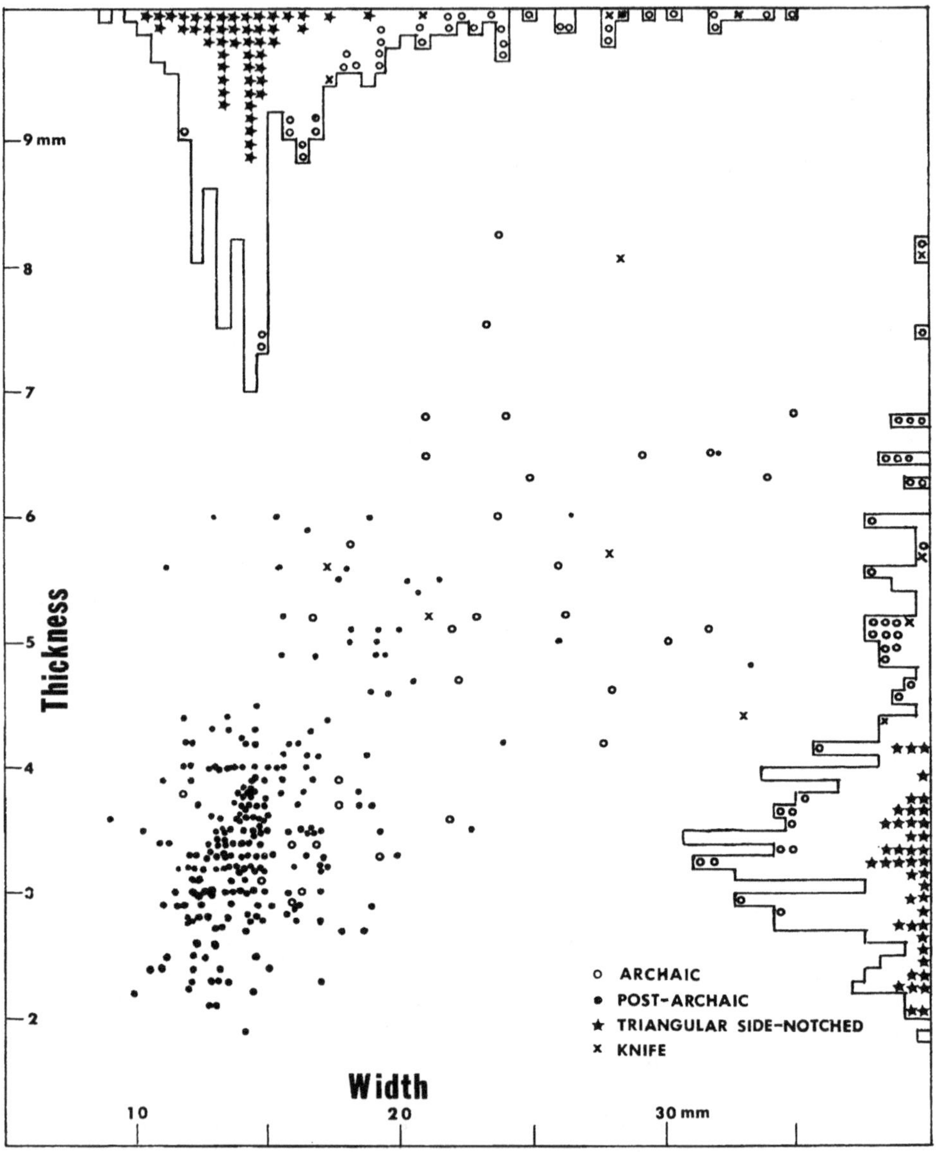

FIG. 13. Distribution of width and thickness of projectile points.

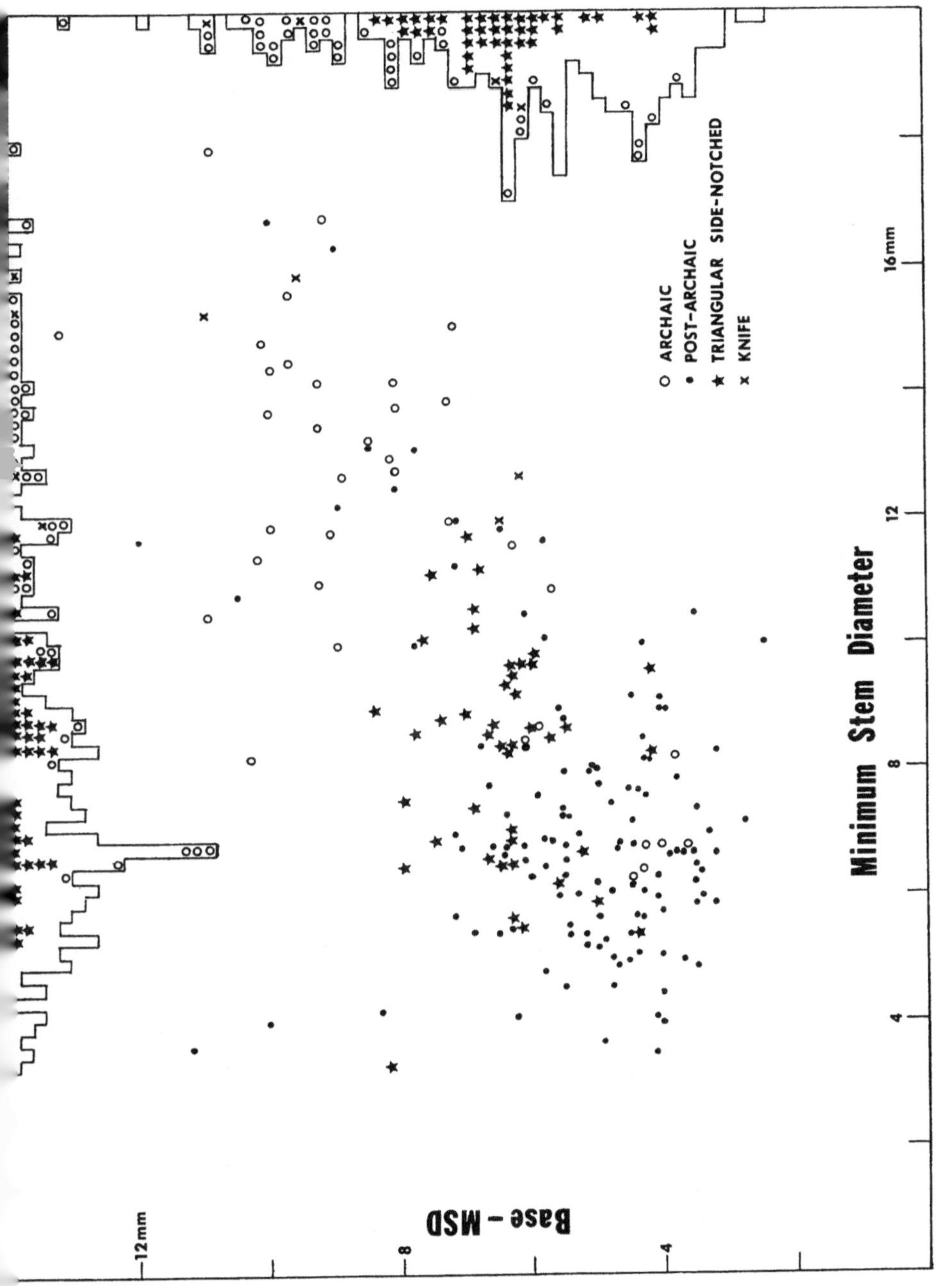

FIG. 14. Distribution of minimum stem diameter and distance from base to minimum stem diameter of projectile points.

The basis of this classification is seen in Fig. 15. Two major form classes are recognized as being of primary importance, deriving from the method of manufacture of the point; the shape of the preform or "blank," and the shape of the notching or other modification for hafting. The simplest projectile point forms are those of the unmodified finished preform appearing in the column at the right side of the illustration. The various forms of hafting modification are shown across the top of the illustration and the combinations of preform and hafting form which actually occur among the projectile points recovered by the survey are shown at the coordinates of the two appropriate forms. The types are designated by the appropriate letter-number combinations. Additional modifications of size and shape beyond the normal range are indicated in the descriptions which follow by the letters S, W, X, Y, and Z, assigned as follows:

S - serrate blade
W - long, narrow (length/width = >1.99)
X - short and wide (length/width = <1.31)
Y - small (length + width = <33.0 mm)
Z - large (length + width = >44.9 mm)

The Y and Z measurements were determined by breaks on a graphic distribution of size. The preforms, designated by letters from A to Q, may be described as follows:

Letter	Blade edge shape	Base edge shape
A.	Moderately convex	Strongly convex
B.	Moderately convex	Slightly convex
C.	Moderately convex	Straight
D.	Moderately convex	Slightly concave
E.	Strongly convex	Straight
F.	Strongly convex	Slightly concave
G.	Straight	Strongly convex
H.	Straight	Slightly convex
J.	Straight	Straight
K.	Straight	Slightly concave
L.	Concave	Slightly convex
M.	Concave	Straight
N.	Straight angular	Concave
P.	Convexo-concave	Slightly convex
Q.	Concavo-convex	Slightly convex

The hafting forms are designated by numbers as follows:

1. No hafting modification
2. Straight, wide stem
3. Expanding wide stem
4. Expanding moderate stem with moderate barbs
5. Expanding moderate stem with pronounced barbs
6. Slightly expanding narrow stem with very pronounced and square-ended barbs
7. Constricted stem
8. Constricted stem with excurvate base
9. Straight, moderately wide short stem
10. Straight, narrow short stem
11. Straight, narrow short stem with moderate barb
12. Expanding narrow short stem
13. Excurvate narrow stem
14. Expanding narrow stem with convex lower edge of barb
15. Moderate 45° corner notches
16. Wide 45° corner notches
17. Moderate 60° corner notches
18. Narrow 60° corner notches
19. Narrow 90° basal notches
20. Small 45° corner notches
21. Narrow 45° corner notches
22. Narrow flared 30° corner notches
23. Expanded 30° corner notches
24. Low moderate side notches
25. Moderate side notches
26. Moderate side notches and basal notch
27. Small side notches
28. Multiple notches

The number in the center of the silhouette indicates the number of examples of that particular form recovered by the survey. The designation of certain of the hafting modifications listed above may be judged as somewhat arbitrary, particularly as concerns the distinction between the barbed, expanding stem types and the inclined expanding notched types. In these cases the relative dimensions of the modification was used to distinguish between "stemmed" and "notched" categories.

Utilizing the attributes distinguished in this classification, I have attempted to discern meaningful differences within the total population of 211 classifiable projectile points and fragments, as well as meaningful associations of these point forms with ceramic assemblages of the phases distinguished in the preceding chapter.

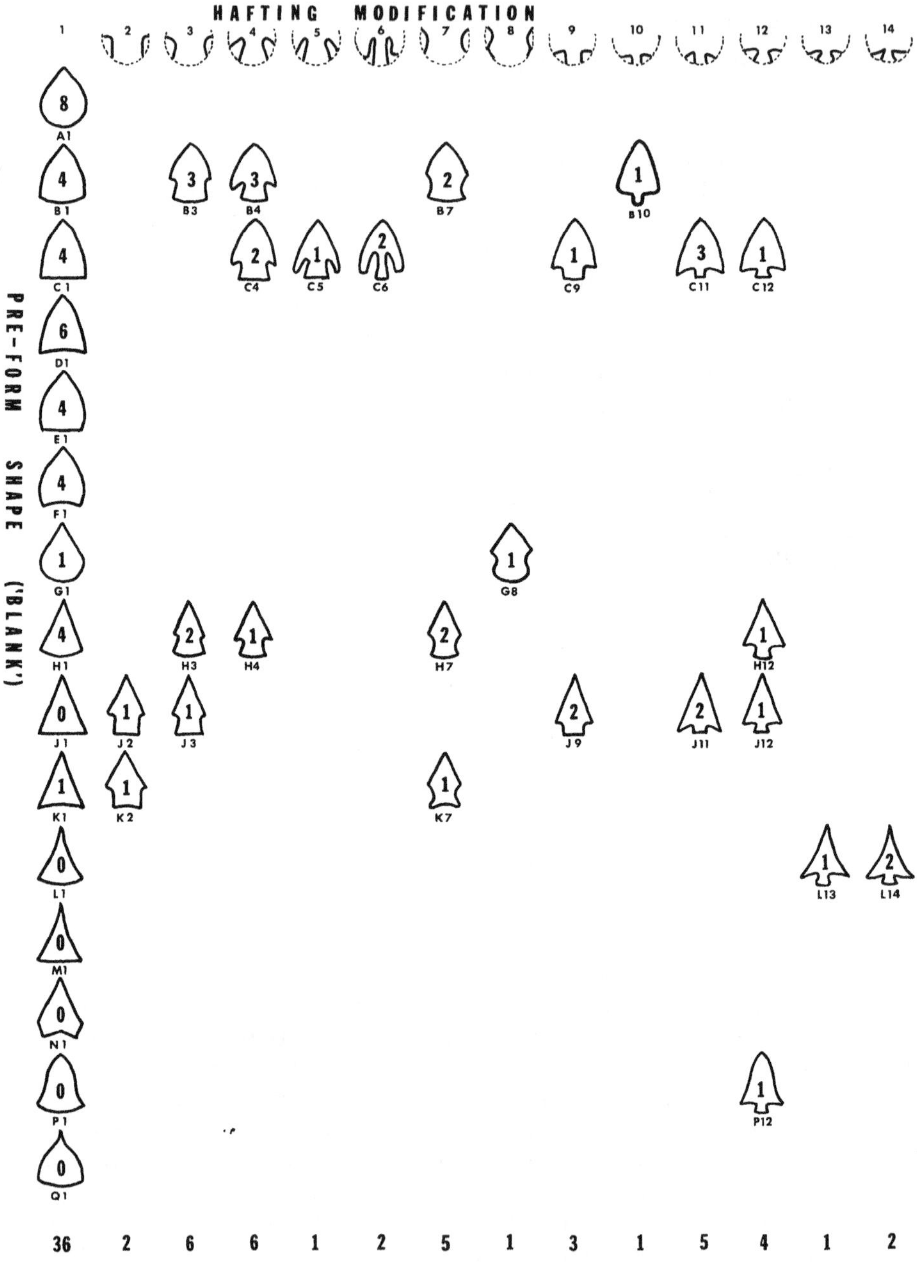

FIG. 15a. Classification for projectile points.

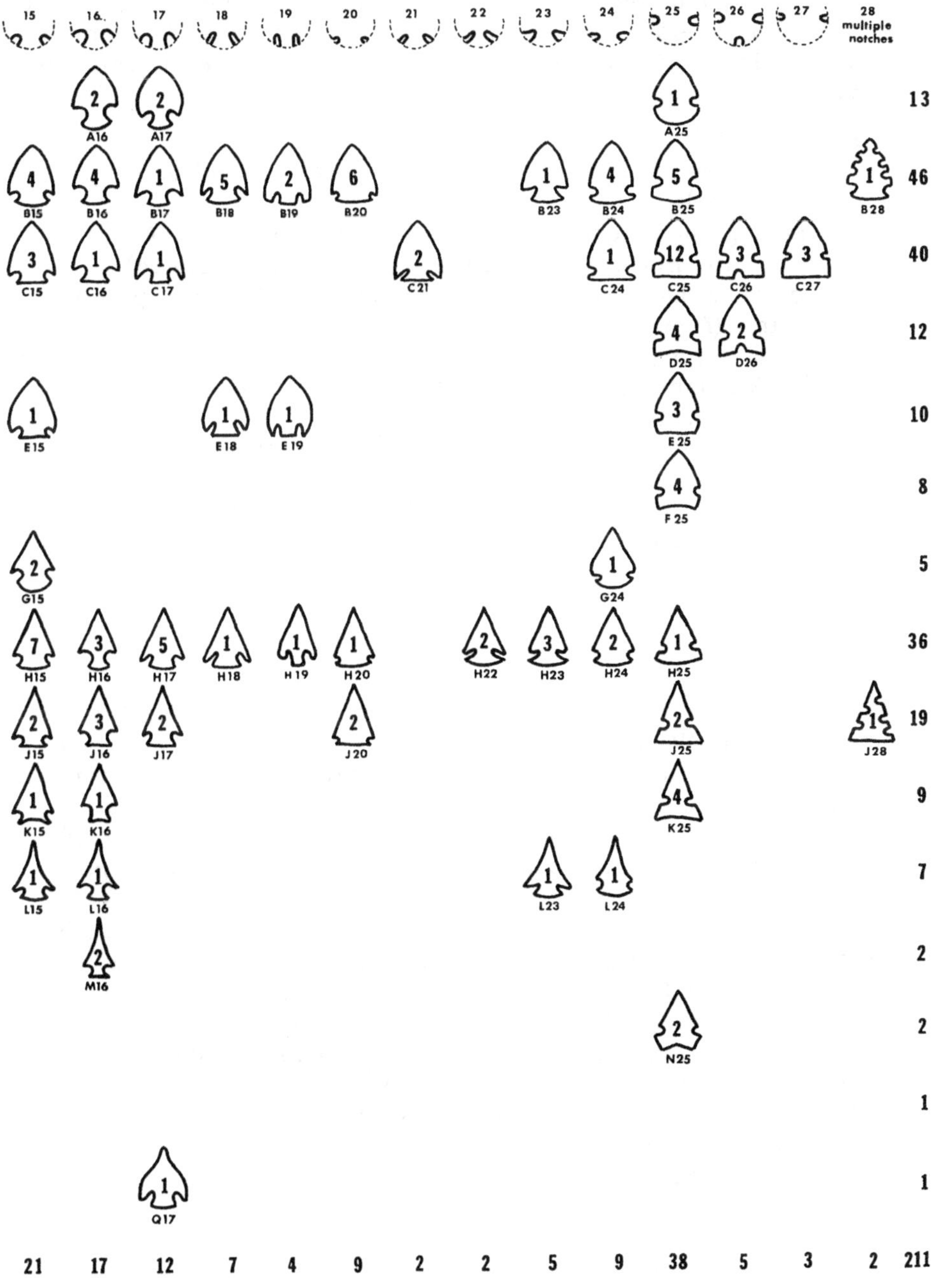

FIG. 15b. Classification for projectile points.

I have attempted to quantify these data in a manner conducive to objective comparison with other populations of projectile points.

The analysis of the total population was concerned with the association of several major categories of variables:

(1) serration
(2) extremes of form (categories W, X, Y, and Z mentioned on p. 94)
(3) hafting modification, grouped as follows: (a) Large-Stem (forms 2-9), (b) Small-Stem (forms 10-14), (c) Diagonal Notch (forms 15-23), (d) Lateral (Side) Notch (forms 24-28)
(4) blade form, grouped as: (a) Convex-edged (forms A-F), (b) Straight-edged (forms G-K), (c) Concave-edged (forms L-M)
(5) base form, grouped as: (a) Strongly Convex Base (forms A, G), (b) Moderately Convex Base (forms B, H, L, P, Q, 83 examples), (c) Straight Base (forms C, E, J, M, 63 examples), (d) Concave Base (forms D, F, K, 18 examples).

Serration

Serration is not significantly associated with any of the extremes of form (W, X, Y, Z) and occurs only rarely with each. This alteration is associated with diagonally notched points to a significant degree, in contrast to other hafting modifications (X^2 = 7.13; significant beyond 1%).[11] Within this group of 79 points 14 are serrate, as opposed to a total of 4 serrate points in the remaining 96 (preforms not included in comparisons for serration). Serration is also strongly associated with straight to concave-edged blades (X^2 = 12.11; significant beyond .1%) since 15 points in this group of 78 are serrate, as opposed to 3 out of the remaining 99 (blade forms of preforms N, P, Q not included in comparison). In addition, serration is associated with moderately convex based points (X^2 = 5.86; significant beyond 2%) with 14 of the 83 points in this group exhibiting serrate blades in contrast to 4 of the remaining 90 points in the sample (preform N not included). On the basis of these tests it is

[11]All X^2 distributions are restricted to 1° of freedom unless otherwise stated, and were calculated with the Yates correction suggested by Moroney (1965: 254).

logical to conclude that most serrate points are diagonally notched with straight to concave blade edges and moderately convex bases, i.e. categories H 15-18, 20-23, L 15, 16 and 23 of the typology presented here. An examination of the points in this category reveals that those with narrow notches (hafting modifications 18-22) have no serration. In the categories that remain only L 23, represented by a single point, does not have an example of serration. These 23 points include 10 of the 18 serrate specimens in the collection, or 55.5% of all serrate points. As would be expected, the significance of the association of serration with this group of points is well beyond the .1% level ($X^2 = 31.36$).

Extremes of Form

The only significant association between extremes of form (i.e. short and wide, long and narrow, small or large) and hafting modifications is between large-stemmed hafting and large-sized points. In this test, as in other tests utilizing extreme form points, only examples complete enough to provide reliable comparative data were used. This reduced the size of the sample to 146 points and 29 preforms. Nevertheless, since 18 of the 22 large-stemmed points were of large size, as opposed to only 15 of the remaining 124 points, the association of these two attributes was most significant ($X^2 = 47.82$; significant well beyond the .1% level). No significant associations were observed between extremes of form and blade form. The distribution of small size related to blade form suggests that about one point in ten in all categories is small, but the distribution does not conform closely enough to be statistically significant. With respect to base shape, the only possible correlation involving points of extreme form is between small size and concave bases ($X^2 = 3.65$; significant only beyond 10%). The distribution of large specimens is sufficiently close to that of the expected population of base forms to suggest that about 2 points out of 9 in all categories are large, but the distributions are not close enough to be significantly correlated.

Hafting Modification

There is a significant preference for convex blades among side-notched points ($X^2 = 12.47$; significant beyond .1%), and for concave bases with the same hafting modification ($X^2 = 17.35$;

significant beyond .1%). A very highly significant correlation exists between diagonal notches and convex bases ($X^2 = 37.04$; significant well beyond .1%). No other correlations of hafting modification and blade or base form appear to be significant.

Blade Form and Base Form

No significant correlations exist between any of the subdivisions of these two groups of attributes. The number of all forms falls within a reasonably expected deviation from the predicted distribution.

Distributions Related to Temporal Differences

Serration

The preference for serration on the blades of projectile points is significantly stronger in the first three sedentary phases, Early 18 Mile through Early Mesita Negra, than in the last three sedentary phases, Late Mesita Negra through Late McKenzie ($X^2 = 6.12$; significant beyond 2%).

Extremes of Form

No significant grouping of long, narrow points occurs by phase. Short, wide points are somewhat more abundant than expected in the Archaic and Late Mesita Negra and Early McKenzie collections, but not significantly so. Small points were completely absent in the collections from Archaic sites and occur in significantly higher quantities than expected in the Lake McKenzie Phase and Post-McKenzie collections ($X^2 = 5.40$; significant beyond 3%). The association of large points with Archaic collections is very highly significant ($X^2 = 42.79$; significant well beyond .1%).

Hafting Modification

Hafting group (a), large-stemmed forms, are significantly associated with Archaic collections ($X^2 = 14.85$; significant beyond .1%). While small-stemmed forms are largely restricted to post-Archaic and pre-Late McKenzie phases this association is only significant at the 10% level ($X^2 = 3.22$). A near mutually-exclusive distribution of corner-notched, group (c), and side-notched, group (d) points was noted. The diagonal-notched points appear to be subject to replacement by side-notched forms beginning in the Early McKenzie Phase. In an analysis restricted to diagonal and side-notched points the association of diagonal-notched forms with Late Mesita Negra and preceding phases and of side-notched forms with McKenzie Phase and post-McKenzie collections was significant well beyond .1% ($X^2 = 51.42$).

Blade Form

The association of concave-edged blades with Early 18 Mile Phase collections is significant beyond the .1% level ($X^2 = 35.17$). The only other significant correlation between blade form and cultural phase can best be expressed as an absence of straight-edged blades in Late McKenzie and post-McKenzie collections ($X^2 = 14.77$; significant beyond .1%).

Base Shape

The predominance of convex-based forms in the first three sedentary phases (Early 18 Mile through Early Mesita Negra) in contrast to all later phases (Late Mesita Negra through post-McKenzie) is significant beyond .1% ($X^2 = 28.59$). Within the post-Archaic phases, straight bases are conspicuously few in the Early 18 Mile Phase ($X^2 = 7.51$; significant beyond 1%). Also within the post-Archaic period there is a marked concentration of concave-based points in the last two phases (Late McKenzie and post-McKenzie) as opposed to the preceding phases ($X^2 = 24.05$; significant beyond .1%).

Discussion

It is clear that distinctive combinations of attributes were favored in particular cultural horizons. It is probable that at least some displacement of points from original context has occurred because of the practice of re-using points made by earlier peoples,[12] but the strong correlations for many attributes and phases seem to indicate that this drift of earlier objects into a later context was not particularly prevalent in the Middle Pecos area in the prehistoric period.

---

[12]A specific example of this usage is given by Opler (1941) for the Chiricahua Apache.

In order to test the cultural significance of the classification I attempted a modified Brainerd-Robinson (Brainerd, 1951) approach to the projectile point data. This procedure involved a separate computation of "indices of likeness" for the phase distributions of preform shape and of hafting modification. These two indices were then combined (with a total possible likeness of 400 rather than 200 as in the traditional usage), and arranged in a matrix to determine the degree of approximation of the projectile point data based on this classification, to the chronological framework based on ceramics. The result given below in Table XIX shows that the best possible arrangement of the post-Archaic data exactly parallels the chronological ordering of the ceramic phases.

TABLE XIX

MATRIX ORDERING OF PROJECTILE POINT PREFORM SHAPE AND HAFTING MODIFICATION

Phase	1	2	3	4	5	6	7
1	X						
2	167.4	X					
3	199.9	256.9	X				
4	133.1	195.3	255.9	X			
5	120.9	160.4	199.8	214.4	X		
6	78.1	129.4	159.5	185.8	254.5	X	
7	61.2	119.3	153.0	186.7	199.7	257.9	X

Phase Key:

1. Early 18 Mile
2. Late 18 Mile
3. Early Mesita Negra
4. Late Mesita Negra
5. Early McKenzie
6. Late McKenzie
7. Post-McKenzie

The significance of this ordering lies in the demonstration that changes in projectile point form, as observed through this classification, are parallel to changes in ceramic style, indicating that both kinds of material can be used as chronological indicators and that each tends to support interpretations based on the other. It also indicates that this particular technique of projectile point classification detects the kinds of attribute changes which are meaningful in cultural chronology and which probably reflect stylistic trends which were meaningful to the manufacturers of the points.

Archaic Points

Points in the collections from Archaic sites are significantly larger than those of later periods, probably reflecting a high proportion of dart points (see Fig. 13). The predominantly heavy stems of points from these collections tend to re-enforce this interpretation, since the heavier shafts of darts would require a stem heavier than that used on a more slender arrow shaft. Hafting techniques are about equally divided between large-stem forms and diagonal-notched forms. Four of the 30 classifiable points (13%) are lateral-notched. Only one small-stem point is present. Of the six large, short, wide points recovered, four are from Archaic sites. Convex blades are favored over straight-edged blades in a ratio of about 2 to 1. Concave-edged blades are not present. Convex bases also seem favored over other forms in a 2 to 1 ratio, with straight bases next in abundance (26%) and concave bases least frequent (7%).

The 24 point types and variants restricted to collections from Archaic sites are:

A16	B18Z (2)	F25XZ	H17Z	K2SZ
B3X	C5Z	G8Z	H19XZ	N25
B15XZ	C9Z	H3	J2Z	N25X
B16Z	C12	H4Z	J9XZ	Q18
B18X	C25W	H7WZ	J16Z	

Early 18 Mile Phase Points

This phase has the highest ratio of serrate points (21%), the highest concentration of moderately convex-based points (92%) and the highest concentration of convex-edged blades (24%), which account for 78% of all blades of this form in the sample. It also includes the highest ratio of large points of any post-Archaic phase, probably reflecting a continuation of Archaic stone-working traditions (or a high proportion of "early point salvage" from Archaic sites), Points from this phase are primarily diagonal-notched, but a higher ratio (and higher number) are of the small-stemmed variety than in any other phase (18%).

An examination of specific point forms reveals that all points but one of the 6 with concave blade edge and convex base are restricted to this phase, suggesting that the one example in the Late Mesita Negra Phase may have been salvaged.

The majority of points in this phase are of moderate size and are either straight or convex-edged, with moderately convex bases. Most of these points are hafted with diagonal notches.

The sixteen point types and variants restricted to this phase are:

B10S	H1Y	H16S	L14 (2)
B19S	H32	H22X	L15S
B25W	H15W	J3Z	L16S
H1	H16 (2)	L13XY	L24

Late 18 Mile Phase Points

These points are not remarkable in any way as regards serration or extremes of form. They are about evenly divided between straight- and convex-edged blade forms, and more than 50% of the specimens are hafted by diagonal notching. Convex bases predominate over straight bases in a ratio of 2 to 1.

The nine point types and variants whose distribution is restricted to this phase are:

A16Y	E18Y	H7
C6X	G15S	H20
C6Z	G24	H24WZ

Early Mesita Negra Phase Points

This sample is perhaps remarkable for the relatively small proportion of points which show extremes of form; only two of the 12 points complete enough for comparison, or 17%. Both of these points are of small size. As regards hafting modification the sample is unique in its high concentration of diagonal-notched forms (87% of modified points), and in the complete absence of large- and small-stemmed points. As in the preceding period, blade forms are evenly distributed between convex-edged and straight-edged specimens. The 2 to 1 ratio of convex to straight base forms noted in the preceding phase seems to hold true for this sample as well.

The eleven point types and variants whose distribution is restricted to this phase are:

B19	E15	H23SY
B25XY	G1	J17
C16	H18	K15
C17	H22	

Late Mesita Negra Phase Points

In contrast to the Early Mesita Negra collections, almost half (45%) of the complete points in this sample are of extreme form, including the second-highest ratio of large points of the post-Archaic phases (22%). As in the preceding three phases, a majority of the hafted points are diagonally-notched and blade forms are almost evenly divided between convex- and straight-edged. In contrast to the preceding two phases, straight and convex bases occur in almost equal numbers.

The fourteen point types and variants whose distribution is restricted to this phase are:

A25	G15	H25S	K16
B7Y	H1WZ	J9Z	L23
B17XY	H1Z	J11X	
C1Z	H17X	J15 (2)	

Early McKenzie Phase Points

As in the Late Mesita Negra Phase collections, almost half (46%) of the points complete enough for comparison are of extreme form. In contrast to earlier phases, a majority of hafted points in this sample (58%), are hafted with lateral-notches, while examples of large- and small-stem and diagonal and multiple-notch hafting are all found among the remaining points. Convex-edged blades are more than twice as abundant as straight-edged blades and straight bases are twice as numerous as convex bases. As might be expected, this phase marks the first appearance, and in some quantity (29%), of lateral-notched points with convex-edged blade and straight base (types C24, C25).

The eight point types and variants whose distribution is restricted to this phase are:

B24XY	C4Z	C24W	J16X
B28	C11Y	H17S	K25

Late McKenzie Phase Points

This sample is remarkable for the large quantity of small points, both with regard to the points of extreme form and to the entire sample. Of the ten points of extreme form, nine are small and account for 28% of the complete points. A great majority of the hafted points in this phase (82%), are lateral-notched, and a similar majority of all the points (85%), have convex-edged blades. Concave and straight bases occur in about equal quantity (about 40% each) and account for four times as many points as do convex bases. The typical points of this phase, then, are lateral-notched with convex blade and straight or concave base.

The eleven point types and variants whose distribution is restricted to this phase are:

A1WY	D1Y	El (3)	K25Y (2)
B20S	D25 (3)	F25Y	K25XZ
C4	D25Y	K7Y	

Post-McKenzie Phase Points

The latest points from the northern Middle Pecos Valley are distinctive in several features. A higher percentage (30%) of complete points are of extreme long, narrow form than in any other phase, and a higher percentage (40%) are small points. This is the only time period in which serrate points are completely absent. All but one of the hafted points (89%) have lateral notches; one of these has multiple lateral notches. All points except one (93%) are made with convex-edged blades. All of the lateral-notched points have either straight or concave bases, and all but three of the points in the sample (78%) have this type of base.

The most prevalent point in this time horizon is similar to the lateral-notched convex-edged blade form of the Late McKenzie phase, with either concave or straight base, but with the additional feature of a single basal notch. These points form 36% of the total sample (five of fourteen) and are completely restricted to this phase.

The ten point types and variants whose distribution is restricted to this phase are:

A1W	C25XY	C26W	D26W	E1Y
B7	C26	C26Z	D26Y	J28Y

Points from Site P24

As was noted in the treatment of the ceramics, Site P24 appears to represent a mixture of all major components of sedentary cultures in the northern Middle Pecos Valley. Thirty identifiable points and fragments were collected from the site and were included in the study. The relatively large number of serrate points (5, or 17%) reflects the presence of the earlier sedentary phases, while the relative abundance of small points (6, or 20%) probably indicates affinities with the later phases. Although diagonal-notched points are the dominant hafted form (64%), the only hafting group not significantly represented is the large-stem category. Four examples of small-stem points (14%), and six lateral-notched points (21%), were collected at the site. The points are almost evenly divided between convex-edged blades and straight-edged blades, which suggests a weighting toward the earlier portion of the sedentary sequence. Moderately convex bases predominate (60%), with straight bases next in importance (37%); there is only a single example of a concave base, which again suggests a weighting toward the earlier phases.

The nineteen point types and variants whose distribution was restricted to this site are:

B1Y	H12W	H24	J20S
B16Y	H17	J11SX	J20Y
B23X	H17Y	J12	K1Y
B24 (2)	H23S	J16XZ	P12
E19Z	H23SZ	J17Z	

Points With Multiple Phase Distribution

Twenty-five point types and variants were distributed over more than a single phase. These points are treated below under the general headings of hafting modification, since this variable seems most closely associated with temporal position.

Preforms

At least one example of each of the five preform types represented was found in the Late McKenzie Phase. No particular pattern of temporal distribution is apparent other than the heavy concentration of the concave-based forms (D, F) in the Late McKenzie and Post-McKenzie Phases. The preforms and phases represented are:

Type	Phases	Type	Phases
A1	Early Mesita Negra Late Mesita Negra (2) Late McKenzie	C1	Late 18 Mile Late Mesita Negra Late McKenzie
A1Z	Archaic Early McKenzie	D1	Late Mesita Negra Late McKenzie (2) Post-McKenzie (2)
B1	Archaic Late McKenzie Post-McKenzie	F1	Early McKenzie Late McKenzie (3)

Large-Stem Points

As might be expected in view of the general characteristics of the phase distributions outlined above, the two large-stemmed forms represented are both large-sized points as well and are confined to the Archaic and Early 18 Mile phase.

Type	Phases
B3Z	Archaic Early 18 Mile
B4Z	Archaic (2) Early 18 Mile

Small-Stem Points

The only small-stem form with a multiple phase distribution is C11, with a single example in the Late 18 Mile and Late Mesita Negra Phases.

Diagonal-Notched Points

These points are almost entirely restricted to the early sedentary phases in the valley. Only one specimen comes from a collection later than Late Mesita Negra, and only two are from Archaic collections. The forms which seem most definitely restricted in time are B20 and H15 which appear concentrated between Late 18 Mile and Early Mesita Negra. It is possible that B18 is restricted to Early 18 Mile and that C15 is restricted to Early and Late Mesita Negra horizons. The distribution of the other forms is too diffuse to attempt chronological restriction. These points and their temporal associations are:

Type	Phases	Type	Phases
A17	Archaic Late Mesita Negra	C15	Early Mesita Negra Late Mesita Negra Site P24

B15	Early 18 Mile Late Mesita Negra Site P24	C21	Archaic Late Mesita Negra
B16	Early 18 Mile Late McKenzie	H15	Late 18 Mile (2) Early Mesita Negra
B18	Early 18 Mile Site P24	H15S	Late 18 Mile Early Mesita Negra Site P24
B20	Early Mesita Negra Site P24 (2)		
B20Y	Late 18 Mile Site P24		

Lateral-Notched Points

In keeping with the previous discussions of the temporal placement of lateral-notched points, it is not surprising that only one example in this group is earlier than the Early McKenzie phase and this point has a convex base. Site P24, as was noted earlier, contains materials ranging from the 18 Mile through the McKenzie Phases. The points and their temporal associations are:

B25	Early Mesita Negra Late McKenzie (2)	E25	Late McKenzie Site P24
C25	Early McKenzie (3) Late McKenzie (6) Site P24	F25	Late McKenzie Post-McKenzie
C27	Late McKenzie (2) Site P24	J25	Early McKenzie Late McKenzie

Summary

My object in this study of projectile points has been to present an objective system of description of this material as collected by the survey, which would be amenable to comparison with populations of projectile points from other areas. In addition, I have attempted to relate this descriptive system to the succession of prehistoric ceramic phases in the valley.

Within the total population of projectile points it appears possible, through the use of metric attributes, to distinguish between arrow points and points of other functions, including dart points and knives. This distinction appears most satisfactorily demonstrated in the correlation of thickness and width (Fig. 13).

If the assumption is valid that points in the strong cluster below a width of 20 mm. and a thickness of about 4.75 mm. are arrow points, then it appears that the bow and arrow had been introduced into the Middle Pecos Valley prior to the end of the Archaic in that area. This may imply that the terminal Archaic in the Middle Pecos Valley is contemporary with Basketmaker III in the Anasazi area. The distribution of the triangular side-notched points in the correlation of *msd* with *b-msd* (Fig. 14) strongly suggests that they are a distinct functional group of arrow points, with the advantage of a longer hafting element below the notches and a wider element between the notches. This may imply a heavier arrow shaft and a more effective lashing to the shaft; this in turn may imply the introduction of a more powerful bow. The triangular side-notched forms appear better designed for penetration than do any of the preceding forms, also suggestive of a more powerful bow, in contrast to that used with the barbed points. These latter appear designed to hold in the quarry after relatively light penetration.

Another correlation, utilizing a combination of metric and qualitative attributes derived from the classification in Figure 15, tends, at least in part, to substantiate the functional difference between arrow points and dart points mentioned above. This is the highly significant correlation between points of large size and the large-stem hafting modification, a hafting technique apparently designed for shafts of significantly larger diameter than those used on arrows. These larger points with wider stems fall outside of the cluster which is postulated to be arrow points on the width-thickness diagram.

Other observations suggest particular restrictions of form (or "rules"), employed throughout the sequence in the manufacture of projectile points. Side-notching was seldom done on a preform that had straight or concave edges. Concave bases are almost entirely restricted to side-notched points. This basal modification in effect adds a barb to the base of a point designed for high penetration. Most diagonal-notching was done on convex-based preforms. Serration tended to be restricted to points of moderate size and shape, with straight blade edges, diagonal-notches, and moderately convex bases.

Within the temporal sequence, several significant associations have been noted. The association of the large point forms with the Archaic period (see Figs. 13, 14) has been demonstrated to be highly significant. The restriction of serration to the earlier sedentary phases also is significant and suggests that the few serrate points found in later phases may have been "salvaged" from earlier sites. The trend toward smaller points in the post-Archaic phases, culminating in the significant association of points of small size with Late McKenzie and Post-McKenzie phase collections, is also important in connection with the postulated greater penetrating ability of the triangular-side-notched points, which were typical of these two latest occupations of the valley. The most striking change in the post-Archaic projectile point sequence takes place between the Late Mesita Negra Phase and the Early McKenzie Phase, with the transition from the diagonal-notched to the side-notched forms. It is my impression that this transition is preceded by a tendency toward "lateralization" of the diagonal notches and less markedly convex bases in the Late Mesita Negra Phase, but I have not attempted to demonstrate this. With the transition from diagonal to lateral notching as clearly marked as our study indicates, it may be possible to relate this change to similar transitions in surrounding areas which have been fitted into an absolute chronology. The only formal attribute which seems restricted enough to postulate a confinement to a single phase is the concave-edged blade, which is very strongly associated with the Early 18 Mile Phase. Straight-edged blades are apparently confined to pre-Late McKenzie horizons. Convex-based preforms were preferred in the early phases of sedentary occupation, with a tendency toward more straight bases in Late Mesita Negra and following phases, and a marked predominance of concave bases restricted to the latest sedentary occupation (Late McKenzie), and the post-sedentary period. Basal notching on side-notched points did not appear in the valley before its abandonment by the sedentary population of the Late McKenzie Phase.

The system of formal classification of points presented in this analysis appears to be related to other cultural changes, as demonstrated by the Brainerd-Robinson matrix; also, it appears to show meaningful changes in projectile point manufacture. These changes, as will be demonstrated, are similar to changes documented in the projectile point sequences of surrounding areas.

Chipped Stone Materials Other Than Projectile Points

No significant temporal correlations were discovered among the chipped stone tools other than a change in small scraping tools in the latest phases of the sequence. In particular, the Late McKenzie and the Roswell Phases are characterized by small, thick end scrapers which frequently exhibit marked wear patterns on the scraping edge with fine striations at right angles to the edge. These scrapers vary considerably in size and shape, but share a steep scraping edge which is shorter than the maximum length of the implement. The smallest specimen from Site P4C was made on the end of a prismatic micro-blade 6.7 mm. in diameter; the largest cutting edge on a scraper from this site is 26 mm. long. Most specimens have cutting edges between 15 and 20 mm. long. The formal distribution of 111 specimens of this type of scraper from Site P4C is as follows:

TABLE XX

DISTRIBUTION OF SHAPE OF SMALL END SCRAPERS FROM SITE P4C

	High Back	Low Back	Total
Straight Edge	8	3	11
Weakly Convex Edge	38	15	53
Strongly Convex Edge	20	13	33
Pointed Edge	11	3	14
Total	77	34	111

The heavy wear on the edges of these scrapers suggests that they were hafted for repeated use. The size of the tools fits well with a description of an implement encountered by the Coronado expedition on the western High Plains, not far from the Middle Pecos Valley. Castañeda describes a "flint as large as a finger tied in a little stick" which is given "an edge with their own teeth" and was used to remove the bison hide at the joints "with a quickness . . . worth seeing and noting" (Winship, 1896: 528).

Prior to these latest sedentary phases the characteristic small scrapers are relatively thin spatulate forms, which in some instances may be modified projectile point preforms.

The most frequent finished chipped stone tools in all phases are simple end scrapers and single-edged side scrapers with straight or convex scraping edges. Flakes with simple retouched edges occur more frequently than finished scrapers.

Ground Stone Materials

The most frequently encountered ground stone tools were fragmentary manos, found on most sites visited by the survey.

They are characteristically relatively small and thick with rounded ends and are convex on one or both grinding edges. Average dimensions appear to be about 120 mm. greatest diameter, 80 mm. lesser diameter, and 45 mm. maximum thickness. Two major types of metates were in use throughout the sedentary sequence in the Middle Pecos Valley. The simplest type of milling stone was a flat slab of native sandstone, casually trimmed on one or more edges and exhibiting evidence of grinding on one or both flat surfaces. The other metate type was basin-shaped, ranging in form from a steep-sided narrow basin to a relatively wide, shallow open-ended form (see Pl. VIII). Small boulder mortars were also used and mortar holes in bedrock were observed on most occasions where outcrops occurred adjacent to sedentary sites.

Small ground stone objects were occasionally encountered in the surface collections. Most frequent of these were small pebbles of white steatite which had one or more smoothed facets. Similar pebbles occur in unmodified form in the terrace gravels along the river. Occasionally this material was used to manufacture beads and pendants. Two small animal effigy beads were found at Site P17. One bead from Site P24 is carved in imitation of an *Olivella* shell. The remaining beads are mostly small and of flat disc shape. One small turquoise pendant was found at Site P4B. Pieces of locally-derived hematite with ground surfaces were frequently encountered.

Artifacts of Other Materials

A few small oval pendants of clamshell (identified by R. J. Drake as *Anodonta grandis* on the basis of specimens from Site P36) were recovered, as was one fragment of a bracelet made from a large marine shell which had been perforated for use as a pendant. Small to medium-sized disc beads of marine and fresh water shell also occur in the collections.

No artifacts of bone were recovered in the surface collections.

Chipped Stone Materials from the Southern Middle Pecos Sites

The chipped stone materials from the Southern Valley sites appear to be generally comparable to those from sites of equivalent phase in the Northern Valley.

Projectile Points

Only two points of identifiable silhouette were recovered from Site P9 (Crosby Phase). One is classifiable as type C16 and the other as A25W. Both of these types occur in Mesita Negra Phases, the Northern equivalent of the Crosby Phase.

Of the six identifiable points from P8 (Roswell Phase), three are unmodified preforms; there is one each of type C, EW, and J. The other points include a single example each of types B25, C25, and H28. Types B25 and C25 are characteristic of the McKenzie Phases in the north, the equivalent of the Roswell Phase. There are no examples of type H28 in the northern collection; however, the generally similar type J28 occurs in a post-McKenzie context. Six less-complete fragments of points from P8 are derived from side-notched triangular points of indeterminate type.

The single identifiable point from Site P7 is of type D25, characteristic of the Late McKenzie Phase in the north and, apparently, of the Roswell Phase in the south.

Other Chipped Stone Materials

The small thick end scrapers which characterize the Late McKenzie Phase in the Northern Valley also occur in sites with Roswell Phase occupations in the south. Twelve examples were collected from Site P8 and five from P7. None were found at Site P9. A fairly thick, bifacially flaked spatulate scraper type occurs at Site P7 and suggests a stage of development between the earlier thin spatulate scrapers and the later thick end scrapers. Three examples were collected at P7. A single specimen of this type of scraper was found at Site L10 at the edge of the Mescalero Scarp. Collections from this site also include triangular side-notched projectile points and fifteen small thick end scrapers identical to those from P8 and P4C.

VI

RESULTS OF EXCAVATIONS IN THE NORTHERN MIDDLE PECOS VALLEY

The excavations conducted during the survey were of necessity on a very small scale. I attempted a series of stratigraphic tests on the individual components of Site P4 in the winter of 1957, and cleared the floor of a surface structure the same season. In 1960 the survey crew made additional stratigraphic tests in 3 ft. test blocks at Site P4 and at Site P24, and attempted to excavate small areas of structures at each of these sites. Finally, in 1965, I carried out a brief test at Site P14. The stratigraphic and architectural excavations are treated separately.

Stratigraphic Tests

The earliest site tested was P14, near the Bosque Redondo. Surface collections from this site in 1960 had failed to yield any sherds and therefore the site was assigned to an Archaic context. The only projectile point collected from the site in that season was small, and typical of 18 Mile points rather than Archaic; and since the site yielded a great quantity of heavy chipped stone materials and very little fine stone material, it appeared desirable to examine it in greater detail. I visited the site late in the summer of 1965, accompanied by James Warnica and Gene McDougal of Portales. We made an additional surface collection which largely duplicated the results of the 1960 visit, but added a few thin preforms of chalcedony that seemed to indicate that the small point was a valid part of the assemblage. There was considerable diversity in the material collected; included were fragments of fossil mammoth enamel (probably derived from the Blackdom Terrace deposits on which the site is situated), a single sherd of brownware tempered with large light-colored particles and similar in character to some of the early brownware of the Rio Bonito area (Jelinek, 1952), and an additional bonus of two late 19th century "liberty-head" nickels. With the help of Warnica and McDougal most of a four-foot square was excavated down to sterile soil (at a maximum depth of about 10 to 12 inches). We recovered about 50 stone flakes, cores, and hammerstones similar to those found on the surface and in no particular sub-surface concentration. The artifacts were accompanied by well-preserved animal bone, suggesting a relatively late date of deposition. During the same visit I excavated a small pit which had been partially destroyed by a ranch road. The pit structure remained intact to a depth of about 1.4 ft. and had a maximum diameter of 3.2 ft. The uppermost surviving portion of the pit was on an eroded slope and was 4.5 ft. below the surface of the original excavation. Near the bottom of this pit we recovered two sherds of the coarse brownware mentioned above and a projectile point of type L14. On the basis of these artifacts and the preservation of the animal bone, the site is included as initial Early 18 Mile Phase rather than Archaic. Both points recovered from the site appear to be arrow points. The ceramics are probably intrusive from the highland area to the southwest of the Pecos Valley.

The initial group of stratigraphic tests at Site P4 revealed that the depth of cultural materials on that site was quite shallow, seldom exceeding 8 to 10 inches. This thin layer of cultural material appears to characterize most sites in the Middle Pecos Valley and is a real obstacle in determining stratigraphic superposition of the cultural phases. The deepest test in the 1960 series reached sterile soil after going through slightly more than 14 inches of cultural deposit (Test 1 at Site P4B). The nature of the sherd relationships in two inch levels in this test suggested that materials down to a depth of about six inches had been disturbed, while sherds below that level exhibited constant ratios of the major types present. As a result of this test, the irregular patterns of relationships in the other shallower tests, and the small quantity of material recovered in the tests, I abandoned the attempt to use these materials to demonstrate stratigraphic relationships. Instead I used the Brainerd-Robinson matrix technique to seriate the groups of combined sherds from each test excavation.

The sherd samples recovered in the 1960 test block excavations are listed in Table XXI. The seriation matrix for these samples, computed by sherd weight, is given in Table XXII. The ordering seems clear with the exception of the relative positions of P4B:2 and P4B:3. The values governing the placement of these two samples are so similar as to indicate no very clear preference for relative age priority. I have chosen the arrangement with least sign changes (18 as opposed to 19) in this matrix. The seriation of sites reflected in this sample ordering is in complete accord with the ordering based on surface samples. The sample ordering was used for the chronological arrangement of

TABLE XXI

SHERD COUNTS FROM TEST PITS IN SITES P4 AND P24

TYPE	P4A:1	P4A:2	P4A:3	P4B:1	P4B:2	P4B:3	P4C:1	P24:1	P24:2	P24:3
Jornada Brown	11	38	50	89	15	8	15	91	43	35
South Pecos Brown	1	4	4	8	10	-	-	4	-	2
Alma Brown	1	8	4	3	1	-	1	2	3	2
Micaceous Brown	8	53	5	147	63	31	15	182	101	35
Roswell Brown	2	7	3	27	8	2	6	13	3	3
McKenzie Brown	-	-	-	-	-	3	65	5	-	-
Red Mesa B/W	-	1	1	-	-	-	-	-	1	-
Crosby B/G	-	-	-	32	1	5	12	20	1	6
M. Pecos B/W	-	-	-	6	1	1	44	8	3	3
Chupadero B/W	-	-	-	-	-	-	6	0	-	1
Other	-	-	-	1	-	2	1	4	1	2
Total	23	111	67	313	99	52	165	329	156	89

TABLE XXII

CHRONOLOGICAL ORDERING OF EXCAVATION TEST SAMPLES FROM SITE P4 AND SITE P24

SAMPLE	P4A:3	P4A:2	P4A:1	P24:2	P24:1	P24:3	P4B:1	P4B:2	P4B:3
P4A:2	110.4	X							
P4A:1	107.7	194.9	X						
P24:2	92.6	179.1	180.3	X					
P24:1	95.3	172.7	172.8	172.1	X				
P24:3	81.2	169.9	172.1	166.2	176.7	X			
P4B:1	84.4	166.8	165.9	157.4	174.9	185.8	X		
P4B:2	51.6	131.2	135.3	136.8	116.7	131.4	133.7	X	
P4B:3	30.2	119.8	122.5	133.8	124.3	134.2	158.6	157.4	X
P4C:1	52.3	58.1	58.2	57.9	69.8	73.7	68.7	37.9	45.1

pollen samples taken from these excavations and discussed in a later chapter.

The sherd samples excavated in the test blocks do not add greatly to our knowledge of the ceramic sequence in the Northern Middle Pecos Valley other than to confirm that subsurface materials reflect the same patterns as the surface collections. There is some indication in these samples that our surface collections may be biased toward higher proportions of the lighter-colored decorated wares (e.g. the higher ratios in excavated samples of McKenzie Brown at P4C and of Middle Pecos Micaceous at P4B). From the consistency of the overall pattern of relationships it would appear that this bias (which apparently survived all efforts at objectivity because of the similarity of brownwares to the soil colors) has been constant from site to site and would not be expected to distort patterns of relationships.

Excavated Structures

The earliest excavated structures are assigned to the Late 18 Mile Phase. In 1956 I excavated a slab-lined storage cyst on Site P4A. The remains of several such cysts were apparent on the site as circular and oval arrangements of eroded edges of upright sandstone slabs. The cyst excavated (Pl. IX) was nearly circular, measuring 4' 8" north-south and 4' 6" east-west. The slab walls were about 18" deep, and the center of the basin-shaped, smoothed floor was about 22" below the present surface. The only features within the cyst were three small post holes and a flat stone set into the floor, perhaps as a footing for a pole to support the roof. The stone pilaster in the floor, and adjacent alignments of stones, suggest that this cyst may be a part of a larger and more complex structure; the basin depression of the floor, and the circular arrangement of adjacent structures, argues against a structure for human habitation. The only materials recovered in the excavation were three small and well-battered hammerstones, a fragment of a mano of indeterminate shape, a large sherd of Jornada brownware and a small fragment of carbonized corncob. The lack of stratification and cultural material in the adobe fill in the cyst suggest that it was deliberately closed.

Several excavations were made on Site P4AB which revealed architectural features. The first of these, in the winter of 1957, was a small test trench which encountered the edge of a structure consisting of inclined slabs of sandstone, apparently mounted above a bench in which post footings could be observed. The small section exposed suggested the edge of a slab-lined pithouse with the floor about 30" below the present ground surface; this floor was covered with a fine layer of ash. Two post holes were exposed in the test trench. One toward the center of the floor was about 4" in diameter, and the other, near the bench and inclined in the direction of the center, was about 3" across. A clear soil horizon was in evidence, dipping from a depth of about 8" below the present surface at the edge of the structure, to about 17" nearest the center of the structure. The bench was 19" below the ground surface, and the tops of the slabs were about 10" deep and inclined sharply toward the center of the structure. There is no surface indication of the presence of this structure, which would have gone unnoticed if not accidentally encountered by the test trench. The sherds from the test in the fill of the structure suggest a Late 18 Mile assemblage, since neither Crosby B/G nor Middle Pecos B/W were present, and two sherds of Red Mesa B/W were encountered. Of the other 25 sherds, 18 were Micaceous, five were Jornada, and two were South Pecos Brown. The high percentage of Micaceous suggests a terminal Late 18 Mile or Early Mesita Negra date for the fill. Three sherds in the sample were found on the floor, and included one example each of Jornada, South Pecos, and Red Mesa; this suggests, on rather tenuous evidence, a Late 18 Mile date for the structure.

During the 1960 season two excavations were conducted on Site P4AB. Because of limited resources and time I did not attempt to excavate the structure previously encountered (Structure 1), but instead began work in an area where upright sandstone slabs in a rectangular arrangement suggested the presence of rectangular surface rooms (Structure 2). A clarification of the period of introduction of this architectural form into the Middle Pecos area would be of importance not only in the local sequence, but to the study of Southwestern prehistory in general.

The first structure encountered in the 1960 excavations proved to be quite different from the expected rectangular surface rooms. After clearing a series of shallow walls, capped with upright sandstone slabs to floor level, and following the floor surface to the limits of definability, a large oval structure was seen to be outlined, shallowly excavated into the present surface (Fig. 16; Pls. X - XI). In basic plan the structure is an oval basin, transected from north to south by a low wall topped with sandstone slabs. This wall is intersected from the west by an additional low wall which isolates a small section of the northwest quarter

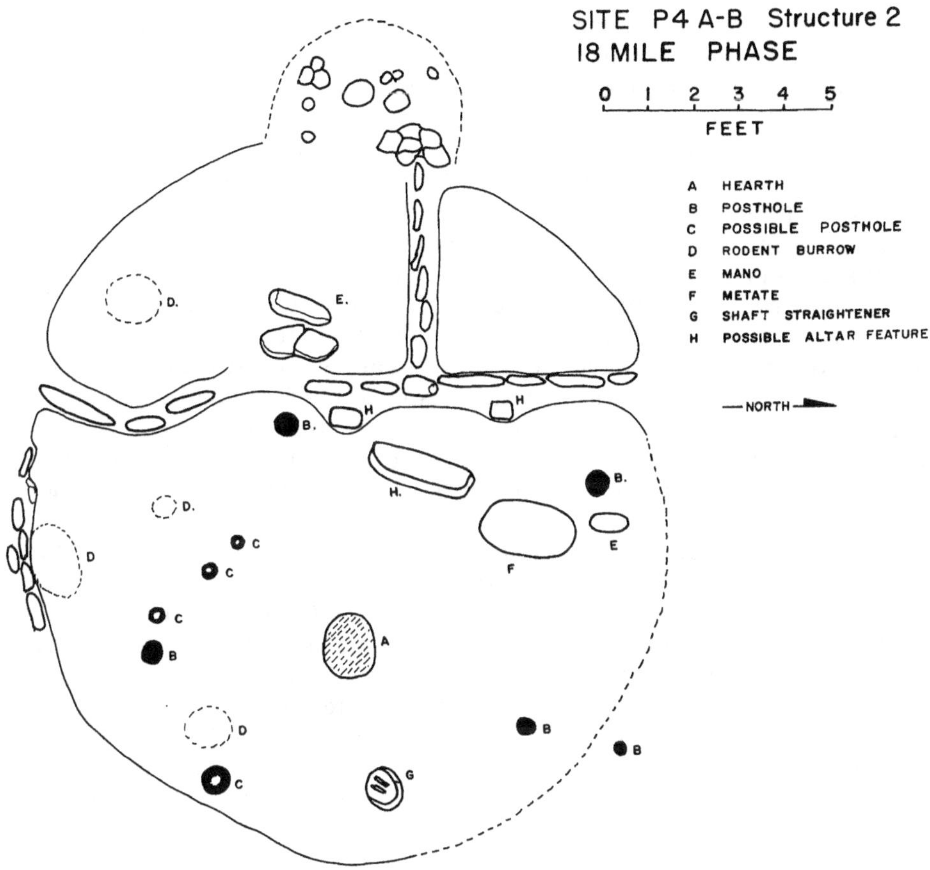

FIG. 16. Plan of Structure 2, Site P4AB.

of the structure. A thin layer of dark earth and ash on the floor confirmed the association of the walls with the basin-shaped structure. An ill-defined irregular small basin at the western extremity of the structure may have been an entryway; no indication of an entry was visible at the eastern extremity, although the shallow depth of the structure here does not preclude an entryway. Four post holes are arranged in a rough rectangle which does not align with the walls. It is possible that some of the pits interpreted as rodent disturbance may have served as post holes in an arrangement of greater symmetry with the interior walls, but this seems unlikely from the clear character of the post holes that were excavated. A poorly defined hearth is present in the eastern end of the structure. The most curious architectural feature consists of two columnar pieces of red sandstone mounted about three feet apart on the east side of the north-south wall, spaced roughly equally on either side of the junction with the wall from the west. In front of these blocks, and approximately centered between them, was a large symmetrically-trimmed slab of white sandstone; this slab was smooth on the outer (eastern) face, and pecked for use as a metate (and very slightly ground) on the face toward the wall. The arrangement strongly suggests an altar. The relatively large size of the structure (approximately 18 by 14 feet, not including the possible entry area) may also indicate ritual function. Although the structure appears to have been deliberately abandoned (e.g. the posts had been removed with the exception of a single rafter-end still in place on the northeast side of the basin) several artifacts of domestic function remained in place on the floor. Near the hearth was a sandstone pebble with two grooves indicating function as a shaft-straightener. To the north of the upright "altar" slab was an inverted flat slab metate, and adjacent to it a thin oval mano, ground flat on both sides; one of the few examples of this form of mano encountered in the survey. In the southeast quarter of the structure was a very large heavy loaf-shaped mano with a single slightly convex grinding surface. Although a few small thick loaf-shaped sandstone manos were encountered on other portions of the P4 site complex, this was by far the largest example of this form of artifact encountered in our study. Sherds encountered in the excavation are summarized in the following table:

TABLE XXIII

SHERDS FROM STRUCTURE 2, SITE P4AB

Type	Fill	Floor	Total
Jornada Brown	47	59	97
Micaceous Brown	44	24	68
South Pecos Brown	26	67	93
Alma Brown	2	2	4
Roswell Brown	15	-	15
McKenzie? Brown	-	1	1
Red Mesa B/W	2	-	2
Local? Pueblo II B/W	-	1	1

The composition of the sherd sample suggests a late 18 Mile date for the structure. Most of the South Pecos Brown sherds seem to belong to one medium-sized olla with a narrow short neck. The sherd tentatively classified as McKenzie Brownware is a relatively soft brownware with crushed quartz temper. The remainder of the tempering elements, however, and the general color and texture of the surface, are not typical of McKenzie.

This excavation continued until the last day of the 1960 season, and I overlooked the measurements necessary to construct a profile. I can, therefore, only estimate the greatest depth of the shallow basin at about 16 to 18 inches, on the basis of the dimensions of the sandstone "altar" slab.

Immediately to the north of Structure 2, a series of 3 small contiguous rectangular rooms (Structure 3) were excavated by Leslie G. Freeman, a member of the 1960 field crew. These rooms were roughly square and averaged about five feet on a side. The floors were about one foot below the present ground surface (Fig. 17, Pl. XII), and the small size suggests that they were storage rooms rather than habitations. A few fragments of eroded upright sandstone slabs suggests that this material may have been incorporated into the bases of all of the walls of the rooms as they were built up above the portions excavated into

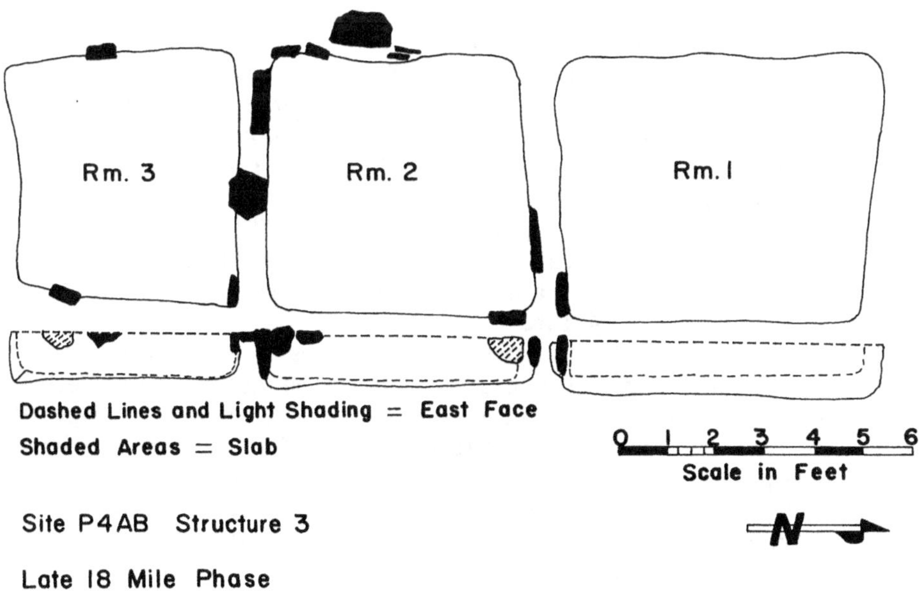

FIG. 17. Plan and profile of Structure 3, Site P4AB.

the ground. No floor features were in evidence. The large hole visible in the photograph was apparently a rodent burrow. Sherds recovered in the excavation can be summarized as follows:

TABLE XXIV

SHERDS FROM STRUCTURE 3, SITE P4AB

Type	Room 1 Fill	Room 1 Floor	Room 2 Fill	Room 2 Floor	Room 3 Fill	Total
Jornada Brown	10	1	5	1	-	17
Micaceous Brown	4	2	5	1	5	17
South Pecos Brown	2	-	-	-	1	3
Alma Brown	1	-	1	-	-	2
Roswell Brown	1	-	-	-	1	2
Red Mesa B/W	-	-	1	-	-	1
Total	18	3	12	2	7	42

These sherds suggest a Late 18 Mile assemblage.

It appears, then, that all structures excavated on Site P4AB contain ceramics characteristic of the Late 18 Mile Phase. No examples of ceramics diagnostic of the Early Mesita Negra Phase (e.g. Crosby B/G and Middle Pecos B/W) are present in a subsurface context, although on the basis of surface collections this component has been assigned to the earliest horizons of that phase.

No structures assignable to the Early or Late Mesita Negra Phase or the Early McKenzie Phase were excavated on any of the Site P4 components. During the winter of 1957 I cleared the floor of an extremely shallow structure on Site P4C (Fig. 18, Pl. XIII). This structure appears to to belong to the Late McKenzie Phase of the P4 Site complex.

The basic plan of the structure includes a central hearth with four posts in a rectangular arrangement; the hearth was well defined and retained the eroded remnants of a clay rim. A possible entryway was outlined on the eastern side of the structure by a slightly depressed area of compact soil. Two small post holes were located on either side of this area. The major post footings were of particular interest since each presented a different aspect in excavation. Post holes B-1, B-2 and B-3 all exhibited some evidence of heat at the floor level. B-1 in the southeast corner was filled with a mixture of ash, charcoal, and cultural

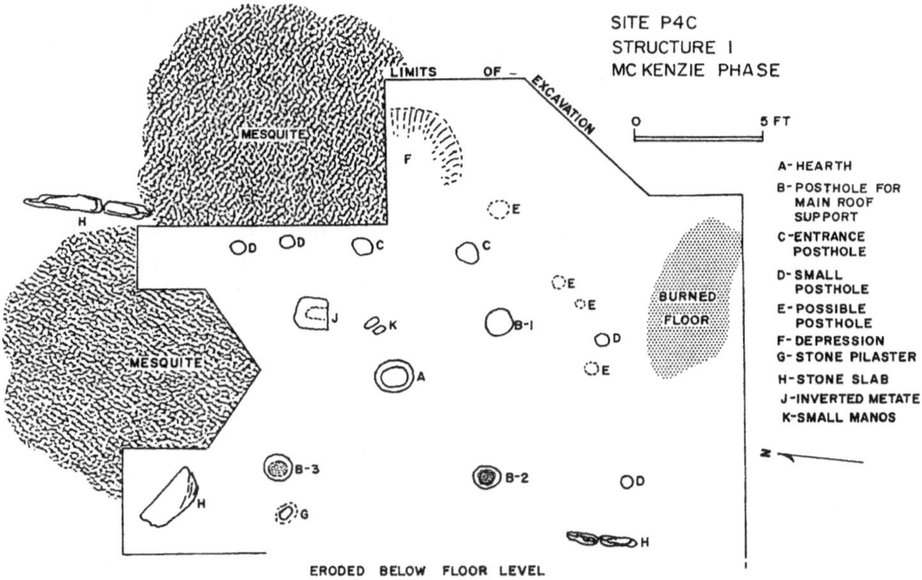

FIG. 18. Plan of Structure 1, Site P4C.

debris, indicating that the remains of the post had probably been removed following the abandonment of the structure. Post hole B-2 revealed the remains of a wooden post still in place, apparently packed with a layer of sand and ashes. A single fragment of baked adobe plaster was recovered in this packing, apparently broken from the hearth from which the ash had been derived. I was hesitant about the interpretation of a deliberate packing of ash and sand around the post until I excavated the northwest post hole (B-3). This hole had been sealed with adobe at some time during the occupation of the structure, and the post supporting that portion of the roof had apparently been supported on a small stone slab embedded in the floor adjacent to the post hole (G). The adobe which had been poured into the hole after the post had been extracted filled a mold in a packing of ash and sand similar to that in the southwest post hole. Additional evidence of concern for the footing of support posts was found in the post holes adjacent to the entrance, both of which contained stone slabs, apparently intended as footings for the posts. One of the small post holes (D) also contained a small stone slab. The fourth major roof support was apparently placed on the underside of a broken fragment of basin metate (J), since this specimen was in an approximately symmetrical arrangement with the roof support post holes, and no post hole was found in this portion of the structure. Heavy growth of mesquite on the north side of the structure prevented complete excavation. To the northeast of this mesquite and at the southeast corner of the structure, a few upright sandstone slabs suggested that the excavated room may have been part of a series of contiguous rectangular surface rooms, now largely eroded away. Evidence that the structure had been destroyed by fire was contained not only in the burned areas of floor adjacent to the post holes, but also in three pieces of baked clay with reed impressions found in the thin layer of earth covering the floor. At no point was this deposit over four inches in thickness, and over the majority of the structure it was much shallower. The southwestern edge of the floor area was terminated by surface erosion. Artifacts recovered in this excavation were typical of the Late McKenzie Phase, and included three fragments of small triangular side-notched points and several of the small thick end-scrapers characteristic of this phase. Sherds found in the entrance area and northern entry post hole included one example each of McKenzie Brown and corrugated brownware, and five sherds of Middle Pecos Black on White. One unusual artifact, recovered near the northwest post hole, was a leaf-shaped biface of dark quartzite, measuring 9.5 x 3.8 cm. The careful flaking and symmetry of this specimen suggest an implement of special function.

One additional structure was excavated at Site P4C in 1960. This was a bell-shaped storage pit located about 10 yards to the southeast of the surface structure. This pit was nearly filled with large fragments of bison bone and a few sherds of pottery. The base of the pit was covered by a slab metate with a slightly concave surface measuring about 6 x 14 inches in greatest diameters. The opening of the pit was 26 inches across in greatest diameter and the pit was 25 inches deep and about 28 inches in diameter at the base, opening out to a diameter of 29 or 30 inches about three inches above the floor. The 16 sherds recovered from the structure include 12 examples of McKenzie Brown, two sherds of Crosby B/G and one sherd each of Broadline R/TC (affinis Three Rivers) and indeterminate Chupadero ware.

During the 1960 season we attempted to excavate structures in two areas of Site P24. The features which at first appeared promising for excavation were the remains of upright sandstone slabs outlining what appeared to be rectangular surface rooms on a small promontory of the site overlooking the river. In subsequent discussion this is referred to as "Structure 1." A careful clearing of these slabs and adjacent areas revealed that the level of the floor of these structures was approximately equivalent to the present soil surface, and virtually all features of the structures with the exception of the wall bases had been destroyed by erosion. We then excavated a small test trench through the area of the wall bases in order to determine the character of the cultural deposits and the depth of sterile soil; this proved to be a layer of gravel about 8 inches below the present surface. At the east end of this trench, in a shallow depression extending into the gravel, we discovered a very fragmentary burial, apparently semi-flexed and partially covered with stones. Rodent disturbance had almost completely destroyed the skeleton and only a few fragments of cranium, mandible, and longbones remained. No artifacts accompanied the burial.

In another area adjacent to the original wall structures we encountered a concentration of large stones, apparently deliberately concentrated as fill in an earlier structure. Four of these stones proved to be metates, complete and fragmentary (Pl. VIII). The structure appeared to have been extensively disturbed; the only clear feature which we were able to define was a hearth lined with small stone slabs, about 10 inches below the present ground surface. The floor of the structure was the sterile gravel encountered by the test trench. To the northwest of the hearth a small sub-floor pit contained the only other burials found in our excavations; the remains of a young woman and a neo-natal infant (Burial 2; Pl. XIV). The adult skeleton was in a semi-flexed position while that of the infant was too poorly preserved to determine position. Two large rocks had been placed in the pit with the adult burial, one above the left shoulder, leaning against the skull, and the other over the pelvis. Here, too, rodent disturbance had been extensive and none of the carpals, tarsals or phalanges were in place at the time of excavation. A portion of the skull (right parietal) had been destroyed, as had the entire pelvic region. No artifacts accompanied the burials.

The sherds excavated in the floor and hearth areas above these burials and in the fill with the pile of heavy stone above the floor (Feature A) are classified in Table XXV.

It is apparent that there is no significant difference in the composition of the sherd samples from the general fill and the fill associated with the group of large rocks and metates. Both samples suggest a date near the end of the Late Mesita Negra Phase. The lack of a well-defined floor above Burial 2 and the pile of heavy rocks above the floor in the vicinity of the burial suggest that the lower structure may have been deliberately filled immediately following the burial, and that this filling is not

TABLE XXV

SHERD COUNTS FROM BELOW STRUCTURE 1, SITE P24

Type	Fill, general	Fill, Feature A	Total
Jornada Brown	28	64	98
Micaceous Brown	28	42	70
S. Pecos Brown	-	1	1
Alma Brown	1	2	3
Roswell Brown	8	15	23
McKenzie Brown	1	2	3
Crosby B/G	4	11	15
M. Pecos B/W	-	3	3
Indet. Chupadero	-	1	1
Total	70	141	211

necessarily associated with the construction of the rectangular surface structure (Structure 1).

One additional structure was partially excavated at Site P24 (Structure 2); it consisted of a semi-circular arrangement of sandstone slabs exposed on the present surface, and a floor level, hearth, and fragmentary walls a few inches under the surface (Pl. XV). Structure 2 was located about 50 feet south of Structure 1. The circular wall of the structure was sufficiently intact to the west and south of the hearth to suggest that the entry was not in that area. However the floor to the north and northeast of the hearth had been completely destroyed, apparently by rodent activity, and no further features could be defined in that area. Remnants of what appeared to be two adobe walls, oriented in a north-south direction, crossed the intact portion of the floor. One was just east of the hearth, and the other at the eastern margin of the floor. Whether these formed part of the original structure or were part of later construction could not be determined with certainty. The floor was not well-defined under these walls, suggesting that they were contemporary with Structure 2. The ceramics recovered from this excavation are summarized in Table XXVI. The shallow depth of the fill in this structure precluded any meaningful separation of sherds from fill and sherds from floor. It is apparent that the composition of this sherd sample differs from the two samples from the fill under Structure 1.

TABLE XXVI

SHERD COUNT OF CERAMICS FROM STRUCTURE 2, SITE P24

Type	Number
Jornada Brown	25
Micaceous Brown	76
South Pecos Brown	4
Alma Brown	2
Red Mesa B/W	1
Crosby B/G	4
Total	112

The higher ratios of Micaceous Brown and South Pecos Brown, and the relatively lower quantity of Jornada Brown, suggest an earlier date, as does the single sherd of Red Mesa B/W. The additional presence of Crosby B/G suggests that the fill in the structure is of Early Mesita Negra origin.

We found excavation at Site P24 to be relatively difficult because of the extensive rodent disturbance in the structures we encountered; also, during the apparently prolonged interval of occupation in the site (probably from the Late 18 Mile to the Early McKenzie Phase), most areas had been used repeatedly for construction, leaving an almost inextricable jumble of remains in the shallow depths to which we limited our excavations. I suspect that deeper structures may exist on Site P24 related to the earlier occupations, but we did not pursue this possibility during our short period of work on the site.

VII

STUDIES CONTRIBUTING TO THE INTERPRETATION OF PREHISTORIC ENVIRONMENT

Two major types of evidence were used in an attempt to reconstruct the environmental conditions of the Middle Pecos Valley during the prehistoric period. A study of fossil pollen was made by Paul S. Martin of the Geochronology Laboratories of the University of Arizona. I studied the vertebrate remains with the aid of collections in the Division of Mammals, University of Michigan Museum of Zoology.

The Pollen Evidence

We collected pollen samples for Martin's study from the test excavations at Site P24 and the major components of Site P4. In addition Martin collected a suite of samples from a vertical cut in the lowest alluvial terrace of the river, a short distance to the south of the U. S. 60 highway crossing, on the west bank of the river, and from several localities in which Pleistocene sediments were exposed (see Chapter I). His report, as prepared in 1962, and revised in 1967, is printed below:

POLLEN ANALYSIS OF PREHISTORIC MIDDENS NEAR FT. SUMNER, NEW MEXICO

Paul S. Martin*

On August 20-21, 1960 a series of pollen samples were collected from (1) archaeological refuse, (2) silts encasing bones of Pleistocene age, and (3) exposed alluvium in the bank of the Pecos River at the town of Ft. Sumner. Pollen was absent from the sediment yielding extinct mammals. Pollen was relatively scarce and fungal spores numerous in postglacial alluvium from banks of the Pecos River. Only samples from archaeological refuse were suitable for analysis.

Although the time sequence in the archaeological middens is relatively short, encompasing roughly the last 1000 years, it includes an interval of important cultural and presumably climatic change. Prior to the 13th century the upper Pecos River was occupied by Pueblo farmers cultivating corn. Alfter the 13th century archaeological record indicates an

*Contribution No. 55, Program in Geochronology, University of Arizona.

interval when bison hunting was an important means of subsistence. The reason why agriculture gave way to hunting and gathering remains obscure, but the economic implications are clear enough. Hunting-gathering is a less productive means of subsistence than raising crops; a cultural reversal is implicit in the archaeological record.

In the hope of discovering more about the cause and consequences of late prehistoric events, pollen samples were carefully chosen to represent three different time periods, from older to younger, as follows: (1) the period of agriculture and Pueblo occupation; (2) the period of bison hunting; (3) the modern (historic) pollen rain. Surface soil samples which should represent the modern pollen rain all contain at least a trace of *Zea* pollen, and must be considered a mixture of prehistoric (fossil) and modern pollen rains. Important differences can be seen in pre- and post-13th Century pollen content of the samples.

Archaeological middens on bluffs above the Pecos River are shallow; all samples were collected within half a meter of the surface of the ground. Active erosion is stripping soil and exposing the middens. Collections were made at three separate sites on the west side of the Pecos River (P4A, P4B, P4C) and at one on the east side of the river (P24-8, A, B. C. E).

Hydrochloric, hydrofluoric, and acetolysis treatments were used to concentrate pollen, with addition of a bleach treatment (Chlorox) to clear excess organic debris. The Chlorox treatment thinned pollen exines and made staining difficult. It is possible that the Chlorox treatment destroyed pine pollen grains (Hafsten 1959).

The most common of the pollen types is that represented by the family Chenopodiaceae plus the genus *Amaranthus*, abbreviated as "cheno-ams." Pollen of the family Compositae can be divided into four types: the genus *Artemisia*, the sub-family Liguliflorae (one grain only), long-spine (spines two microns or longer in length) and short-spine (spines less than two microns) types. The short-spine Compositae include mainly wind-pollinated species, such as *Ambrosia* and *Xanthium*. The long-spine types should include various insect-pollinated genera.

Applying size criteria of Martin and Schoenwetter (1960) the pollen of the grasses (Gramineae) could readily be distinguished from pollen of *Zea*. *Zea* (maize) pollen appeared in all but one of the samples. Crosses shown on Fig. 1 indicate levels in which corn pollen was not found in the regular 200-grain sample but was discovered in a sample of approximately 1000 pollen grains. Pollen of *Ephedra* was characterized by many furrows; the grains lacked hyaline lines running at angles to the furrows. *Ephedra* pollen can be referred entirely to the species *Ephedra torreyana*, which is common in eastern New Mexico.

Tree pollen is scarce and limited to the genera *Pinus*, *Juniperus*, and *Quercus*. Pine pollen is more abundant and better preserved in the surface samples. Five surface samples contained 12 broken and 29 entire pine pollen grains; 11 occupation levels contained 21 broken and 15 entire pine pollen grains.

Other pollen types encountered during analysis included the genus *Erioginum* (buckwheat), the family Malvaceae (mainly pollen of the *Sphaeralcea* type), *Tidestroemia*, *Typha* (both tetrads and monads), Liliaceae, Euphorbia, and Onagraceae. Unknowns were scarce (Table XXVII).

Accepting archaeological provenience as a basis for the stratigraphic arrangement shown in Fig. 1, we can recognize the following changes:

Site	Chenopodiaceae -*Amaranthus*	Gramineae	Compositae (short spine)	Compositae (long spine)	*Artemisia*	*Ephedra*	*Pinus*	*Zea* in 200	*Eriogonum*	Malvaceae	*Tidestroemia*	*Typha*	Liguliflorae	Liliaceae	*Euphorbia*	Onagraceae	*Quercus*	*Juniperus*	Unknowns	Sample size (N)	Σ less Cheno-ams + *Zea*
P4C Test 1	108	38	18	21		2	9			1							1		2	N 200	
P4B " 1	139	27	18	9	1	2	3	2			1	3								205	
P4A " 2	84	30	45	16	3	2	15		1						1	1		1	1	200	
P4A " 3	77	26	73	13	5	2	2												2	200	
P4B " 1	93	67	22	13			3	4		1						1			1	205	
P4C " 1	70	103	4	13		4	1	1	1	2										200	129
" " "	110	56	12	16		3	1	6							1					205	94
P4B " 3	151	17	3	4	3		3	14											5	200	35
P4B " 1	133	34	1	15	1	1	$\frac{1}{3}$	12											2	200	55
" " "	108	56	3	8	1	0	1	21		1				1					1	201	72
" " "	155	22	1	17	0			2		2									1	200	43
P4A " 2	142	19	21	8	4	2	1	1			2									200	57
P4A " 3	102	34	26	11	17	2	2	5				1						1		201	94
P4 A-B	148	31	6	8	1	4			1			1							2	202	54
P4 A-B	124	32	27	7	3	5	4						1							203	79
P24 A	188	4	6				1				1								2	202	14
P24 B	163	26	3	5	1	1						1								200	37
P24 C	138	12	12	14	4	4	4	1	8										3	200	61
P24 E	159	12	12	6		4	2		5			1							1	202	

TABLE XXVII

POLLEN COUNTS FROM TEST SAMPLES FROM SITES P4 AND P24

(1) Cheno-ams diminish in the younger (post-13th Century) samples. This change is used as the basis for distinguishing two pollen zones in Fig. 1. (2) There is a suggestion of a strong increase in grass pollen in the bison hunting period (1300-1500). The 10 cm level of P4C, test 1, may be the only sample which properly represents the local pollen rain above the Pecos River during the bison hunting period. (3) There is some suggestion that the short-spine Compositae have increased since occupation ended. (4) Pine pollen is more abundant at the surface where it averages 6.6 percent in five levels. In the prehistoric samples it averages 1.5 percent per level. (5) Although *Zea* occurs in virtually all samples, it is clearly most abundant on the west side of the Pecos River at site P4B, test 1 and test 3. Scarcity of *Zea* in site P24A-E is not readily explained, but the high frequency of cheno-ams from P24A-E indicates a period of occupation corresponding to Pollen Zone 2 on the west side of the river.

Interpretation. The Chenopodiaceae with *Amaranthus* are camp followers, indicators of disturbed ground. It is not surprising to find a reduction in their pollen after occupation ends. The abundance of corn pollen in P4B, test 3 and test 1, does not prove that *Zea* was cultivated close to the occupation site. Both prehistoric and modern maize fields contain very little *Zea* pollen; the record of more than one or two percent *Zea* pollen may mean that tassels or even raw pollen was carried into the site. *Typha* pollen is also unlikely to be wind-borne a great distance, and was probably carried by man to the sites.

Can the change in pollen types between Zones 1 and 2 be explained in terms of climatic change? The slight but significant increase in pine pollen suggests an expansion of pine communities in mountains upwind of the fossil locality. Apart from a possible cooler, wetter climate there are at least two other hypotheses which might explain the pine rise found in surface samples. One is an expansion of pine woodland following Pueblo abandonment of the four-corners region, upwind of the Pecos Valley. The sudden abandonment of northern Arizona and northern New Mexico in the thirteenth and fourteenth centuries may have resulted in an expansion of both pinyon *(P. edulis)* and ponderosa *(P. ponderosa)* with a regional increase in forest tree pollen.

A second possible explanation underscores one of the major difficulties in the use of percentage data. This is the fact that any single percentage variable in the pollen count is dependent on the sum of the other percentages. Let us assume there was a constant pine pollen fall-out at the Pecos River sites during the last 1000 years. A relative increase in pine would nevertheless appear in the record if there were a reduction in local pollen production among the non-arboreal plants growing on or near the site. As weedy plants are likely to have been more abundant near the sites during occupation and as they are superior pollen producers, a decrease in their pollen production following abandonment is likely.

The stratigraphic change is clear enough, a relative drop in pollen of cheno-ams, of *Zea* and a rise in *Pinus*. But none of the changes seen in the pollen counts *require* a climatic explanation and it is not obvious to me how one might choose between climatic and cultural variables and their (probable) interaction. Nor is the expansion of *Bison* westward decisive evidence of expansion of grassland along the Pecos River. Apart from the fact that large mammals are euryoeic - typically found in a variety of habitats under a variety of climates - the striking thing about *Bison* in the last 1000 years is its *absence* from a vast area of apparently suitable habitat, the grassland of the Mexican Plateau and adjacent parts of the Southwest. Bison numbers were lowest in those parts of North America where prehistoric human populations were large and where corn agriculture was well developed. I would regard the late prehistoric expansion of bison around the periphery of its range after the 13th Century as the consequence of cultural, not climatic deterioration.

Quite probably a climatic upset, perhaps a shortening of the growing season, triggered the decline of the Pueblos and their allies throughout the Southwest in the 13th-15th centuries. But it is not at all clear that the fossil evidence of change which the archaeologist has so diligently sought and occasionally found is the direct result of whatever caused prehistoric crop failure.

LITERATURE CITED

Hafsten, U.
1959 Bleaching + HF + acetolysis - a hazardous preparation process. Pollen et Spores 1: 77-79. Paris

Martin, P. S., and J. Schoenwetter
1960 Arizona's oldest cornfield. Science 132 (3418): 33-34. Washington.

The sequence of palynological deposition, based on the ceramic seriation of the test excavations from which the samples were derived, is seen in Fig. 19. The surface samples (those collected from a depth of less than 10 cm.) are shown at the top of the diagram and the sub-surface samples are graphed below with appropriate texturing to indicate the associated cultural phase. The P4A samples represent a Late 18 Mile horizon, those from P4B and P24 represent a Late Mesita Negra horizon, and those from P4C represent the Late McKenzie Phase.

I have discussed the interpretation of this pollen sequence, in relation to the artifact materials represented in each of the test excavations, in a previous publication (Jelinek, 1966a). The results of this study indicate that a climatic change may have been responsible for the changes in pollen ratios through the sequence; in particular, that a shift toward slightly more favorable growing conditions may have encouraged the spread of the predominantly grassland vegetation of the Mescalero Pediment and western Llano Estacado into the Middle Pecos Valley, toward the end of the Late Mesita Negra Phase. The modified pollen sequence based on this study is seen in Fig. 20.

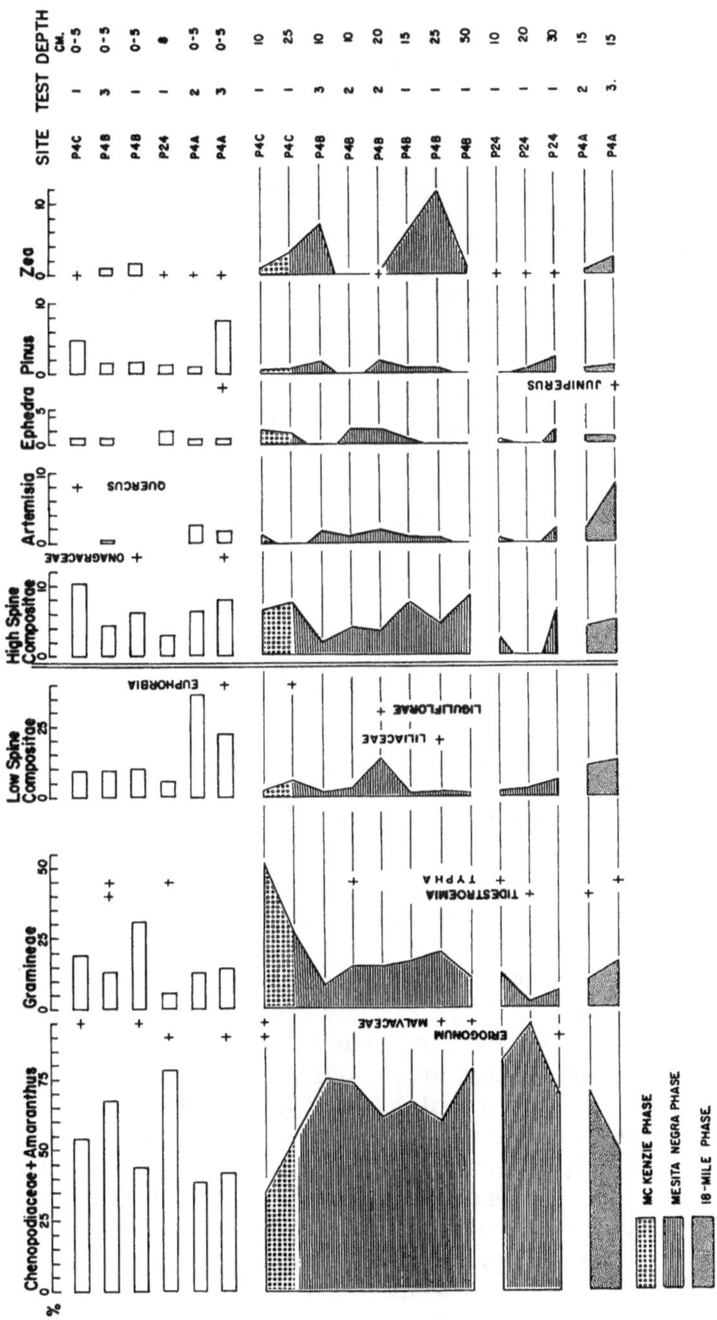

FIG. 19. Sequence of pollen samples from tests.

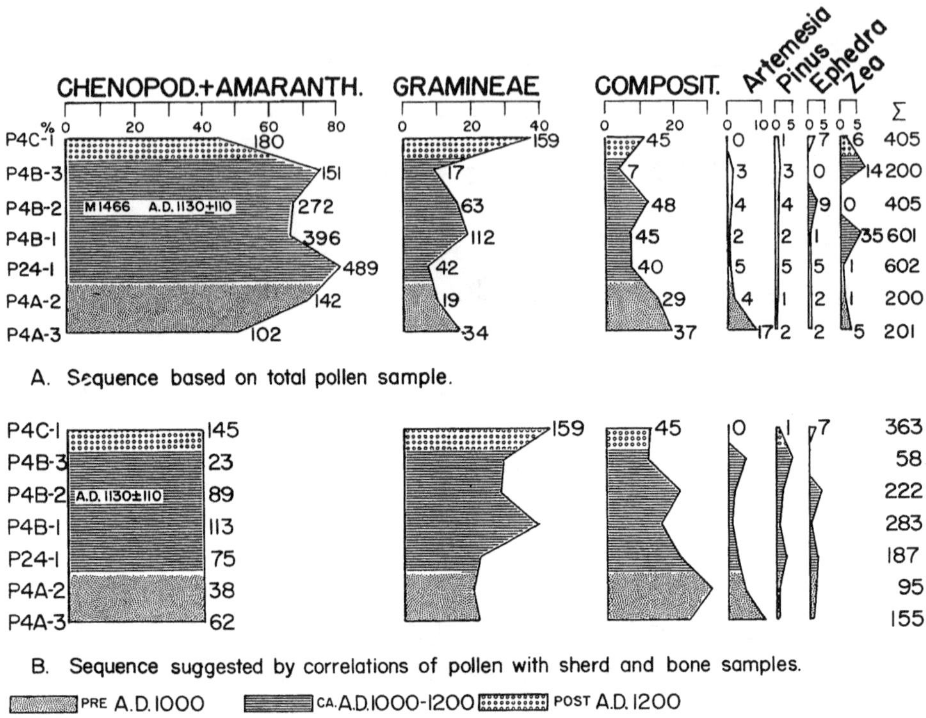

FIG. 20. Pollen sequence interpreted on the basis of pollen-artifact correlations. *From:* Arthur J. Jelinek, "Correlation of Archeological and Palynological Data," *Science*, Vol. 152 (3728), page 1508. Copyright 1966 by the American Association for the Advancement of Science.

The Vertebrate Evidence

Most of the vertebrate remains recovered in the excavations are listed in the chart in Fig. 21. The remains from the test at P14 have not been fully tabulated, but both *Bison* and *Cynomys* are known to be represented in the sample. Since these forms are characteristic of the grassland habitat of the area to the east of the valley their presence is of some importance. Both forms, however, are also represented in the material from Site P24.

In the Late 18 Mile Phase (including the P4AB Structures), the most abundantly represented group of animal bone is from the jackrabbits and cottontails. The remains of hard- and soft-shelled turtles are frequent, while large herbivores are represented by a few bones of antelope and possibly deer.

SITE	P4A					P4AB			P24							P2	P4B					P4C				Σ
	TESTS					STRUC.			TESTS			STRUC.		BU.			TESTS			ST.		TE.	CYS.			
Provenience:	1	2	3	'57	Σ	2	3	Σ	1	2	3	1	2	2	Σ	'57	1	2	3	1	Σ	1	1	'57	Σ	
Sylvilagus	—	1	1	—	**2**	—	4	**4**	22	5	12	10	1	2	**52**	·	46	3	2	—	**51**	5	—	5	**10**	119
Lepus	—	—	1	1	**2**	1	11	**12**	14	3	13	13	1	—	**44**	**3**	128	3	2	—	**133**	18	1	2	**21**	215
Cynomys	—	—	—	—	·	—	—	·	—	—	—	4	—	1	**5**	·	—	—	—	—	·	—	—	—	·	5
GEOMYIDAE	—	—	—	—	·	—	—	·	1	—	—	—	—	—	**1**	·	1	—	—	—	**1**	—	—	—	·	2
Antilocapra	—	—	—	1	·	1	1	**2**	1	—	2	1	—	—	**4**	·	5	—	—	—	**5**	—	—	—	·	11
Odocoileus	—	—	—	—	·	—	—	·	—	—	—	—	—	—	·	·	2	—	—	—	**2**	—	—	—	·	2
Deer/Antelope	—	3	—	—	**3**	—	—	·	—	—	1	2	—	—	**3**	·	14	—	—	—	**14**	—	—	1	**1**	21
Bison	—	—	—	—	·	—	—	·	—	1	—	—	—	—	**1**	·	—	12	—	—	**12**	60	36+	115	**211**	224
Taxidea	—	—	—	—	·	—	—	·	—	—	—	—	—	—	·	·	2	—	—	—	**2**	—	—	—	·	2
TESTUDINES	—	1	—	—	**1**	—	—	·	—	—	—	—	—	—	·	·	4	—	—	—	**4**	—	—	—	·	5
Hard Carapace	1	2	1	—	**4**	—	1	**1**	11	3	4	2	—	—	**20**	6	13	4	1	—	**18**	—	—	—	·	49
Soft Carapace	—	2	2	—	**4**	—	—	·	1	—	1	—	—	—	**2**	·	3	1	—	—	**4**	—	—	—	·	10
SERPENTES	—	—	—	—	·	—	—	·	6	1	—	—	—	—	**7**	·	—	—	—	—	·	—	—	—	·	7
TOTAL BONE FRAGMENTS	3	17	37	2	**59**	23	89	**112**	187	45	130	137	7	3	**500**	**9**	515	161	23	32	**731**	1619	734	123	**2476**	**3887**

FIG. 21. Vertebrate remains recovered in excavations.

The Early Mesita Negra Phase is represented by two samples from Site P24; Test 2 and Structure 2. In these samples, rabbit remains are again most common, with hard-carapace turtle also frequent, and one specimen of *Bison.*

In the Late Mesita Negra Phase, represented by the remaining excavated samples at P24 and the tests from P4B, rabbits are again the dominant element of the faunal assemblage, and the Testudines the second most important element. Antelope are well represented and Bison remains were frequent in Test 2 at P4B. Other forms present include prairie dog, badger, and pocket gopher. Several snake vertebrae were encountered in Test 1 at P24.

None of our samples represent the Early McKenzie Phase, which is particularly unfortunate in view of the dramatic change in composition of the faunal remains in the succeeding Late McKenzie Phase. Here, in samples from Site P4C, it is clear that *Bison* is the dominant form of food refuse. The total of 224 definitely identified examples of *Bison* bone from the site is certainly far below the total quantity of *Bison* bone represented in the refuse. It is probable, for instance, that all of the 734 fragments of bone from the storage cyst are of *Bison,* since no bone fragments of a character different from those identified as *Bison* were encountered. It is interesting to note that of the 243 identified fragments of bone, only one is of deer or antelope; and not one of the 2476 bone fragments from the site could be identified as hard or soft shelled turtle. This suggests that these animals were not considered desirable when *Bison* was available.

The coincidence of the appearance of large quantities of *Bison* in the food refuse on the P4C site and the marked rise in proportion of grass pollen strongly suggests that a slight climatic change in this area on the eastern margin of the Southwest semi-desert environment, and the western margin of the High Plains grasslands, produced conditions which allowed a dramatic shift in wild food resources as the bison followed the expanding margins of the grasslands down to the Pecos River.

There is little in either the faunal or pollen evidence to suggest that the Pecos Valley of the late prehistoric period differed greatly in environmental conditions from the reports of the early explorers (see Chapter II). It does appear, on the basis of the absence of *Prosopis* in the pollen record, that mesquite was not present in the valley as late as the Late McKenzie Phase. It is clear that this form of vegetation was much in evidence at the time the first explorers entered the valley in the 16th Century. Considering the known mechanisms by which this plant has spread in the historic period it may be possible to equate the introduction of mesquite with the migration of bison herds through the valley. A polished mesquite stump in the possession of R. E. McKenzie of Fort Sumner in 1960 appeared to have approximately 300 growth rings, which would tend to verify the presence of mesquite in the valley as early as the first Spanish exploration and well before early herds of domestic livestock were present in the area.

VIII

THE PREHISTORIC CULTURAL SEQUENCE IN THE MIDDLE PECOS VALLEY

The materials described in the preceding chapters are of considerable help in understanding the activities of prehistoric man in the Middle Pecos Valley. This chapter will attempt to integrate these materials with our knowledge of cultural activity in surrounding areas to produce a comprehensive view of the place of the Middle Pecos sequence in the prehistory of western North America.

The Paleo-Indian Period

Direct evidences of Paleo-Indian occupations in the valley are limited to five projectile point bases and a single Folsom-type channel flake. All of the point bases are similar to those from well-documented sites of the "Plano" horizon in the Paleo-Indian sequence. The time period represented by these materials is between about 8000 B. C. (for the channel flake) and 6000 B. C. for the latest Plano industries. No deposits of apparent Late Pleistocene age other than occasional exposures of the Lakewood terrace were encountered in the valley. The character of these terrace deposits is not favorable for Paleo-Indian sites, since they appear to consist almost entirely of aggradational surfaces of rapidly accumulating coarse sediment on the stream floor. Tributary drainages appear to have been scoured free of Late Pleistocene sediments, at least as far as they have been revealed by present erosion. On the basis of our reconnaissance I would guess that, aside from the possibility of a peculiar situation of local preservation, the chances for an *in situ* Paleo-Indian sequence in the Middle Pecos Valley are slim.

The prehistory of surrounding areas, however, suggests that the valley was occupied through the entire known sequence of western Paleo-Indian culture. To both east and west we have well-documented accounts of Clovis (or "Llano") occupations (Sellards, 1952; Haury, Sayles, and Wasley, 1959). In addition, only a short distance to the west, in the Estancia Basin, the Lucy Site (Roosa, 1956) has yielded evidence of an apparent contact (or transition) between a Sandia and a fluted point tradition. The concentration of water resources in the Pecos drainage, considerably greater in the terminal stages of the Pleistocene than at present, undoubtedly furnished an attraction for large game, which in turn probably drew Paleo-Indian hunters.

The Archaic Period

The range of Archaic materials in the sites visited by the survey indicates a wide time span. Probably the earliest materials are examples of "J" points (Ellis and Campbell, 1952) from Site L6 (Pl. XVI H). It is possible that these two examples have been salvaged from earlier sites, since the smaller one has been re-fashioned into a graver. A single San Jose point (Agogino and Hester, 1956) was found at site P38 (Pl. XVI I). It is made of a multicolored chalcedony which does not appear in any of the other Pecos Valley collections. Since many Bosque Redondo Navajo sherds are present on this site, I think it is possible that the Navajo may have brought this point from the northwestern New Mexico area. The possibility of the native occurrence of San Jose points in the valley is favored by the presence of specimens of this type in a site on the western Llano Estacado (L9) and in a collection made by Warnica from a site in the valley (W41) about 35 miles south of Fort Sumner (Jelinek, 1960; 173). The latter site collections include Mesita Negra Phase and post-McKenzie Phase materials.

In 1960 (*op.cit.*) I postulated the existence of a Late Archaic "Yeso Phase," named after Site P5 on Yeso Creek, a few miles west of the Pecos River. After examining a greater number of aceramic site localities in and around the Pecos Valley, and in other areas of the Southwest, I am now less inclined to treat the collections from this site as a particular assemblage. While I remain confident that late Archaic materials are present in context in the valley in sufficient quantity for an eventual definition of such a phase, I do not feel that the present evidence justifies a definition. In this same context, I would like to mention the frequent occurrence of crudely chipped stone "tools" and objects along the top of the western edge of the Mescalero Pediment and in similar topographic positions in the valley. The simple workmanship displayed on these objects and their location at the top of high terraces is likely to suggest to the inexperienced student that these specimens represent a culture of great age, and in fact I seriously considered this question in my initial examination of these localities. I have observed, however, that these objects are almost always associated with outcrops of heavy gravel, including all of the types of stone used in the industry. And, having observed and practiced rudimentary stone-chipping, I conclude that most of these objects are rejected or briefly used cores which were cast aside after a few test flakes had been struck, in favor of more suitable material. Factors favoring this interpretation are the fresh (unpatinated and otherwise unaltered) flake scars on the cores and the presence of many cortical flakes in the area. In general, the gravels found at lower elevations in the valley are finer in texture, which, with the denser vegetation expected at lower elevations in the prehistoric period, would encourage the utilization of the higher outcrops throughout the late prehistoric occupation.

The only aceramic flaking industry encountered in the valley which appears sufficiently distinctive and localized to warrant separation from other industries was found along stream drainages in the northern Bitter Lake Wildlife Refuge west of the river. These sites, at the front of the northern slopes of the Dunahoo Hills, are characterized by tremendous numbers of flakes on a fine-grained highly altered chert. The chert flakes are all patinated to a creamy tan color and some exhibit distinct banding in light shades, but a fresh fracture reveals that the interior is light to dark gray. The chracter of the flakes is quite distinct from the flakes of all other localities in the valley. They are predominantly quite thin and elongated, with relatively few cortical flakes and frequent examples of flakes of bifacial retouch (Bordes, 1963; Jelinek, 1966b). It seems clear that the manufacturers of this industry were using local outcrops of fairly large nodules of chert, probably from the Chalk Bluff formation, and were doing a great deal more direct percussion with a fairly heavy soft (or "cylindrical") hammer than is evident in other valley sites. Few points or fragments were encountered on these sites, but most of those recovered in the same material as the flaking suggest a late Archaic context. This industry is tentatively designated here as the "Dunahoo Complex" after the small range of hills to the south of the sites.

The general character and specific range of forms of Archaic points in the survey collections is covered in Chapter V of this report. Most of the points are too generalized in form to be assigned to specific time horizons or phases known from studies elsewhere. In addition to the J points and San Jose points mentioned earlier, the short pentagonal side-notched points with indented bases (type N25 and N25X Pl. XVI, A, B) appear to be similar in form to points from Signal Butte in the Central Plains (Strong, 1935; Pl. 25:1*e*) and to points associated with the Chiricahua Stage of the Cochise Culture (Dick, 1965: Fig. 21; 1,m). And finally, the large short diagonal-notched points, with straight to convex blade edges and convex bases (Pl. XVI, D, E) found at Site W11, close to Site W9 on the Mescalero Pediment in the southern valley, suggest similarities to the point described by Steen (1959) in his definition of the "Clayton Complex" from northeastern New Mexico. This complex appears to be associated with an extinct variety of bison and has yielded a radiocarbon date of 5280 ± 1000 B.P.

Scrapers associated with Archaic collections from Site P5 resemble those figured by Fenenga and Cummings (1956a: Fig. 148, n-q) from Site LA2709, a short distance west of the Pecos River in the southern valley. The point figured from this site is also typical of late Archaic specimens from other areas of the valley.

In general, there seems to be little to distinguish the Archaic cultural manifestations in the Middle Pecos Valley from those of surrounding areas, as they are presently documented. From the presence of San Jose and J points in the earlier Archaic horizons it appears that the cultural affinities of the valley were more with the Southwest than the Plains. The type N25 forms can be interpreted either as forming a link between the southwestern and plains forms at one horizon or as merely showing influence from one to the other. The late Archaic is generally similar in its artifact content to the Archaic of west Texas, such as is represented at the Little Sunday site (Hughes, 1955); it is similar also, in chipped stone materials, to Basketmaker sites in the northern Southwest.

The presence of points at Site P5 which fall within the cluster attributed to arrow points in Fig. 13 suggests that the bow and arrow had appeared in the Middle Pecos Valley prior to the appearance of ceramics. The locations of most late Archaic sites also suggest that cultivation had not yet appeared. The appearance of the bow and arrow in the Anasazi tradition seems clearly documented during Basketmaker III (c. A.D. 600). If we assume, on the basis of succeeding influences, that the major cultural stimuli in the Pecos Valley in this period were from the west, we can assume that the terminal Archaic cultures in this area lasted at least until A. D. 600, and quite possibly somewhat later.

The Early 18 Mile Phase

This is the first cultural phase in which artifact materials and site locations suggest relatively permanent settlements in topographic situations suitable for the practice of maize cultivation. The small number of sites assignable to this phase and the relatively small quantity of ceramics recovered from each site suggest an initial adaptation of an economy based on cultivation, while the small sherd collections which characterize most of these sites suggest that a fully sedentary southwestern way of life was not yet in effect. I would interpret the large quantities of crudely-chipped stone tools on Site P14 as largely indicative of wild plant-processing, on the basis of a tendency toward larger quantities of chipped stone in stratigraphic collections showing less bone. These ratios are seen in the table below, in which the test samples treated in the study of pollen-artifact correlations (Jelinek, 1966a) are ranked according to quantity of stone material.

TABLE XXVIII

RATIOS OF STONE AND BONE FRAGMENTS IN STRATIGRAPHIC SAMPLES

Locus	Stone	Bone	Stone/Bone
P4C-1	414	1619	.26
P4B-1	332	515	.65
P24-1	242	178	1.36
P4A-3	136	37	3.68
P4B-2	110	161	.68
P4A-2	81	17	4.76
P4B-3	67	23	3.43

There is some indication of a general age gradation in this table, perhaps reflecting bone preservation differences with age; however, the preservation of bone is roughly comparable among all of the Site P4B samples, and between the P4B and P4C samples, indicating that this factor is not apt to account for most of the differences observed in the table. Since chipped stone in this table shows a tendency to decrease as animal bone increases (probably reflecting a practice of butchering away from the site) and chipped stone is not known to be used in processing domesticated plants, it is assumed that the chipped stone on these sites largely reflects use on wild plant resources.

The few sherds found in the excavation and surface sample from Site P14 appear to represent contact with sedentary cultivators to the west, and are probably indicative of the kinds of contacts which first brought the techniques of maize cultivation into the valley. The projectile point from the excavation is typical of the convex-edged forms restricted to this phase.

The presence of these points associated with plain brownwares and a few sherds of Lino Gray in this phase gives a reasonable indication of the time horizon of the Early 18 Mile Phase. The presence of similar points at Shabik'eshchee Village (Roberts, 1929: Pl. 28, p, r), Jeddito 264 (Daifuku, 1961: Fig. 15 d), and in the La Plata District (Morris, 1939: Pls. 125, 126) in a Basketmaker III-Pueblo I context, suggests a date for this form at about A. D. 700-800 in the Anasazi area. At this time Lino Gray was the dominant utility ware in the eastern portion of the Anasazi area, and its presence in the Middle Pecos Valley with these projectile points tends to support a date for the Early 18 Mile Phase in the late 8th Century, or early 9th Century A.D. In view of our limited knowledge of the area between the valley and northwestern New Mexico I would place this phase in the time interval from the early to late 800's.

The only reported site which appears to equate with this period in the eastern portion of the Anasazi area is LA2579, a pithouse village near Gran Quivira (Fenenga, 1956a; Green, 1955), at which Jornada Brown was the dominant ceramic type (63%) and Lino Gray was of secondary importance (15%). The circular pithouse reported by Fenenga from this site is quite generalized in form, with a clay-rimmed hearth surrounded by four major roof supports and a ventilator opening from the southeast. Irregular, cylindrical, and bell-shaped cache pits were also reported for the site.

To the southeast of the Middle Pecos Valley, in the Jornada tradition of the Mogollon culture (Lehmer, 1948), the Capitan Phase is equivalent, at least in part, to the Early 18 Mile Phase. At the Three Posts site, a Capitan Phase site in the Bonito Valley (Jelinek, 1952), plain brownwares were the only ceramics collected; associated with two projectile points with convex blades, moderate barbs, and a large expanding stem similar to an example figured by Roberts (1929: Pl. 28 m) from Shibik'eshchee Village. Two other plain brownware sites were also reported in this area (Jelinek, *op. cit.*), one of which yielded fragments of two vessels of a coarse, polished redware.

The presence of these sites to the east of the Middle Pecos Valley suggests a gradual spread of a sedentary way of life based on maize cultivation, from the centers of development of the Mogollon and Anasazi traditions into this area during the 8th Century A. D. and to the eastern limits of the natural resources which could support such an economy (the Pecos Valley) in the following century. There is some evidence (e.g., Site P14) that local groups of food collectors did adopt this new way of life; and, on the other hand, there is nothing which suggests a migration of outside peoples with a developed agricultural system into the valley in this period.

The Late 18 Mile Phase

This is the first phase in which well-established small sedentary communities make their appearance in the valley. The phase is chiefly distinguished on the basis of the ceramic assemblage, which includes the first appreciable quantity of reduced-fired decorated ceramics, in the form of intrusive Red Mesa B/W. During this phase the local Middle Pecos Micaceous Brown type of Jornada Brownware gradually becomes the dominant utility ware, replacing the more generalized Jornada Brown. South Pecos Brown continues to be well represented as a minority type in this phase. The limited data available suggests that small necks were favored on ollas of this ware; this, along with the hard-fired paste, may indicate that South Pecos Brown vessels were used as water containers. This interpretation appears to be supported by the decrease in popularity of South Pecos Brown with the appearance of ollas of the relatively hard-fired local graywares in the Early Mesita Negra Phase.

Projectile points in Late 18 Mile Phase collections are mostly diagonally notched, with convex bases and convex to straight blade edges. They are of moderate size and are almost all apparently arrow points.

Architectural forms associated with this phase include slab-lined storage cysts, slab-lined pithouses, the large peculiar shallow pithouse structure from Site P4AB, and small contiguous-roomed rectangular structures, slightly excavated into the ground and incorporating small vertical sandstone slabs in the wall bases. These architectural forms are similar to those of the Basketmaker III-Pueblo I periods in the Anasazi area.

The pollen evidence from Site P4A appears to favor an initial occupation of the site area in Late 18 Mile Phase times. Test 3 at this site, which was the earliest sample in the seriation, shows the highest ratio of *Artemesia* of any sample, and the lowest ratio of Cheno-Am pollen of all samples but the latest McKenzie Phase. This probably indicates that *Artemesia* near the site had not yet been heavily utilized for fuel or removed from cultivated areas, and that the very heavy disturbance, producing large quantities of Cheno-Am pollen, had not yet taken place. Conditions in the valley may have been slightly less moist; this is indicated by the high ratio of compositae relative to grasses (Fig. 20). I would interpret the presence of hard-shell turtle remains (probably desert tortoise) in the refuse as an indication of relatively impoverished conditions.

The most closely comparable culture phase outside of the Middle Pecos Valley is represented by the Taylor Draw site near Carrizozo, New Mexico, excavated by Stewart Peckham (personal communication). The major ceramic types of this site are Jornada Brown utility ware and lesser quantities (c. 5%) of Red Mesa Black on White. Projectile points are diagonally notched with convex bases. The architectural forms from Taylor Draw include numerous slab-lined storage cysts, arranged in rows, and several deep pithouses. The similarity of this site with the description of the Late 18 Mile Phase suggests that a single tradition may account for both developments. It is interesting, in this regard, to note that no similar sites have yet been reported for the highland area between Carrizozo and the Pecos Valley. Sites of comparable age in the highlands appear to lack Red Mesa B/W, and while their architecture is known to include pithouses (Jelinek, 1952; 147), the specific forms remain undescribed.[13] It appears that in the area to the east of the Rio Grande, Anasazi influence (as represented by Red Mesa B/W) was strongest in the lower topographical areas, while the Mogollon of the highland areas remained beyond any significant Anasazi contact.

The temporal position of this phase has been determined largely on the basis of the intrusive Red Mesa B/W ceramics. This type has a wide geographical distribution and in all areas its manufacture seems to be associated with a Late Pueblo I to Pueblo II culture. In the Chaco Canyon area Pueblo II has recently been placed between about A.D. 900 and 1050 (Vivian and Mathews, 1965: 29). We can infer (Vivian, 1965: 40-41) that the manufacture of Red Mesa B/W at Chaco Canyon took place between

---

[13] Lehmer's (1948; 85) assignment of the lower structure at Site LA2000, excavated by Jennings (1940), to the Capitan Phase, seems unwarranted in view of the presence of El Paso Polychrome, Chupadero B/W and Three Rivers R/TC in the structure. The structure, apparently a rectangular pithouse, was not completely excavated.

about A.D. 870 and sometime shortly after 950. On this basis, and with the probability of some lag in the manufacture of this type in areas between Chaco Canyon and the Pecos Valley, I would place the Late 18 Mile Phase between about A.D. 900 and 1000.

As in the preceding phase, there is no evidence in the artifact materials of a dominance of outside traditions over the local tradition; and therefore there is no reason to believe that the people of the Late 18 Mile Phase were not direct descendants of earlier populations of the valley. By this time, however, cultural influences from the expanding Northern Rio Grande tradition (Wendorf and Reed, 1955: 140) had begun to affect the basic Mogollon pattern of the Middle Pecos tradition.

The Early Mesita Negra Phase

It is clear from Fig. 9 that in the Northern Valley relatively large sites of the Mesita Negra Phase are more abundant than sites of similar size for all other phases combined. These Mesita Negra sites are about evenly divided between the Early Phase and Late Phase.

The Early Mesita Negra Phase marks the first appearance of reduced-fired wares (or graywares) of native manufacture in the valley. The fact that these types appear to directly succeed Red Mesa B/W and are contemporary with Socorro B/W (as evidenced by intrusive sherds) seems to prove Mera incorrect in his statement that Chupadero developed from Socorro B/W and spread to the east (Mera, 1935: 30). In fact, if the succession of Socorro to Chupadero in the Rio Grande Valley is valid, the evidence would support an origin of Chupadero in the eastern area and a relatively late spread to the west. The inference of Stubbs (in Smiley, Stubbs, and Bannister, 1953: 58) that Chupadero B/W developed directly from a local earlier Pueblo tradition, with influence from Mimbres B/W, may be more correct, although Mimbres influences do not seem likely in the Middle Pecos area.

The brownware ceramic tradition in this phase shows a marked dominance of Middle Pecos Micaceous Brown, with Jornada and South Pecos Brown continuing in diminished quantity. Roswell Brown continues to appear in about the same quantity as in the preceding phase. The first few sherds of Chupadero B/W appear as intrusives.

The most frequent encountered intrusive ceramic type in this phase is Red Mesa B/W, indicating a close relationship of the ceramics with the Late 18 Mile Phase. Other intrusive types include Cebolleta, Socorro, Mimbres, and Reserve Black on White, and Broadline Red on Terra Cotta. One sherd which may possibly be Santa Fe B/W was found at the latest site assigned to this phase (P13).

The projectile points associated with collections of this phase are generally similar to those in the Late 18 Mile Phase; of moderate size and shape, diagonally notched, with convex base and straight to convex blade edges. The few forms peculiar to this phase have been listed earlier.

The only structure which can be assigned to this phase was Structure 2 at Site P24, a shallow floor outlined by a semi-circular arrangement of sandstone slabs, with a central hearth and possible internal partitions of adobe.

None of the environmental evidence collected in the tests can be assigned to this phase with the exception of two rabbit bones collected in the excavation of the above-mentioned structure. The similarity between the pollen counts of Late 18 Mile and the earliest Late Mesita Negra tests suggests little change in vegetation during this period.

No sites of comparable period have been excavated or reported from the area between the Middle Pecos Valley and the Rio Grande. This Phase appears to be contemporary with the later period of Lehmer's Capitan Phase (Lehmer, 1948: 85).

The instrusive ceramics suggest a time horizon from about A.D. 1000 to the early 1100's, based upon the dates given by Stubbs (in Smiley, Stubbs and Bannister, 1953: 58) for the Rio Grande area.

The Late Mesita Negra Phase

With regard to ceramics, this phase is marked by an increase in the quantity of native graywares, and by a marked decline in Micaceous Brown utility ware as the phase developed. The few sherds of McKenzie Brown mark the beginning of an almost complete replacement of Micaceous Brown by this new type in succeeding phases. The pronounced rise in quantity of Roswell Brown may indicate increased contact with the south, either in the form of economic exchange, or perhaps, even in the presence of women from that area in the northern Middle Valley. The first appearance of Chupadero B/W in significant quantities in this phase corroborates the more intensive relationships with the southern valley.

Intrusive ceramics from outside of the Pecos Valley again demonstrate relationships with the Middle and Northern Rio Grande Valley. Definite examples of Santa Fe B/W are present, as are sherds of Cebolleta and Socorro B/W and Broadline Red on Terra Cotta. Sherds of Red Mesa B/W present in Late Mesita Negra collections are assumed to be remnants of intrusives from earlier phases. It is interesting to note that intrusive black on white sherds from the west account for only 1.22% of the sherds recovered in sites assigned to this phase, while in the Early Mesita Negra Phase this percentage was 2.06, and in the Late 18 Mile Phase, Red Mesa B/W accounted for 4.87% of the ceramics collected. This seems to represent a gradual decrease in contact with the Rio Grande area. It is possible that this decreased contact was due to an increasing number of intervening settlements in the Jornada-Chupadero tradition whose intrusive ceramics have gone unrecognized in the Pecos Valley samples.

Projectile points in this phase are more varied in size and relative dimensions than in the Early Mesita Negra Phase. Straight and convex blade edges occur in equal amounts and the formerly predominant convex bases are now only roughly equal in number to straight bases. Most points are diagonally notched.

Architecture definitely associated with this phase is limited to the poorly-defined sub-surface features of Site P24, Structure 1, It appears that sub-surface dwellings may still have been utilized in this phase, since all of the fill in this structure appears to be of Late Mesita Negra origin. The burials encountered in this context show that inhumation was practiced, with a semi-flexed position apparently preferred. A few heavy stones were placed over the deceased and no grave goods were included in the burials.

Environmental evidence from this phase shows a gradual shift toward more grasses, apparently reflecting slightly increased precipitation (Fig. 20). This increase in grasses is at the expense of the Compositae; these latter tend to increase with slightly dryer conditions in the Middle Pecos area. The very slight overall rise in pine pollen during this phase may also represent a slight rise in precipitation. Highest percentages of maize pollen occurred during the Late Mesita Negra phase, but, as Martin suggests, probably indicate ritual activity involving maize pollen rather than intensity of cultivation. The very high quantity of cheno-am pollen due to cultural activity in this phase (Jelinek, 1966a) probably does indicate the maximum sedentary utilization of the P4 and P24 site complexes in this period. In the vertebrate remains, the dominance of *Lepus* over *Sylvilagus*, and the presence of *Cynomys* and *Bison* in this phase, all suggest a greater proximity of grasslands than do preceding faunas. The continuing importance of hard-shelled turtle (or more probably tortoise) remains in the midden debris suggests that meat was not easily available in the Middle Pecos area.

As in the preceding phase, no excavated sites have been reported for the area between the Middle Pecos Valley and the Rio Grande which appear to be contemporary with this phase.

The dating of the Late Mesita Negra Phase again depends largely upon the dates determined elsewhere for the intrusive ceramic types. The latest type to appear in the Late Mesita Negra Phase is Sante Fe B/W. Stubbs (in Smiley, Stubbs, and Bannister, 1953: 58) dates the manufacture of this type between about A.D. 1200 and 1350. However, at the only site in the report (LA114, Arroyo Negro) in which Santa Fe B/W is the latest type reported, a total of 137 tree-ring specimens have been dated between A. D. 1045 and 1145 (*ibid.:* 22). Of these specimens, 41 were dated between 1127 and 1133, and 29 were dated at 1145. The authors state: "All of these specimens are small charcoal fragments and probably represent cooking fires, etc., rather than construction beams". (*op. cit.*). These dates indicate that Santa Fe B/W may have been in use as early as the first half of the twelfth century. The majority of evidence favors the time interval selected by Stubbs for the period of widest use of this type; thus, this period may be assumed to have been the time from which the sherds recovered were imported to the Middle Pecos Valley. Therefore, the Late Mesita Negra Phase was probably in existence at least into the early years of the thirteenth century. A single radiocarbon date on fragments of *Bison* bone from Test 2 at the Site P4B gave a date of A.D. 1130 ±110 (M-1466), perhaps indicating that the earlier range of this phase was in the early twelfth century. Lehmer's chronology chart (Lehmer, 1948: 89) indicates that this time period is equivalent to the Three Rivers Phase of the Northern Jornada Mogollon culture. The absence of Three Rivers R/TC in the Late Mesita Negra Phase (although Broadline R/TC is present) and Stubb's date for Three Rivers R/TC, between 1150 and 1300 (in Smiley, Stubbs and Bannister, 1953: 58) may indicate that the dates of A.D. 1100 to 1200 are too early for this phase, and that Late Mesita Negra is equivalent to the latest Capitan Phase. No examples of Santa Fe B/W were recovered from sub-surface samples on Site P4B or Site P24, which suggests that this type arrived late in the period.

The Early McKenzie Phase

This phase is represented by only three sites in the northern valley. This may reflect a reduced population in the valley during the phase or may indicate that the phase was of short duration. I tend to favor the latter interpretation, since the sites are widely spaced through the northern valley. All three of the sites are relatively large; a pattern which contrasts with the preceding phase, in which six of the 11 sites reported yielded fewer than 100 sherds. There is some evidence that Sites P1 and P21 which have primarily Early McKènzie Phase occupations may also have earlier occupations. Further, it is probable that a small Late McKenzine occupation has been masked by the predominant Late Mesita Negra materials at Sites P4B and P24, since the proportion of McKenzie Brown in the surface collections is not matched in the stratigraphic samples from either site.

The ceramic assemblage of this phase is similar to that of the Late Mesita Negra Phase except for higher percentages of McKenzie Brown and Middle Pecos B/W in this phase. The use of Roswell Brown continues to be heavy, and Chupadero B/W is present in about the same quantity as in the preceding phase.

Intrusive black on white ceramics account for only .26% of the sherds at the three sites, and if Red Mesa B/W is removed from consideration as obviously intrusive from earlier levels, the four remaining sherds account for only .18% of the sherd count. Of these four sherds, one is of Cebolleta B/W and is probably from an earlier horizon. The remaining three consist of two definite and one doubtful example of Santa Fe B/W. These few sherds demonstrate a dramatic decrease in contact with the ceramics of the Rio Grande area. A single sherd of Wingate B/R from Site P1 is certainly from an earlier occupation.

The projectile points of the Early McKenzie Phase present a marked departure from the Mesita Negra forms. This phase is characterized by the first appearance in quantity of triangular points with straight bases, convex blade edges, and lateral notches. A definite preference for convex over straight blade edges, and straight over convex bases, is apparent in all points of this phase.

Architecture in this phase includes rectangular, slab-based surface rooms, as observed at Site P25. It is possible that the surface structure excavated at P24 belongs to this phase, since it clearly succeeded the subsurface structures with Late Mesita Negra fill.

No evidence was collected relating to environment during the Early McKenzie Phase.

No excavated sites or surface sites have been reported in the area between the Pecos Valley and the Rio Grande in a time period comparable to this phase.

The dating of the Early McKenzie Phase is made more difficult by the absence of a reasonable amount of intrusive ceramics. The suggested short time span and the presence of Santa Fe B/W argue for a date in a span of a few decades following the Late Mesita Negra Phase. A date near A.D. 1250 seems plausible. This date probably indicates that the Early McKenzie Phase is temporally equivalent to an early stage of Lehmer's Three Rivers Phase of the Northern Jornada Mogollon (Lehmer, 1948: 85-86).

In view of the inferences based upon ceramics, the change in projectile point form is most interesting. The transition from diagonal-notched points with convex bases to triangular lateral-notched forms has been documented for much of the Southwest. Perhaps the best dated transition is in the Chaco Canyon area. Judd (1954: 255) felt that at Pueblo Bonito the corner-notched forms could be associated with the earlier and more conservative "Old Bonitan" occupation areas, and the side-notched points related to the "Late Bonitan" occupations and to later masonry forms. Side-notched points from Pueblo Bonito appear to be predominantly of the types B24 and H24 of this report, with low side notches, and are frequently of the "W" (long, narrow) variant (*ibid.:* Pls. 73A, 74B). One point each with straight, concave, and notched base are included in an illustration captioned "Miscellaneous arrowheads, including those of aberrant form" (*ibid.:* Pl. 73B). At the nearby site of Pueblo del Arroyo, Judd reports that all but two of the 32 points recovered were of the side-notched variety, and of these 16 had a convex base, while 14 had a straight to slightly concave base (Judd, 1959: 138). These points appear to differ from the side-notched points of Pueblo Bonito in having the notches higher on the blade (*ibid.:* Pl. 40 d-j). The occupation of Pueblo del Arroyo was, after the initial period of construction, of Judd's (1954: 21) "Late Bonitan" variety. Vivian and Mathews' recent outline (1965: 108-110) of the simultaneous occupation of Chaco Canyon by three phases (McElmo, Hosta Butte, and Bonito), would equate Judd's Old Bonitan with the Bonito Phase and his Late Bonitan with the McElmo Phase. In their report on the McElmo Phase site of Kin Kletso (*op. cit.*), Vivian and Mathews' note (*ibid.:* 85) that 90% of identifiable points were side-notched. Of these, points with straight bases predominated, those with slightly concave bases were next, and those with convex bases were least frequent. The final construction period in the Bonito and McElmo Phase sites at Chaco Canyon has been dated at A.D. 1124 and the final date of occupation at about A.D.1178 (*ibid.:* 113). Initial construction at Kin Kletso is thought to date to about A.D. 1050 (Bannister, 1965: 171). The major period of construction at Pueblo del Arroyo was between A.D. 1090 and 1110 (*ibid.:*188-189). This would seem to indicate that several styles of side-notched points were in use in Chaco Canyon in the same period of the late eleventh and early twelfth centuries. Judd's interpretation of conservative tendencies in the Bonito Phase population could suggest that the convex-based side-notched forms were more closely associated with that group. This seems in accord with the distribution within the three sites mentioned above. From this evidence it appears that the transition from corner-notched to side-notched points in the Chaco area had taken place by about A.D. 1050. Our evidence from the Pecos Valley indicates that a similar transition there did not occur until about A.D. 1250.

In the Rio Grande area between Chaco Canyon and the Middle Pecos Valley two sites have been reported which may be relevant to this transition. At LA2567 five triangular side-notched points were discovered at a site with a time range from Pueblo II through Pueblo III (Fenenga, 1956b). One of these was found in stratigraphic context in a house with a sherd assemblage which may indicate occupation from Late Pueblo II to Early Pueblo III. The date suggested by most of the ceramic evidence is between A.D. 1100 and 1150; however, a date as late as A.D. 1250 would not be impossible. A date between 1150 and 1250 is suggested for a triangular side-notched point with straight base from Site LA2569, on the basis of associated ceramics in the room in which it occurred (Fenenga and Cummings, 1956b).

The conclusion here derived from the data on this transition in projectile point forms is that by the time triangular side-notched projectile points came into use in the Middle Pecos Valley, they had long been used in the heart of the Anasazi area, and had probably also been used in the Rio Grande Valley for nearly 100 years. The lag in diffusion of this form of projectile point emphasizes the peripheral nature of the Middle Pecos settlements with regard to the Puebloan (Reed, 1946) cultures to the east, and seems to confirm the reduced contact with this area apparent in the ceramics.

To the northeast of the Middle Pecos Valley, the Upper Republican assemblage of the west Central Plains suggests that in this area as well small triangular side-notched points were in use several centuries before they first appear in the valley (Wedel, 1959: 402-3, Pl. 62).

No data are available for the area of the Plains immediately to the east of the Llano Estacado during this period. On the Llano it appears that at this time most cultural activity was an eastward extension of the Pecos Valley Phases (Krieger, 1946: 80; Jelinek, 1960: 188).

The Late McKenzie Phase

The restriction of this phase to a single relatively large site (P4C) and to a few additional small sites within the survey is evidence in itself of the dramatic cultural changes which were taking place in the Middle Pecos Valley during this period.

The predominance of Middle Pecos B/W in the surface collections indicates a marked shift in patterns of ceramic usage; for the first time in the sequence, brown utility wares are a minor element in the ceramic assemblage. The slight overall increase in relative number of grayware olla sherds in this phase (Table XII) may indicate a preference for more (or larger) water containers. The sudden disappearance of Roswell Brown from the inventory at the P4 site complex is puzzling, especially since this type was still being manufactured in the apparently equivalent Roswell Phase in the southern valley. Perhaps a commodity previously imported in these vessels was no longer in demand in the northern area. Chupadero B/W, however, increases in frequency and was presumably largely derived from the south. Corrugated brownware appears in significant quantity in this phase for the first time.

Intrusive ceramics are difficult to appraise at Site P4C; an earlier occupation may be responsible for sherds of Red Mesa B/W and a Local (?) Pueblo II B/W, as well as the sherds of Kwahe'e B/W. The Santa Fe B/W sherds are probably associated with the late McKenzie ceramics. The presence of Los Lunas Smudged and Pitoche Rubbed-ribbed may also relate to an earlier occupation, since the primary association of these types in the Rio Grande is with Socorro B/W; the latter is a type not represented at P4C, although it occurs in collections from P4B and P4AB. Two sherds questionably identified as Socorro were recovered from Site P31, as was a single sherd of St. Johns Polychrome. The only other intrusive sherd associated with this phase is a single example of Three Rivers R/TC from Site P64. Even if the example of Pitoche Rubbed-ribbed and Los Lunas

Smudged are included in the Late McKenzie sample, sherds from the Rio Grande area form less than .56% of the sample. If these sherds are excluded, the percentage falls to less than .14% of the total, less than in any other phase following the Early 18 Mile Phase.

The projectile points of the Late McKenzie Phase continue the trend established in the Early McKenzie Phase toward lateral notching; over 80% of the points are of this form. In contrast to the preceding phase, none of these points has low lateral notches, and about half of the lateral-notched points have concave bases, while the remainder have straight bases. Almost all points have convex-edged blades. The number of points and fragments relative to sherds is greater for this phase than for any preceding phase. An additional distinctive element of the chipped stone assemblage of this phase is the small, thick, steep-edged end scraper, which occurs in abundance at Site P4C and is present at all sites of this phase.

The architectural remains associated with this phase indicate the use of surface structures, probably of contiguous-room rectangular form, with support posts for the roof. The wood for the posts in this phase as in preceding phases may have either been salvaged from driftwood from river floods or been transported a considerable distance, since the arboreal pollen represented throughout the sequence in the valley is negligible. The single surviving post in the structure at Site P4C appears to be of juniper (V. Jones, personal communication). The relatively elaborate treatment accorded the bases of the posts lends support to the idea that they were a rare commodity. The bell-shaped cache pit at Site P4C is similar to a structure of earlier date reported by Fenenga (1956a: 227, Fig. 149) from Site LA2579. The pit from P4C differs from the LA2579 structure in that its point of greatest constriction is at the surface (due to erosion?), and in the addition of a stone floor made from a slab metate.

The environmental evidence from this phase provides some of the most dramatic evidence for the interpretation of cultural development in the entire prehistoric sequence in the valley. The marked rise of grass pollen in this phase corresponds to a drop in cheno-am pollen and in *Zea* pollen. This would seem to indicate a less intensive sedentary utilization of the P4 site area and a decrease in cultivating activities. That the rise in grasses is independent of these factors is indicated in the compensation for cultural effects on pollen production seen in Fig. 20. This increase in grasses is matched by a dramatic increase in the utilization of bison by the people of the Late McKenzie Phase at

Site P4C. This great increase in quantity of animal remains, particularly of *Bison*, suggests drastic changes in patterns of economic activity within the community. The complete absence of remains of Testudines in this phase probably signified the end of poverty of meat resources. The anatomical representation of the *Bison* bone from Site P4C includes a high ratio of limb bones and ribs relative to fragments of skull, vertebrae, and pectoral and pelvic girdles, and much of the bone appears to be from relatively young animals. Both of these lines of evidence suggest that butchering was done at some distance from the site and that only those most easily transported portions of lighter animals were brought into the site. The high proportion of projectile points and the many small end scrapers show a heavier concentration on hunting and game-processing activities than are present in the earlier phases.

A major change in the basis of subsistence, such as occurred here, needs clarification. The alternatives seem to be whether a change to natural conditions less favorable to cultivation forced the Middle Pecos peoples to engage in more intensive utilization of extant wild resources, or whether there was an intrusion of a new resource (i.e. *Bison*) in sufficient quantity to encourage the abandonment of the marginally successful cultivation which had been practiced in the valley, in favor of hunting. The pollen evidence appears to favor the latter alternative, since there is no evidence of less favorable growing conditions in this record, and some evidence, in the increased ratio of grasses, that a slightly higher rate of precipitation was in effect than in the preceding several hundred years. It seems probable that the bison followed the grasslands as they expanded into the valley and thus became available in increasing quantity to the McKenzie Phase people. That this expansion of *Bison* may be part of a larger overall expansion of the species is suggested by the evidence reported by Bell (1962: 27-28) that few bison remains occur in sites in Oklahoma prior to the period of A.D. 1000 to 1200, and by the somewhat earlier utilization of *Bison* to the north on the Central Plains in the Upper Republican Aspect. In the Northern Plains bison are utilized in quantity as early as the Monroe Focus at the Dodd Site (T. E. White *in* Lehmer, 1954: 166) which has been radiocarbon dated to A.D. 719 $\pm$ 150 (M608). This evidence suggests that the adaptation of *Bison* to a grassland environment, presumably following the sort of adjustment to woodland conditions favored by the more "primitive" *B. b. athabascae*, was most successful only toward the close of the late prehistoric period. It is assumed that the initial expansion of *Bison* into the grasslands was made possible by the disappearance of the Pleistocene equidae, which had previously utilized this niche. With the introduction of arid conditions throughout the western plains following the Pleistocene the *Bison,* then transitional in morphology between *B. occidentalis* and the living *B. b. athabascae*, were forced out of all areas except the northernmost plains and the highlands of the eastern Basin-Range country, exemplified by a find near Bat Cave (Dick, 1965: 92). With the return of more favorable moisture conditions these relatively small populations expanded into the increasing grasslands. This re-expansion of the Great Plains population appears to have reached the eastern edge of the Southwest by the late thirteenth century, although expanding elements of the refugee highland populations had made their appearance in scattered areas of the Mogollon region in earlier periods (Dick, 1965: 90-92). The activities of expanding human communities in these areas apparently reduced most of the smaller bison population in the Southwest by about A.D. 1200 to 1300 (Reed, 1955). On the plains, the great bison herds continued to expand, reaching the eastern woodland areas only shortly before European contact. Rostlund (1960) has suggested that the expansion of *Bison* into the Southeast was aided by the depopulation of that area due to European diseases.

All evidence, then, seems to favor an intrusion into the Middle Pecos Valley sometime in the McKenzie Phases of resources of sufficient promise to persuade the peoples living in that area to abandon their traditional pattern of cultivation in favor of bison hunting. The continuation of the ceramic tradition without evidence of eastern influence, and the dissimilarity of the small end scrapers with the specific forms of similar tools of Plains cultures suggests an *in situ* adaptation to a pattern of bison hunting in the Middle Pecos Valley.

The chronological position of this transition is based on several aspects of the ceramic assemblage. First, the presence of Santa Fe B/W, Pitoche Rubbed-ribbed, Los Lunas Smudged, Three Rivers R/TC, and St. Johns Polychrome in collections from sites of this phase, suggest a date in the early to mid-thirteenth century. The presence of brown corrugated utility wares other than those mentioned above, and the absence of the earliest Rio Grande Glazes in these sites, suggests a date late in the thirteenth or early in the fourteenth century. A thirteenth century date seems supported by the El Paso Polychrome and Three Rivers R/TC intrusives in sites of the Roswell Phase in the southern valley. The ceramic assemblage, stone industry, and quantities of bison bone weathering from exposures on these sites all suggest contemporaneity with the Late McKenzie Phase.

Several radiocarbon dates are available for materials relevant to the dating of the Lake McKenzie Phase. The first date to be run was a sample from the wooden post in the structure at P4C. This sample (M-742) gave a date of A.D. 1100 ± 200. It is probable that the wood selected for the date represents all portions of the log, since the post was poorly preserved and badly fragmented. In addition, the habit of re-using posts and the uncertain derivation of the original timber must be considered. All of these factors tend to favor an earlier date for the specimen than the occupation of the structure. The other sample from the site is bison bone from the storage cyst. This sample (M-1372) dates A.D. 1380 ± 100. The late thirteenth century favored by the ceramic evidence is within the standard deviation of both radiocarbon dates from this site; for the reasons discussed above the second date is presumed to provide better evidence for the date of the Late McKenzie occupation. An additional date from a sample of bison bone (M-1326) from a deeply buried cultural horizon on Yeso Creek about 20 miles west of the Pecos River is A.D. 1360 ± 100. This indicated that the site is not terminal Pleistocene, as had been originally expected, but that it dates to a period of bison hunting which corresponds to the Late McKenzie Phase in the Pecos Valley.

In summary, the radiocarbon evidence does not appear to contradict a date between A.D. 1250 and 1350 for the Late McKenzie Phase.

Post-McKenzie Phase Occupations

Materials assigned to this horizon appear to represent temporary camps, generally in localities not favored by the sedentary population. The presence of sherds of Rio Grande Glazeware and other Puebloan ceramics on these sites indicates a later time period than the Late McKenzie Phase and a general orientation toward the Rio Grande area. An apparently post-McKenzie occupation on Site P3, which left sherds of a corrugated olla of McKenzie brownware and six sherds of Rio Grande Glaze I Red, indicates that some continuity probably exists between the cultures of the early post-McKenzie population and the Late McKenzie peoples.

The more frequent use of obsidian for implements in post-McKenzie Phase sites also indicates increased contact with the northern Rio Grande area.

The projectile points of this period are frequently distinct from those of the McKenzie phases through the addition of a basal notch on the triangular side-notched points. No examples of this point style were recovered in either McKenzie or Roswell Phase collections.

The only post-McKenzie Phase site on which structures were observed was Site P11, on which small stone circles suggesting tipi rings were in evidence. A detailed report on the site by Jelinek and Warnica is in preparation.

The time range of the Rio Grande Glazes from sites on the Llano Estacado to the east of the Middle Pecos Valley (Jelinek, 1960: 204-205) suggests that the valley was traversed by groups in contact with the Rio Grande Pueblos up to the early historic period.

A Summary of Prehistoric Cultural Developments in the Middle Pecos Valley

Hunters of the terminal Pleistocene undoubtedly utilized the resources of the Middle Pecos drainage, although almost no trace remains of their occupation. All direct evidence is confined to relatively late Paleo-Indian artifacts, none of which was in stratigraphic context. Evidence of post-Pleistocene food collectors is more abundant and is most frequently encountered in areas somewhat removed from the river. None of these localities appears to have material in stratigraphic context, however. The late Archaic collecting pattern appears to be similar to that reported for sites of a similar period in the Southwest in terms of artifact types. Projectile points similar to those from the Rio Grande area have been encountered, with small milling stones and abundant crude percussion-flaked implements. A few projectile points from these collections suggest contact with areas to the east and south of the Llano Estacado (e.g. the Edwards Plateau), but these distinctive types are clearly rare in the Middle Pecos region. By the latest Archaic the bow and arrow seems to have been in use in the valley, suggesting a date equivalent to Basketmaker III.

The earliest evidence of sedentary communities shows an assemblage generally similar to that of the latest Archaic, accompanied by examples of the earliest ceramics in the valley. The ceramic tradition which begins in this phase (Early 18 Mile) is closely related to the early Jornada Mogollon Capitan Phase of the Sacramento Highlands to the southwest of the Middle Pecos

Valley, and is tentatively dated at A.D. 800-900. The pattern of cultivation in the valley must have been quite different from the practices in the highland area, since valley crops probably depended largely on the spring floods from the Sangre de Cristo and other ranges whose melting snow drained into the upper Pecos, while summer rains must have played a more important part in highland cultivation. Perhaps as a reflection of these differences in basic patterns of farming, there is relatively little evidence of contact between the highland region and the Pecos Valley in the succeeding period. Instead, the most easily observed evidence, the ceramics, indicates fairly strong contacts with cultural groups in the Middle and Northern Rio Grande areas. Suggestions of such contacts with the Anasazi area are found in the projectile point forms and a few sherds of utility ware in the preceding period, but in this phase (Late 18 Mile), similarities extend to general patterns of architecture, as well as projectile points. The character of the sites and the pollen evidence suggest that this phase marks the earliest appearance of small well-settled communities adjusted to an existence largely dependent upon farming. The ceramic evidence suggests a date of A.D. 900 to 1000 for this phase. The first appearance at this time of small rectangular contiguous structures, only slightly excavated into the ground, suggests a lag of about 100 years in the diffusion of architectural patterns from the Anasazi area.

The two succeeding phases (Early and Late Mesita Negra) are equated with the widest utilization of the valley, probably reflecting the densest population. Faunal evidence from Late Mesita Negra excavations suggests that game was not abundant during this phase. At this time of most intensive farming activity, contact with the Rio Grande area, as reflected in ceramics, gradually dwindled to a few insignificant sherds. Whether this less intensive contact was due to intervening settlements with a ceramic tradition similar to those on the Middle Pecos, or whether patterns of exchange between the northern and southern Middle Valley gradually filled the needs previously satisfied from outside of the valley, is not clear. It is possible that contact interpreted as Rio Grande may have been restricted to the outliers of the Rio Grande cultural tradition in the Upper Pecos Valley. In that event, the "internalizing" of the Middle Pecos tradition would correspond to the crystalization of the Pueblo III pattern oriented toward the area west of the Pecos River in the Upper Valley. The Early Mesita Negra Phase appears to date from about A.D. 1000 to the early 1100's, while the Late Mesita Negra Phase apparently lasted until about A.D. 1200 or 1250.

Following this period of intensive farming in the valley, a transition in basic economic pattern seems to have taken place in less than 100 years. This transition from farming to bison-hunting is accompanied by environmental evidence suggesting slightly more moist conditions which allowed a spread of grass-lands into the vicinity of the valley, and archaeological evidence from surrounding areas which indicates that the expansion of the Great Plains bison herds into the area adjacent to the Middle Pecos Valley may have been taking place about this time. Thus, even though the palynological evidence indicates that conditions for farming during this period did not deteriorate and may even have slightly improved over the preceding period, the peoples of the Middle Pecos area instead developed a pattern of bison hunting. This pattern appears to have led them into a nomadic existence which, on the basis of some post-McKenzie Phase sherds, continued in the Middle Pecos area for a short period before leading them elsewhere, undoubtedly out onto the High Plains. The exact period of this transition cannot yet be definitely dated, but the best evidence now available indicates a period of no more than a century between about A.D. 1250 and 1350 for the abandonment of the sedentary patterns of the earlier farming communities.

The identity of these Middle Pecos farming peoples, in terms of historic Indian populations, is one of the most intriguing problems to rise from these data. The long period in the development of the Middle Pecos tradition when strongest contacts were with the Rio Grande tradition, and the generally common Archaic tradition underlying both areas, suggests that a common language background may also have been present for the two areas. In terms of Middle and Northern Rio Grande contacts the most likely language group with this time depth is Tanoan. In terms of Plains Indians, the only group demonstrably related linguistically to the Tanoan languages is the Kiowa (Trager, 1951; Trager and Trager, 1959; Swadesh, 1963). It is interesting to note that the Tanoan language closest to Kiowa is that of Jemez, the only surviving Towa Pueblo (Trager and Trager, 1959: 1079). The language of Pecos Pueblo, on the Upper Pecos River, was also Towa, and when the pueblo of Pecos was abandoned the survivors of Pecos took refuge with the Jemez for that reason. In terms of primitive routes of communication the Upper Pecos was the easiest area of access within the Northern Rio Grande tradition for the Middle Pecos peoples, and it is likely that this is the area with which greatest communication took place. Estimates have been made, using the controversial glottochronological techniques, of the interval since Kiowa separated from the other

Tanoan languages. Swadesh (1963: 265) estimates the interval at about 2800 years, with a maximum of 3300 years. Trager (1951), who has greater familiarity with the two languages, estimates that the separation took place no later than A. D. 1000, and probably somewhat earlier. This estimate is, of course, in close accord with the period of decreasing contact between the Middle Pecos and the Rio Grande traditions. It seems likely that the isolation of the Middle Pecos peoples since the Archaic period had led to divergent language patterns by this time. On the basis of present evidence, it does not appear that a transition from a Puebloan to a Plains way of life took place in the area to the north of the Middle Pecos Valley; cultural developments in that area are quite different (Lutes, 1959). At present the Pecos Valley is the only place along the eastern frontier of the Puebloan area where a transition from a characteristically Southwestern cultural pattern to a pattern characteristic of a Plains hunting culture can be demonstrated to have taken place. On the basis of this evidence it seems very likely that the Puebloan peoples of the Pecos Valley were the cultural ancestors of the Kiowa of the Plains.

Aside from the question of the historical identity of these peoples, there is a problem of a more general interest. In terms of most theories of cultural change, the transition from a theoretically superior technological level (simple cultivation) to a lower level (food collecting) in the face of an environmental shift favorable to the higher type of activity is difficult to explain. Probably the essential factor in determining the course of cultural development in this instance was the extremely marginal existence of the farming economy in the Middle Pecos area. If conditions were at all similar to those of the historic period the only areas of the valley in which cultivation was possible were the portions of the flood plain adjacent to the river channel. If the river flowed slowly down a meandering channel, as is suggested by some of the air photos, the water table would probably have been high enough for cultivation on the flood plain surface. Undoubtedly the inundation and silting of the seasonal floods every spring were also favorable to cultivation. The disadvantage of this type of cultivation would have come with unusually heavy summer rains, when a rise in the river level could wipe out most of the planted fields, as happened in the lower portions of the Bosque Redondo during the reservation period. Since the heaviest summer rains in this area fall in July and August and the first frost averages October 24 (Von Eschen, 1961: 29), these conditions made cultivation in the valley a hazardous undertaking. At the same time a fairly intensive use of the valley floor for cultivation must have reduced the quantity of game in the area, since the valley floor seems to have been the area of thickest concentration of animal life in the historic period. The quantity of tortoise bone in the Mesita Negra sites attests, I believe, the lack of available game in the area. The occasional large mammals, deer or bison, which were obtained by the Middle Pecos people would have been of considerable importance to them, and when the bison began to appear in the valley in some quantity they must have presented a better prospect for these marginal farmers than a continuation of their tradition of cultivation. This may have been particularly true if the slight increase in moisture suggested by the pollen record was in the form of summer rains, increasing the likelihood of destructive floods.

The Pecos River valley lies on the border of the Southwestern and Plains culture areas, as known from the historic period, with distinct subsistence patterns of agriculture and bison-hunting. Therefore, information on possible cultural relationships in this region was one of the objects of this study. The sequence that has been outlined here, however, is of interest in that it documents a dramatic technological change, and that this change was an *in situ* development based in an essentially Southwestern tradition with no apparent contact with Plains traditions. The maximum utilization of the area by the Middle Pecos agriculturalists seems to have been during the period from about A.D. 1000 to 1200. There followed a relatively short period, probably less than a century, during which bison became an important source of food. Then the valley was abandoned by the bison hunters except for infrequent visits by later hunters and gatherers.

The extent and rapidity of the change in economic orientation of the Middle Pecos population may be unique in prehistoric Western America.

LITERATURE CITED

Agogino, G. and J. Hester
1956 A reevaluation of the San Jose non-ceramic cultures. El Palacio 63 (1):6-21, Santa Fe.

Bailey, L. R.
1964 The Long Walk. Pp. xiii + 252, Los Angeles: Westernlore.

Bailey, V.
1913 Life zones and crop zones of New Mexico. North American Fauna 35, pp. 100, Washington.

Bannister, B.
1965 Tree-ring dating of the archaeological sites in the Chaco Canyon region, New Mexico. Southwestern Monuments Association Technical Series 6, part 2, pp. 117-201, Globe.

Bell, R. E.
1962 Precolumbian prairie settlement in the Great Plains. Great Plains Journal 2 (1):22-28, Lawton.

Bernard, M.
1942 Climatic characteristics and data. *In* U. S. National Resources Planning Board. The Pecos River Joint Investigation, pp. 1-21, Washington.

Bordes, F.
1961 Typologie du Paléolithique Ancien et Moyen. Publications de L'Institut de Préhistoire de L'Université de Bordeaux, Memoire No. 1, pp. 85 + 108 plates, Bordeaux.

Brainerd, G. W.
1951 The place of chronological ordering in archaeological analysis. American Antiquity 16 (4):301-313, Salt Lake City.

Brooks, C. E., and F. D. Reeve, editors
1948 Forts and Forays, James A. Bennett: a dragoon in New Mexico 1850-1856. Pp. 85, Albuquerque: University of New Mexico Press.

Calhoun, J. S.
1851 Letters to the Hon. Luke Lea, Commissioner of Indian Affairs. Annual Report of the Commissioner for Indian Affairs, 1851, pp. 195-199, Washington.

Carleton, J. H., Brig. Gen.
1864 Letter to Brig. Gen. Lorenzo Thomas, Adjutant General. Report of the Commissioner for Indian Affairs, 1863, pp. 110-111, Washington.

Carleton, J. H.
1867 Letter to W. McCleave, July 18, 1865. U. S. Congress Joint Special Committee to Inquire into the Condition of the Indian Tribes. Condition of the Indian Tribes, pp. 229-230, Washington.

Carter, G. F.
1945 Plant geography and culture history in the American Southwest. Viking Fund Publications in Anthropology 5, pp. 140, New York.

Clark, J. A.
1865 Letter to M. Steck, October 21, 1863. Report of the Commissioner for Indian Affairs, 1864, pp. 208, Washington.

Colton, H. S., and L. L. Hargrave
1937 Handbook of northern Arizona pottery wares. Museum of Northern Arizona Bulletin 11, pp. 267, Flagstaff.

Cremony, J. C.
1868 Life among the Apaches. Pp. 322. San Francisco and New York: A. Roman & Company.

Daifuku, H.
1961 Jeddito 264: a report on the excavation of a Basket Maker III-Pueblo I site in northeastern Arizona with a review of some current theories in southwestern archaeology. Papers of the Peabody Museum of Archaeology and Ethnology, Harvard University 33(1), pp. xii + 98, Cambridge.

Davis, N. M.
1868 Report to Hon. N. G. Taylor, Commissioner of Indian Affairs, Sept. 15, 1868. Annual Report of the Commissioner for Indian Affairs, 1868, pp. 159-162, Washington.

Delgado, F.
1866 Report to the Commissioner of Indian Affairs, September 10, 1865. Report of the Commissioner of Indian Affairs, 1865, pp. 160-164, Washington.

Dice, L. R.
1943 The Biotic Provinces of North America. Pp. 78, Ann Arbor, University of Michigan Press.

Dick, H. W.
1965 Bat Cave. School of American Research Monographs 27, pp. xiv + 114, Santa Fe.

Dittert, A. E., Jr., and R. J. Ruppé, Jr.
1951 The archaeology of Cebolleta Mesa: a preliminary report. El Palacio 58(4):116-129. Santa Fe.

Dodd, T. H.
1867 Report to Col. A. B. Norton, Superintendent of Indian Affairs, Santa Fe, New Mexico, August 28, 1866. Report of the Commissioner of Indian Affairs, 1866, pp. 148-150. Washington.

1868 Report to Superintendent of Indian Affairs for New Mexico, June 30, 1867. Report of the Commissioner of Indian Affairs, 1867, pp. 198-203, Washington.

Ellis, F. H., and J. M. Campbell
1952 The Atrisco sites: Cochise manifestations in the Middle Rio Grande Valley. American Antiquity 17:211-221, Salt Lake City.

Espenshade, E. B., Jr.
1960 Goode's world atlas. Pp. 288, Chicago: Rand McNally.

Fenenga, F.
1956a Excavations at site LA 2579, a Mogollon village near Grand Quivira. *In* Wendorf, F., Fox, N., and O. L. Lewis, eds., Pipeline Archaeology, pp. 226-233, Santa Fe and Flagstaff.

1956b Excavation at site LA 2567. *In* Wendorf, F., Fox, N., and O. L. Lewis, eds., Pipeline Archaeology, pp. 233-241, Santa Fe and Flagstaff.

Fenenga F., and T. S. Cummings
1956a The eastern section of the Permian-San Juan project. *In* Wendorf, F., Fox, N., and O. L. Lewis, eds., Pipeline Archaeology, pp. 216-226, Santa Fe and Flagstaff.

1956b LA 2569: Cerros Majinos, a Late Pueblo II-Early Pueblo III village on the Rio Puerco near Los Lunas, New Mexico. *In* Wendorf, F., Fox, N., and O. L. Lewis, eds., Pipeline Archaeology, pp. 242-255, Santa Fe and Flagstaff.

Fiedler, A. G., and S. S. Nye
1933 Geology and ground-water resources of the Roswell artesian basin, New Mexico. U. S. Geological Survey Water-Supply Paper 639, pp. 372, Washington.

Frazer, R. W.
1965 Forts of the west. Pp. 246. Norman: University of Oklahoma Press.

Frye, J. C., and A. B. Leonard
1952 Pleistocene geology of Kansas. Kansas Geological Survey Bulletin 99, pp. 230, Topeka.

Gidley, J. W.
1901 Tooth characters and revision of the North American species of the genus Equus. Bulletin of the American Museum of Natural History, 14(9):91-142. New York.

Graves, J. K.
1867 Report to Commissioner of Indian Affairs. Report of the Commissioner of Indian Affairs, 1866, pp. 131-137. Washington.

Green, Earl
1955 Excavations near Gran Quivira, New Mexico. Bulletin of the Texas Archaeological Society 26, pp. 182-185. Austin.

Hammond, G. P.
1929 Expedition into New Mexico made by Antonio de Espejo 1582-1583, as revealed in the journal of Diego Pérez de Luxán, a member of the party. Quivira Society Publications 1, pp. 143. Los Angeles.

Hammond, G. P., and A. Rey
1940 Narratives of the Coronado expedition 1540-1542. Coronado Quarto Centennial Publications 2, pp. 413. Albuquerque.

Harrington, E. R.
1957 Sinkholes, bottomless lakes, and the Pecos River. Scientific Monthly 84(6):302-308. Washington.

Haury, E. W.
1936 Some southwestern pottery types: series IV. Medallion Papers 19, pp. 49. Globe.

Haury, E. W., Sayles, E. B., and W. W. Wasley
1959 The Lehner mammoth site, southwestern Arizona. American Antiquity 25(1):2-30. Salt Lake City.

Hawley, F. M.
1939 Additions to descriptions of Chaco pottery types. *In* Kluckhohn, C., and P. Reiter, eds., Preliminary report on the 1937 excavations, Bc 50-51, Chaco Canyon, New Mexico. University of New Mexico Bulletin 345, pp. 49-53. Albuquerque.

Hawley, F. M.
1950 Field manual of prehistoric southwestern pottery types (revised). University of New Mexico Bulletin 291, pp. 126. Albuquerque.

Hay, O. P.
1913 Notes on some fossil horses with descriptions of four new species. Proceedings of the United States National Museum 44(1969):569-594. Washington.

Hibbard, C. W.
1952 Vertebrate fossils from Late Cenozoic deposits of central Kansas. University of Kansas Paleontological Contributions: Vertebrata 2:1-14. Lawrence.

1955 Pleistocene vertebrates from the Upper Becerra (*Becerra Superior*) formation, Valley of Tequixquiac, Mexico, with notes on other Pleistocene forms. Contributions from the Muséum of Paleontology, University of Michigan 12(5):47-96. Ann Arbor.

1958 Summary of North American Pleistocene local faunas. Papers of the Michigan Academy of Science, Arts and Letters 43(1957 meeting), pp. 3-32. Ann Arbor.

Hibbard, C. W., and D. W. Taylor
1960 Two late Pleistocene faunas from southwestern Kansas. Contributions from the Museum of Paleontology, University of Michigan 15(1):1-223. Ann Arbor.

Hibbard, C. W., Ray, D. E., Savage, D. E., Taylor, D. W., and J. E. Guilday
1965 Quaternary mammals of North America. *In* Wright, H. E., Jr., and D. G. Frey, eds., The Quaternary of the United States, pp. 509-525. Princeton: Princeton University Press.

Holden, J.
1952 The Bonnell Site. Bulletin of the Texas Archaeological and Paleontological Society 23:78-132. Lubbock.

Hughes, J. T.
1955 Little Sunday: an Archaic site in the Texas Panhandle. Bulletin of the Texas Archaeological Society 26:55-74. Austin.

Jelinek, A. J.
1952 Pottery of the Rio Bonito area of Lincoln County, New Mexico. Bulletin of the Texas Archaeological and Paleontological Society 23:147-167. Lubbock.

1958 Archaeological materials from the Middle Pecos River Valley, New Mexico. Papers of the Michigan Academy of Science, Arts and Letters 43 (1957 meeting), pp. 159-168. Ann Arbor.

1960 An archaeological survey of the Middle Pecos River Valley and the adjacent Llano Estacado. Doctoral Dissertation, University of Michigan, pp. 285. Ann Arbor.

1962 Use of the cumulative graph in termporal ordering. American Antiquity 28(2):241-243. Salt Lake City.

1966a Correlation of archaeological and palynological data. Science 152(3728):1507-1509. Washington.

1966b Some distinctive flakes and flake tools from the Llano Estacado. Papers of the Michigan Academy of Science, Arts and Letters 51 (1965 meeting), pp. 399-405. Ann Arbor.

Jennings, J. D.
1940 A variation of southwestern Pueblo culture. Laboratory of Anthropology Technical Series Bulletin 10, pp. 1-12 + 7 pl. Santa Fe.

Johnson, W. D.
1901 The High Plains and their utilization. Annual Report of the U. S. Geological Survey 21(4):601-674. Washington.

1902 The High Plains and their utilization. Annual Report of the U. S. Geological Survey 22(4):631-669. Washington.

Judd, N. M.
1954 The material culture of Pueblo Bonito. Smithsonian Miscellaneous Collections 124, pp. xii + 398. Washington.

1959 Pueblo Del Arroyo, Chaco Canyon, New Mexico. Smithsonian Miscellaneous Collections 138(1), pp. vii + 222. Washington.

Kelley, J. C.
1937 The route of Antonio de Espejo down the Pecos River and

across the Trans-Pecos Region in 1583: its relations to West Texas archaeology. West Texas Historical and Scientific Society Publication 7, pp. 7-25. Alpine.

Kidder, A. V.
1924 An introduction to the study of southwestern archaeology. Papers of the Phillips Academy Southwestern Expedition 1, pp. vii + 151. New Haven.

Krieger, A. D.
1946 Culture complexes and chronology in northern Texas with extension of Puebloan datings to the Mississippi Valley. University of Texas Publication 4640, pp. 366. Austin.

Küchler, A. W.
1964 Potential natural vegetation of the coterminous United States. American Geographical Society Special Publication 36, pp. 156 + map. New York.

Labadi, L.
1864 Report to Commissioner of Indian Affairs, October 10, 1863. Report of the Commissioner of Indian Affairs, 1863, pp. 424-427. Washington.

1865 Report to Commissioner of Indian Affairs, October 22, 1864. Report of the Commissioner of Indian Affairs, 1864, pp. 202-205. Washington.

1866 Report to Felipe Delgado, Superintendent of Indian Affairs, New Mexico, September 30, 1865. Report of the Commissioner for Indian Affairs, 1865, pp. 173-176. Washington.

Lance, J. F.
1959 Faunal remains from the Lehner Mammoth Site. American Antiquity 25(1):35-39. Salt Lake City.

Lehmer, D. J.
1948 The Jornada branch of the Mogollon. University of Arizona Bulletin 19(2), pp. 99. Tucson.

1954 River basin surveys papers No. 7 — archaeological investigations in the Oahe Dam area, South Dakota 1950-51. Bureau of American Ethnology Bulletin 158, pp. 190.

Little, V. A., and D. F. Martin
1942 Cotton insects of the United States. Pp. 130. Minneapolis: Burgess.

Lutes, E.
1959 A marginal prehistoric culture of North Eastern New Mexico. El Palacio 66(2):59-68. Santa Fe.

Maerz, A., and M. R. Paul
1930 A Dictionary of Color, pp. 207. New York: McGraw-Hill.

Martin, P. S., and J. B. Rinaldo
1950 Sites of the Reserve Phase, Pine Lawn Valley, western New Mexico. Fieldiana: Anthropology 38(3):403-577. Chicago.

McCabe, F.
1896 Report of the census, condition, etc. of the Navajo Indians. The War of the Rebellion: a Compilation of the Official Records of the Union and Confederate Armies, ser. 1, 48(1): 524-529. Washington.

McCleave, W.
1867 Letter to Genl. J. H. Carleton, July 14, 1865. U. S. Congress Joint Special Committee to inquire into the condition of the Indian tribes. Condition of the Indian Tribes, pp. 312. Washington.

McCluney, E.
1962 A new name and revised description for a Mogollon pottery type from southern New Mexico. Southwestern Lore 27(4): 49-55. Boulder.

McMains, P. M., and L. W. Hill
1942 History of irrigation development. *In* U. S. National Resources Planning Board, The Pecos River Joint Investigation. Report of Participating Agencies, pp. 134-149. Washington.

Mera, H. P.
1931 Chupadero Black on White. Laboratory of Anthropology Technical Series Bulletin 1, pp. 3 + 7 pl. Santa Fe.

1935. Ceramic clues to the prehistory of North Central New Mexico. Laboratory of Anthropology Technical Series Bulletin 8, pp. 43 + 17 pl. Santa Fe.

1938 Reconnaissance and excavation in southeastern New Mexico. Memoirs of the American Anthropological Association No. 51, pp. 70 + 24 pl. Menasha.

1940 Population changes in the Rio Grande glaze-paint area. Laboratory of Anthropology Technical Series Bulletin No. 9, pp. 41. Santa Fe.

1943 An outline of ceramic developments in southern and southeastern New Mexico. Laboratory of Anthropology Technical Series Bulletin 11, pp. 20 + 1 pl. Santa Fe.

Mera, H. P., and W. S. Stallings, Jr.
1931 Lincoln Black on Red. Laboratory of Anthropology Technical Series Bulletin 2, pp. 10 + 4 pl. Santa Fe.

Merriwether, D.
1854 Report to Commissioner of Indian Affairs. Annual Report of the Commissioner of Indian Affairs, 1854:166-177. Washington.

Metcalf, C. L., and W. P. Flint
1962 Destructive and useful insects (4th ed.), pp. 1087. New York: McGraw-Hill.

Miller, B. B.
1966 Five Illinoian molluscan faunas from the southern Great Plains. Malacologia 4(1):173-260. Ann Arbor.

Morgan, A. M.

1942 Water resources: geology. U. S. National Resources Planning Board, The Pecos River Joint Investigation, pp. 28-38. Washington.

Moroney, M. J.

1965 Facts from figures (3d edition, revised), pp. 472. Baltimore: Harmondsworth.

Morris, E. H.

1939 Archaeological studies in the LaPlata District. Carnegie Institution of Washington Publication 519, pp. xxiv: 298 + 321 pl. Washington.

Motts, W. S., and R. L. Cushman

1964 An appraisal of the possibilities of artificial recharge to ground-water supplies in part of the Roswell Basin, New Mexico. U. S. Geological Survey Water-Supply Paper 1785, pp. 86. Washington.

Norton, A. B., Col.

1867 Report to Commissioner of Indian Affairs, September 28, 1866. Report of the Commissioner of Indian Affairs, 1866, pp. 144-148. Washington.

1868 Report to Commissioner of Indian Affairs, August 24, 1867. Report of the Commissioner of Indian Affairs, 1867, pp. 189-195. Washington.

Opler, M.

1941 An Apache Life-Way, pp. 500. Chicago: University of Chicago Press.

Parker, G. L., and C. G. Paulsen

1942 Water resources. U. S. National Resources Planning Board, The Pecos River Joint Investigation, pp. 22-26. Washington.

Peckham, S.

1957 Highway salvage archaeology no. 12: three pithouse sites near Albuquerque, New Mexico. Highway Salvage Archaeology 3:39-70. Santa Fe.

Pope, Bvt. Capt. J.

1854 Report of exploration of a route for the Pacific Railroad near the thirty-second parallel of north latitude from the Red River to the Rio Grande. Explorations and Surveys for a Railroad Route from the Mississippi River to the Pacific Ocean 2, pp. 185. War Department, Washington.

Reed, E. K.

1946 The distinctive features and distribution of the San Juan Anasazi culture. Southwestern Journal of Anthropology 2: 295-305. Albuquerque.

1955 Bison beyond the Pecos. Texas Journal of Science 7(2): 130-135. San Marcos.

Renaud, E. B.
1937 Northeastern New Mexico. The Archaeological Survey of the Western High Plains, Ninth Report, pp. 69. Denver.

Roberts, F. H. H., Jr.
1929 Shabik'eshchee Village, a Late Basket Maker site in the Chaco Canyon, New Mexico. Bureau of American Ethnology Bulletin 92, pp. viii + 164. Washington.

Roosa, W. B.
1956 Preliminary report on the Lucy site. El Palacio 63(2): 36-49. Santa Fe.

Rostlund, E.
1960 The geographic range of the historic bison in the Southeast. Annals of the Association of American Geographers 50(4):395-407. Lawrence.

Schroeder, A. H.
1962 A re-analysis of the routes of Coronado and Oñate into the plains in 1541 and 1601. Plains Anthropologist 7(15): 2-23. Lincoln.

Schroder, A. H., and D. S. Matson
1965 A Colony on the Move, pp. 196. Santa Fe.

Sellards, E. H.
1952 Early Man in America, pp. 211. Austin: University of Texas Press.

Smiley, T. A., Stubbs, S., and B. Bannister
1953 A foundation for the dating of some late archaeological sites in the Rio Grande area, New Mexico: based on studies in tree ring methods and pottery analyses. University of Arizona Bulletin 24(3). Pp. 66. Tucson.

Stallings, W. S., Jr.
1931 El Paso Polychrome. Laboratory of Anthropology Technical Series Bulletin 3, pp. 13 + 3 pl. Santa Fe.

Steck, M.
1865 Report to the Commissioner of Indian Affairs. Report of the Commissioner of Indian Affairs, 1864, pp. 180-187. Washington.

Steen, C. R.
1959 The Pigeon Cliffs site, Union County, New Mexico. Paper delivered at the 24th Annual Meeting of the Society for American Archaeology, May 2, 1959. Salt Lake City.

Strong, W. D.
1935 An introduction to Nebraska archeology. Smithsonian Miscellaneous Collections 93(10). Pp. 323. Washington.

Swadesh, M.
1963 Nuevo ensayo de glotocronologia Yutonahua. Anales, 1962, Instituto Nacional de Antropologia e Historia 15(44):263-302. Mexico.

Taylor, D. W.
1960 Late Cenozoic molluscan faunas from the High Plains. U. S. Geological Survey Prof. Paper 337, pp. 94. Washington.

Trager, G. L.
1951 Linguistic history and ethnologic history in the Southwest. Journal of the Washington Academy of Science 41:341-343. Washington.

Trager, G. L., and E. C. Trager
1959 Kiowa and Tanoan. American Anthropologist 61(6):1078-1083. Menasha.

U. S. Congress Joint Special Committee to inquire into the condition of the
1867 Indian Tribes. 1867 Condition of the Indian Tribes, pp. 532. Washington.

U. S. National Resources Planning Board
1942 The Pecos River Joint Investigation: Reports of Participating Agencies, pp. 407 + 34 pl. Washington.

Usher, J. P., Secretary of the Interior
1865 Letter to W. P. Dole, Commissioner of Indian Affairs. Report of the Commissioner of Indian Affairs, 1864, pp. 207. Washington.

Vivian, G.
1965 The Three-C site, an Early Pueblo II ruin in Chaco Canyon, New Mexico. University of New Mexico Publications in Anthropology 13, pp. 48. Albuquerque.

Vivian, G., and T. W. Mathews
1965 Kin Kletso, a Pueblo III community in Chaco Canyon, New Mexico. Southwestern Monuments Association Technical Series 6(1):1-115. Globe.

Von Eschen, G. F.
1961 The climate of New Mexico. Business Information Series 37. Pp. 72. University of New Mexico Bureau of Business Research. Albuquerque.

Wedel, W. R.
1959 An introduction to Kansas archaeology. Bureau of American Ethnology Bulletin 174, pp. xvii + 723. Washington.

Wendorf, F., and Reed, E. K.
1955 An alternative reconstruction of northern Rio Grande prehistory. El Palacio 62 (5-6):131-173. Santa Fe.

Wheat, J. B.
1955 Mogollon culture prior to A. D. 1000. Memoirs of the Society for American Archaeology 10, pp. 242. Salt Lake City.

Wheat, J. B., J. C. Gifford, and W. W. Wasley
1958 Ceramic variety, type cluster, and ceramic system in southwestern pottery analysis. American Antiquity 24(1): 34-46. Salt Lake City.

Williams, J. W.
1959 Coronado, from the Rio Grande to the Concho, reprinted from The Southwestern Historical Quarterly 43(2), pp. 31. Austin.

Winship, G. P.
1896 The Coronado expedition. Annual Report of the Bureau of American Ethnology 14:329-613. Washington.

PLATE I

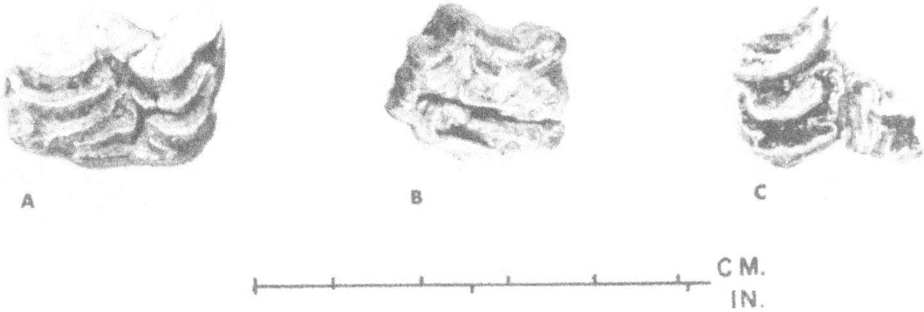

D

A-C. Occlusal surfaces of teeth of *Equus* from Locality U8 in Blackdom Terrace deposits near Fort Sumner.

D. Badly eroded mandible of *Mammuthus imperator* (Leidy) at Locality U6 on top of Blackdom terrace near 18-Mile Bend. Arrow is one foot long.

PLATE II

Tilted beds of Kansan (?) age in Blackdom Terrace deposits at Locality U7.

PLATE III

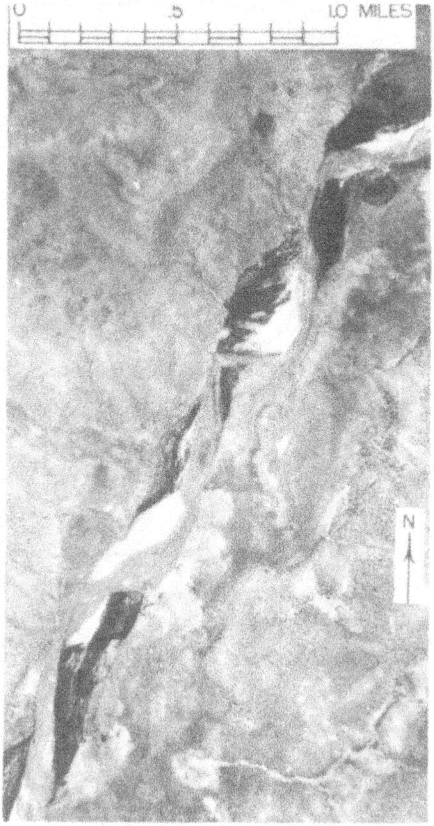

A

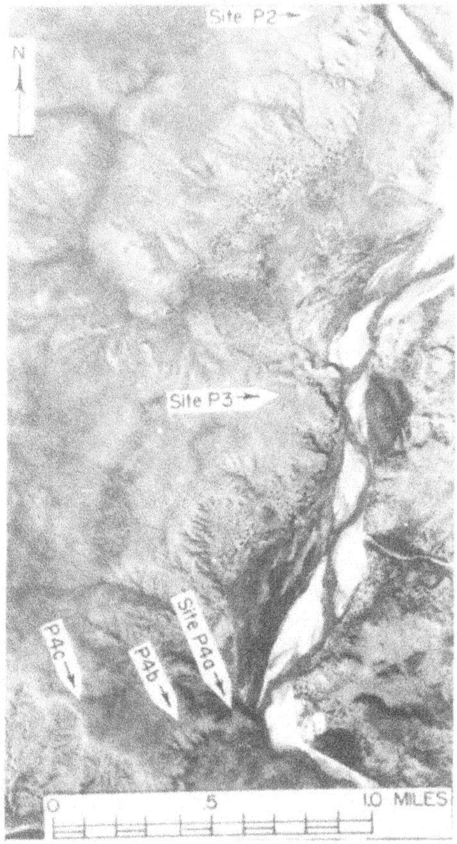

B

A. Air photo of Pecos Valley about 10 miles north of Roswell. Recent meander channels on Lakewood Terrace visible east of present channel.

B. Air photo of Pecos Valley near Fort Sumner showing typical pattern of site distribution on high promontories adjacent to stream channel. (U.S. Department of Agriculture, Soil Conservation Service base photographs).

PLATE IV

Sherds of Crosby Black on Gray illustrating typical design motifs; A-L, Site P4B; M-Q, Site P9.

PLATE V

Sherds of Middle Pecos Black on White from Site P4C illustrating design motifs. Note design outline in fine dark line on A,B, with broader lines added later in thinner paint. C,D,G,H,K,M,T are bowl sherds; Q a single strand lug; U a canteen lug.

PLATE VI

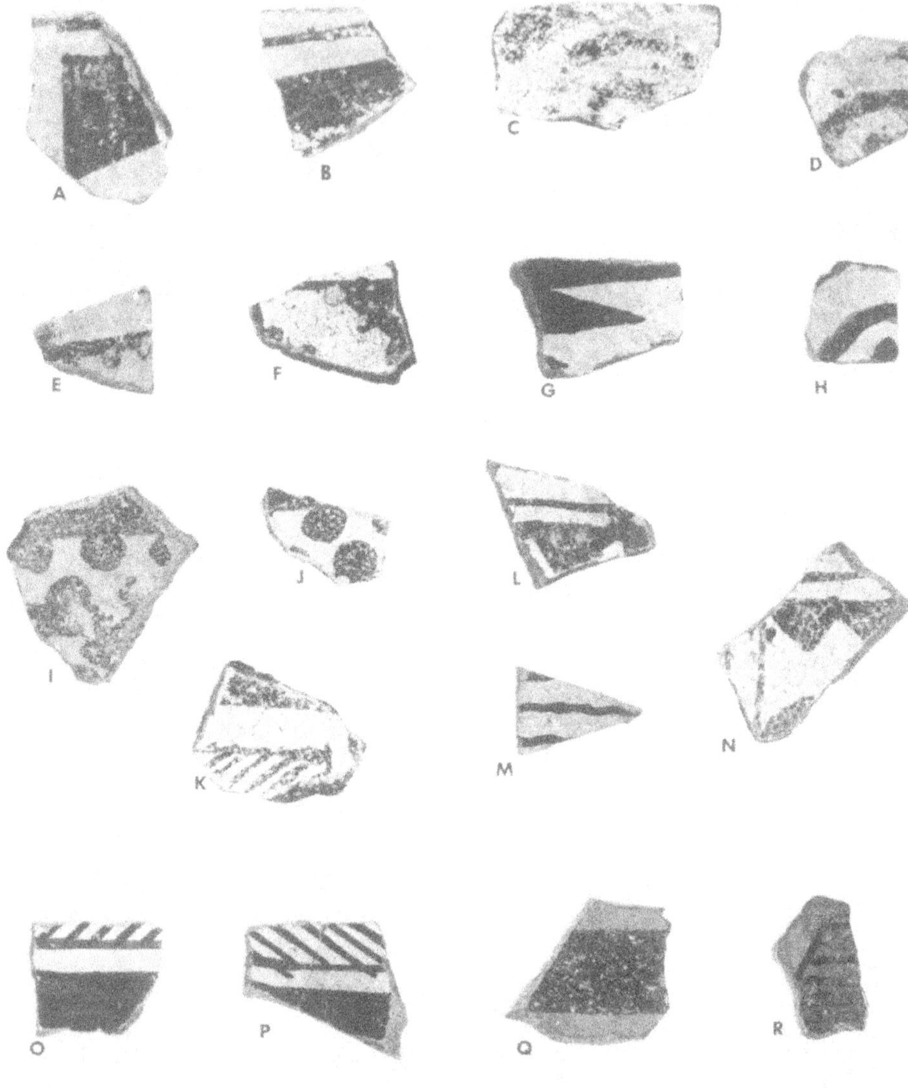

Sherds of intrusive ceramics. A-H, L-N Red Mesa Black on White from Sites P4A and P4AB; I-K "Local Pueblo II" Black on White, I,J from Site P4B, K from Site P4C; O,P Reserve Black on White from Site P4AB; Q,R Santa Fe Black on White from Site P4C.

PLATE VII

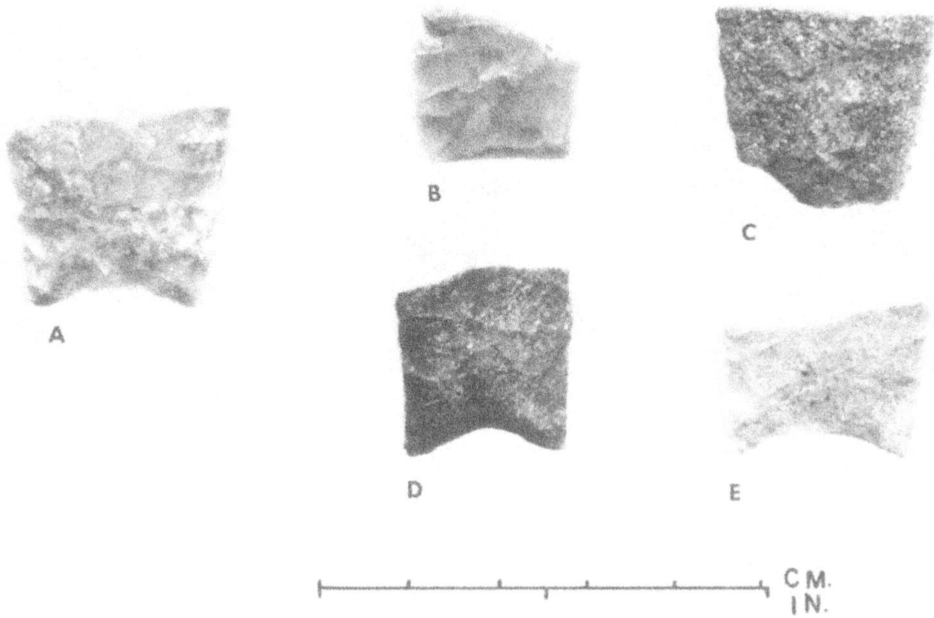

Paleo-Indian projectile point bases: A,B Site P28; C Site P7; D Site P24; E surface of Blackdom Terrace, west bank, a few miles south of Fort Sumner.

PLATE VIII

Metates from fill of Structure 1, Site P24. Example at far right is nearest to trough form of any observed in valley. Late Mesita Negra Phase.

PLATE IX

Slab-lined storage cyst with post holes in smoothed adobe floor excavated in 1956 at Site P4A. Maximum diameter 4 ft. 8 in. Sunlight from west. Late(?) 18-Mile Phase.

PLATE X

Structure 2, Site P4AB; view from north. Arrow is one foot long. Late 18-Mile Phase.

PLATE XI

Structure 2, Site P4AB; view from east showing sandstone slab and upright sandstone blocks in cross-wall suggesting altar features. Late 18-Mile Phase.

PLATE XII

Structure 3, Site P4AB; viewed from south. Late 18-Mile Phase.

PLATE XIII

A

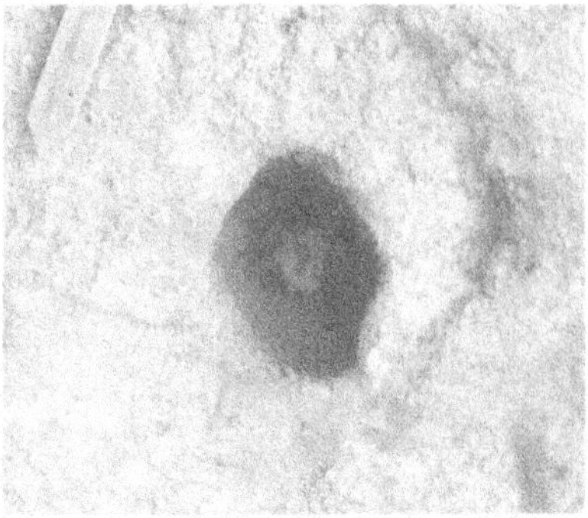

B

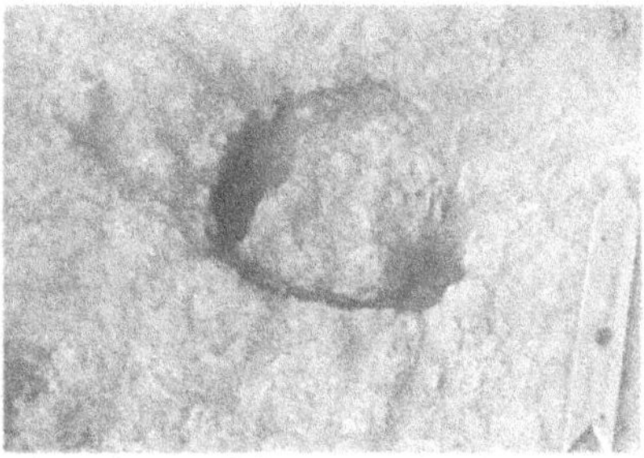

C

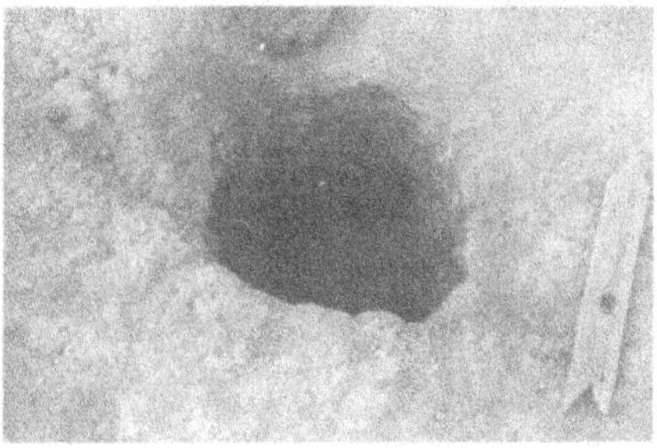

D

Architectural features, Structure 1, Site P4C. McKenzie Phase.

A. Hearth; note sand compacted by recent cow tracks across original ground surface west of hearth. Arrow one foot from tip to notch.

B. Remains of wooden post packed in sand and ash in southwest post hole.

C. Northwest post hole with adobe core in place in sand and ash packing.

D. Northwest post hole with adobe core removed (tip visible top center).

PLATE XIV

A

B

Burial 2, Site P24. Late Mesita Negra Phase.
A. View from south showing position of stones in burial pit.
B. View from west with most of fill removed from burial pit. Fragmented skull of infant visible above patella.

PLATE XV

Structure 2, Site P24; view from east. Plastered hearth is just above large stone at center. Floor apparently destroyed north of this area. Possible cross-wall runs north-south just beyond large stone. Early Mesita Negra Phase.

PLATE XVI

Archaic projectile points: A-C,G,J-L, Site P5; D,E, Site W11; F, Site P27; H, Site L6; I, Site P38.

www.ingramcontent.com/pod-product-compliance
Lightning Source LLC
LaVergne TN
LVHW050021250826
846302LV00008B/47